A
BOOK OF BOMBAY

A BOOK OF BOMBAY

JAMES DOUGLAS

GYAN

Published by

GYAN

Gyan Publishing House
5, Ansari Road
Daryaganj, New Delhi-110002
Phone: 011-47034999, 9811692060
E-mail: books@gyanbooks.com

Distribution Network
gyanbooks.com
India, USA, Canada, UK, Australia, France

ISBN : 978-81-212-9652-6 (PB)
First Published, 1882

2nd Impression 2023

Printed at: Gyan Press, Delhi.

A BOOK OF BOMBAY
Author: JAMES DOUGLAS

SEVAGI

A
BOOK OF BOMBAY.

BY

JAMES DOUGLAS.

1883.

CONTENTS.

CHAPTER I.

BOMBAY MARRIAGE TREATY.

PAGE

Article XI.—Instrument of Possession .... 3—20

CHAPTER II.

WESTERN INDIA IN 1583.

The Man about Town—King of Ballagat—The Master-Mariner—Decline and Fall—The Inquisition—Miscellanea—Archæological Note on Linschotten .... 23—46

CHAPTER III.

BOMBAY BEGINNINGS.

Mortuary Returns—Exchange—Profits of Trade—The Cotton Trade—The Imports—Freights—Jovial Times—Bombay Green—Never Taken—A Sneaker of Bombay Punch—A Home in Bombay in 1694 .... 49—78

CHAPTER IV.

GERALD AUNGIER, GOVERNOR OF BOMBAY.

Who he was—What he did—Traits—His Silver Chalice—Where he lived—His House—Conclusion .... 81—98

CHAPTER V.

SEEVAJEE.

PAGE

His Country—His Birth—His Person and Character—His Accomplishments—Part Second—Traits Bad and Good—His Two Great Crimes—His Master Passion—Seevajee's Coronation—His Death .... 101—124

CHAPTER VI.

KANOJEE ANGRIA AND THE PIRATES OF WESTERN INDIA.

Early Navigation—Angria's Kolaba—Fleet of Seevajee—The Commerce assailed by the Pirates—What he cost us—His Crowning Achievement—Vengeance—The English Pirate—The Police of the Indian Seas—Their Cruelties—The Last of the Angrias—Their Old Haunts—Conclusion—Supplementary Note .... 127—156

CHAPTER VII.

BOMBAY, 1750.

Grose's Account—When Grose Landed—Mr. Grose asked to Supper—A Few Ladies—Subjects of Conversation—The Government House—A Colossal Sundial—The Bombay of 1750—Hornby's Vellard—The Fort—The Dockyard—Cartography of Bombay—The Towers of Silence—First Parsee in Europe—A Plucky Woman—Elephanta—His Portrait of Kanojee Angria—Raighur—Bullion and Exchange—Native Character—Malabar Hill. 159—194

CHAPTER VIII.

The Book of Gombroon, 1752-53.

PAGE

History not Antiquarianism—Mortality Bills—The Inkstand—Etcetera—The Lord of the Hot Countries—Four Gradations of Service—People were here before us—The English Sirnames of Bombay ....197—214

CHAPTER IX.

Horatio Nelson: or Bombay 1775 ....217—226

CHAPTER X.

Napoleon Bonaparte at Suez, 1798.

Suez—His Visit and Schemes—Crosses the Red Sea —State of Feeling in Bombay—The Suez Canal —The Forbes' Loans—Conclusion ....229—246

CHAPTER XI.

The Duke of Wellington in Bombay.

A Love-passage—The Duke's Nose—The Duke of Wellington in Bombay and Western India—The Duke in India—The Bombay of his Period —A Great Dearth of Materials—The Duke's Triumphal Entry into Bombay—The Condition of the People—Why was Arthur Wellesley here—His Celebrated March to Poona—Duel; Discipline at Nagar—Native Opinion of the Duke—Traits—Here are Two Notabilia—Was the Duke at Matheran—The Duke of Wellington's Bombay Residence..249—280

CHAPTER XII.

MOUNTSTUART ELPHINSTONE.

PAGE

Items—His Popularity—Portrait—Political—Eccentricities—His History of India—Governors of Bombay—Religious—Character and Accomplishments—Biographical .... 283—302

CHAPTER XIII.

SIR JOHN MALCOLM.

Priliminary—Calf Country—The Soldiers' Return—In Paris—A Big Day—Dinner to the Ettrick Shepherd—Governor of Bombay—Reductio ad Absurdum—Vi et Armis—Person—Conclusion 305—326

CHAPTER XIV.

SIR JAMES MACKINTOSH; OR BOMBAY 1804 TO 1812.

Bombay a Dull Place—The Diary and Letters of Mackintosh—He did Good Work in Bombay—A Quiet Day at Parell—A Noisy Day at Taralla—Calls—On the Judgment Seat—An Unspoken Bombay Sermon—Mackintosh and Wilson ...329—352

CHAPTER XV.

POONA AND THE PESHWAS.

A Retrospect ....355—368

CHAPTER XVI.

SEEVAJEE'S FORTS.

TORNA ....371—381

THE FORT OF RAJMACHEE, NEAR KHANDALA.

The Bombay Forts—The Road to it—The Look-out—Condition of the People—Streams ....382—397

THE FORT OF RAIGHUR.

PAGE

Raighur Ho—View of Nagotna Creek from Bombay—Pachad and the Staircase—Position—Descriptive—Architecture—A View from Raighur—Why Seevajee Chose Raighur—The English Embassy—Nil Desperandum—The Burst of the Monsoon—TheCoronation—Portrait—How they Spend the Time—A Transaction in Piece-Goods—Seevajee and the English—Its Memories ......398—434

CHAPTER XVII.

BEEJAPOOR.

Meadows Taylor—The Accommodation—Tombs—Doves—Sheep and Dogs—Famine—The Country about Beejapoor—Globe-trotters ....437—456

CHAPTER XVIII.

THE MARTYRS OF TANNA.

Note on the Gold of Ophir.......................................459—470

CHAPTER XIX.

THE HON'BLE E. I. COMPANY'S FIRST SHROFF IN GUJARAT.

Trawadi Shri Krishna Arjunji Nathji of Surat......473—482

CHAPTER XX.

JAMES FORBES.

His Book—Arrival in Bombay—Ways and Means—His Library—James Forbes and the Ladies of Bombay—Diana and the Cobra—The Execution of Gassi Ram—Natural History of Bombay—Notable Things—The Oriental Memoirs—The Apostle—His Attachment to Bombay—Home—Forbes's View from Malabar Hill ....485—516

CHAPTER XXI.

PAGE

Dr. Wilson ....519—542

CHAPTER XXII.

BOMBAY DIRECTORY—1792.

The Honorable Mayor's Court—The Honorable Court of Appeals—List of Merchants ....545—550

CHAPTER XXIII.

TWELVE VIEWS OF BOMBAY.

The Doctor, 1673—The Philosopher, 1804—The Traveller, 1812—The Soldier, 1818—The Bishop, 1825—The Governor, 1830—The Geologist, 1855—The Cicerone, 1859—The Presbyter, 1866—The Editor from a Balloon, 1877—The Agriculturist, 1879—Sir Richard Temple, 1879 ....553—558

CHAPTER XXIV.

BOMBAY, SOCIAL AND POLITICAL, TWELVE VIEWS.

An Eye-witness, 1690—The Muslim, 1694—The Statesman, 1707—The Political Economist, 1775—The Civilian—Ces gens la, 1765-83—La femme Anglaise—Mackintosh's Bombay, 1804-11—The Missionary, 1811—The Persian—The Chota Sahib, 1830—L'Inde Occidentale Poona, 1832—The Censorious, 1854—Excelsior........................561—566

PREFACE.

We make no apology for presenting these sketches in a collected form to the reader. They have already been kindly received through the press by the Bombay public; and the Bombay Government and the Director of Public Instruction have generously awarded their patronage to the publication, for which I thank them. They are the work of an unprofessional pen, during intervals of leisure.

"I am a plain man, and I think if I had pitten my materials into better hands, I would have dune better."*

No doubt of it; but they must now go forth as they are to the public, with all their sins upon them.

They have been written in the interests of good government.

They do not aspire to the dignity, the philosophy, or even the rigid accuracy of History, and

* Elliot Warburton in *Darien*.

pretend to no special sources of information but what are open to the public.

They presume, however, by way of endeavour, to illustrate one of the noblest episodes in the Colonial History of England, the rise and growth, amid many difficulties, of a great city on the shores of Asia, with some account of the men who have distinguished themselves in its History.

Why do men, after a long residence in a foreign country, set such store on their place of abode? The answer is *Patria est ubicunque bene est.*

But Bombay over and above this has special and great attractions.

For beauty of situation it is "the joy of the whole earth," unrivalled, at all events, in the Eastern dominions of Queen Victoria.

Its geographical position is also unrivalled. When Sir JAMES MACKINTOSH resided in Bombay, it was considered the most obscure corner of India. The Suez Canal has now made of it the key of Asia.

The Time in which we live seems to bridge two vast eras, and we stand midway between the old and the new. We have witnessed the end of one era, and are now the spectators of another, the era of steamers, railways, and telegraphs, and have seen what no generation has seen before, nor will ever see again.

It is at such a time that one sits down to remember that Bombay has a history before the opening of the Suez Canal, and I have written to little purpose if these essays fail in conveying to the reader an exhibition of moral strength and a tenacity of purpose unexampled in the History of Colonisation.

The spectacle of this lone and isolated community, battling for existence for a hundred years, and upholding the banner and the honour of England, is a noble one, and not devoid of moral grandeur. Strange to say it attracted little or no attention at home.

In the Diary of JOHN EVELYN, one of the most accomplished men of his day, and who was in the thick of politics, 1660 to 1705, that is, during the reigns of Charles II., James II., and William III., and which embraces every notable event of his time, there is no mention of Bombay, and yet this was the time during which were laid the foundations of our dominion in Western India.

One word more. The writer has kept steadily before him the condition of the people. Are the subject peoples better or worse off than they were under the former native governments of

Western India? A question of much import, and of more import to the native populations of these countries, than it is even to the ruling class. The answer which is contained in these papers is this, that the Governments we supplanted in Western India were unequal to the task of guaranteeing life and property to their subjects; that they were out of the pathway of human progress, and did not assist in any way the onward march of Civilisation. This is not an English view of the subject, but is and must be the view of every man who can distinguish right from wrong, or the difference between a good government and a bad government. It thus resolves itself into a matter of fact, not a matter of conjecture. The writer has no interested motive to serve in these essays. He is not a servant of the Government of India.

According to the verdict of History it was perfectly open to him in view of the facts to write either one way or the other.

The facts left no other course open to him, than to denounce these Governments as the enemies of mankind.

What destiny is reserved for this great community of Bombay, God only knows. Population and opulence have increased, and may increase with giant strides, but we can scarcely imagine a time when the story of its early history will cease to interest, or its example be without effect upon future generations.

I write this from the Bay of Naples, which recalled to Sir John Malcolm, the glorified image of his beloved Bombay.

June 10*th*, 1882.

BOMBAY MARRIAGE TREATY.

CHAPTER I.

BOMBAY MARRIAGE TREATY.

The Portugalls have choused us it seems on the Island of Bombay.—*Samuel Pepys.*

The train of circumstances which ended in the establishment of the English in Bombay is certainly as wonderful as anything on record. A group of grey-headed sinners living in London, and another group living in Lisbon, decree that the island of Bombay shall constitute part of a dowery of a Portuguese girl who shall marry Charles II., King of England. The island is 12,000 miles away, and none of them have seen it, except on the map. It does not matter. The deed is done, and, as sayeth the clown in the circus—"Here we are!"

What we were bound to receive was Tangier,

Bombay and £500,000. Tangier nearly fell into the hands of the Moors. We ultimately received Bombay without its dependencies, and the money payment dwindled down to £200,000 in bills, with some bills of lading of sugar and coffee cargoes to be realised in London. It is related that shortly after this time a gibbet was erected at Lord Clarendon's gate by the populace of London, on which was printed—

Three sights to be seen
Dunkirk, Tangier, and a barren Queene.

For anything we were the better they might have added "Bombay Green," without injuring the rhyme or reason of the inuendo. And had the public known as much as we know now, it would have been there. The whole business was a pure swindle. At this very moment there lay in the strong box of Clarendon a secret article of the marriage treaty, the existence of which was carefully concealed from the public, by which, in consideration of these forts and the gold that fell into the lap of Barbara Palmer, we were bound neck and heel to fight the battles of Portugal through thick and thin in India. In this way, without our consent being asked or given, were our lives and liberties signed away. Hume and

Macaulay doubtless knew of this secret article, but neither they nor James Mill allude to it, and it is strange that Mackintosh, whom we claim as a Bombay man, passes it over in silence. We are indebted to Bruce, the paid and painstaking annalist of the East India Company, for searching out the details which we now give, with the regret that such a disgraceful document should smudge one page of the History of England. Had the statesmen of Portugal been strong enough to exact its stipulations (they soon became effete), or had our relations with Holland remained the same as they were when the treaty was signed, we would have seen a new and startling evolution of events. The Portuguese in India apparently soon knew of it. When hard pressed by the Mahrattas at Bassein, in 1739, they sent a wail across the water. But our tender mercies were cruel. On the security of some old brass guns and church plate, a unique collateral security, we advanced them Rs. 15,000. Governor Hornby knew of this *secret* treaty, and refers to it, for in 1780, when they again asked assistance, he refused it, and told them to pay us the money already due to us. We are indeed told by a recent historian* that this bond of alliance or marriage treaty is the foundation of all our territorial possessions in the East Indies, and remains unbroken to the present day. We are sorry to hear it, and don't believe it, as far as this secret article is concerned. Both lawgiver and historian unite in common to treat it as a dead-letter and consign it to oblivion.

The foundation of English dominion in Bombay lies in the 11th article of the *Marriage Treaty,* concluded 23rd June, 1661, between his Majesty Charles II., King of Great Britain, and Alfonsus VI., King of Portugal. Here it is:—

ARTICLE XI.

That for the better improvement of the English interest and commerce in the East Indies, and that the King of Great Britain may be better enabled to assist, defend, and protect the subjects of the King of Portugal in those parts, from the power and invasion of the States of the United Provinces, the King of Portugal, with the assent and advice of his Council, gives, transfers, and by these presents, grants and confirms, to the King of Great Britain, his heirs and successors, for ever, the port and island of Bombay, in the East Indies, with all the rights, profits, territories, and appurtenances whatsoever thereunto belonging, and, together with the income and revenue, the

* *Lives of the Queens of England.—Agnes Strickland*, 1851.

direct, full, and absolute dominion and sovereignty of the said port, island, and premises, with all their royalties, freely, fully, entirely, and absolutely. He also covenants and grants that the quiet and peaceable possession of the same shall, with all convenient speed, be freely and effectually delivered to the King of Great Britain, or to the persons thereto appointed by the said King of Great Britain, for his use, in pursuance of this cession, the inhabitants of the said island (as subjects of the King of Great Britain, and under his sovereignty, crown, jurisdiction, and government) being permitted to remain there, and to enjoy the free exercise of the Roman Catholic religion, in the same manner as they do at present. It being always understood, as it is now declared, once for all, that the same regulation shall be observed for the exercise and preservation of the Roman Catholic religion in Tangier, and all other places which shall be ceded and delivered by the King of Portugal into the possession of the King of Great Britain, as were stipulated and agreed to on the surrender of Dunkirk into the hands of the English ; and when the King of Great Britain shall send his fleet to take possession of the said port and island of Bombay, the English shall have instructions to treat the subjects of the King of Portugal, throughout the East Indies, in the most friendly manner, to help and assist them, and to protect them in their trade and navigation there.

The *Treaty of Surrender and Delivery* to Humphrey Cooke on the 18th February, 1665, was unearthed a quarter of a century ago from the archives of Goa by Major T. B. Jervis. This treaty was signed in a large house of the Lady Donna Ignez Miranda, widow, elsewhere designated the lady proprietrix of Bombay, and possessed of the manor right thereof. It was never ratified by the sovereigns of England or Portugal, but constitutes the public deed by which before witnesses we took possession of the port and island of Bombay. It is a document of antique phraseology, and guards against the possibility of mistake as to who Cooke was, by informing posterity that Humphrey Cooke's name in the Spanish and Portuguese language would be *Inofre* Cooke.

Dominion absolutely, *i.e.*, to hold and to have, does not exist in it, for its first right, the right of taxation, we mean beyond what the Portuguese thought proper, is denied to us. We only give the

INSTRUMENT OF POSSESSION.

Possession was accordingly given and delivery made of the port and island of Bombay, which comprehends in its territories the villages of Mazagon, Parell, Worlee, &c., and the said Governor Humphrey Cooke accepted and received the same in the name of his Serene Majesty the King of Great Britain, in the manner and form laid down in the instructions from the Viceroy, Antonio de Mello e Castro. By all and every declaration, clause, and condition in the said instructions, which are fully expressed and declared, he promised (in the name of his Majesty the King of Great Britain) to abide ; and, saying, assuring, and promising so to do, he took personally possession of the said port and island of Bombay, walking thereupon, taking in his hands earth and stones thereof, entering, and walking upon its bastions, &c., and performing other like acts, which, in right, were necessary, without any impediment or contradiction, quietly and peaceably, that his Majesty the King of Great Britain might have, possess, and be come master (also his heirs and successors) of the said island.

And the inhabitants thereof, gentlemen and proprietors of estates within the circuit and territories of the said island, who now pay foras to the King our Master, shall pay the same henceforth to his Majesty the King of Great Britain. And the same L. M. de Vasconcellos, S. Alvares Migos, and the Governor Humphrey Cooke, have ordered this instrument to be drawn up, and copies thereof given to parties requiring it, and that the same shall be registered in the book of the tower of Goa, and in that of the chamber of the city of Bassein, and of the factory of the said city, and at all other suitable places ; and that the necessary declarations shall be recorded in those books, that at all times may appear the manner in which this possession was given and delivery made. And as they thus ordered this public instrument to be prepared, they, the said L. Mendes de Vasconcellos, &c. &c., have put their names thereto in testimony of their having made the said delivery, and the Governor Humphrey Cooke, his, in testimony of his having accepted possession, &c., &c.—(Signed) ANTONIO MONTIERA DE FONCECA,

Notary Public of the city of Bassein, &c.*

The *Secret Treaty* was of course an article of the Marriage Treaty. It is thus described by Bruce, in his *Annals of the East India Company*, vol. ii., page 105: "By the secret article of this treaty the King of England obliged himself to guarantee to the King of Portugal the possessions of that crown in the East Indies; and to mediate a peace between Portugal and the States General, with the object that the respective possessions of the two nations in that quarter might be ascertained, and then explained that *should the States General refuse to accept of such mediations, the King would employ his forces and fleets to compel the States General to accede to these conditions and to obtain restitution to the Crown of Portugal of such Portuguese settlements in the East Indies as the Dutch might subsequent to this treaty become possessed of.*" The italics are ours.

Our readers from this will see that if we have occasion to deal hardly with the Portuguese in

* Proceedings of the Bombay Geographical Society, Report on the Landed Tenures of Bombay, by T. Warden, Esq.—Communicated by Major T. B. Jervis.

the seventeenth century, the English Government of the same period is not a whit behind them in this; that they knew the right and did the wrong. When we came in 1662 to take over this precious dowery the Portuguese would not give it to us. We expected the islands, but they held on to them like grim death; we asked for Colaba, but it was then an island, and we dare not touch it. Salsette, Trombay, Caranja, Elephanta, Butcher, and Hog Islands were all in the same category. We all know that in consequence of this obstinacy 400 Englishmen were left to rot on the barren isle of Angediva. This was the first price, the original purchase-money of Bombay. It was a ghastly infeftment. The island of Bombay was really then of very little value, and an idea may be formed of its resources from the fact that we had a difficulty in raising at first an annual revenue out of it of £2,800, and so late as 1728 we let the whole of Malabar Hill on lease (to a cow-feeder we presume) at a rental of Rs. 130, and the island of Colaba at a proportionate amount. It was *the harbour* that attracted our attention, and the vain attempts we made in Cromwell's time to get possession of it show that there were men even then, with no Suez Canal looming in the distance, who foresaw that Bombay, from its geographical position, was destined to become the key of India. What is now the city must have been a very poor place when the Portuguese came to it in 1532, for our Chief Justice, Sir Michael Westropp, tells us* that it is not even mentioned in the Treaty of Bassein, made that year in favour of the Portuguese, and Dr. Da Cunha tells us there was only one native village, that of Kalpadavee, on the island.† We presume he excepts Walkeshwur which must have had a gathering of holy men round it for centuries and accommodation for many pilgrims who came to it from the Malabar Coast.

The head-quarters of the Portuguese in the Konkan was at Bassein. It was there the General of the North resided and not in Bombay, where we will suppose there was little room for colonial enterprise or few incitements to it. Be that as it may, the dominion of the Portuguese over Bombay, when we came to it, had lasted one hundred and thirty years, a period ample enough to see what stuff they were made of. The world knows that it was not a good dominion.

* 21th June, 1875.

† At Asiatic Society, July 1881.

It produced nothing and has left us nothing, except a portion of that wreck of humanity that still lies stranded on the shores of Western India. So far as Bombay is concerned there is nothing to show that the Portuguese, armed as they were with all the rights that sovereignty implies, were here. Neither road, nor bridge, nor aqueduct, nor tank.* The vestiges of their dominion have passed away as completely as did those of the Vandals in Africa. What we fell heir to by the Treaty of 1661, when Cooke took over the island in 1665 on his own responsibility, and with all the hampering conditions which we afterwards repudiated, we will endeavour to show. Here is the inventory from authentic sources of what we actually received with the island of Bombay :—

1. A four square house, some part of the walls of which may still exist in the arsenal, and which afterwards became our Government House. 2. The garden which surrounded it, verdant with slippered pantaloons, fardingales of frowsy women from Europe, and the *sarries* of " the pampered jades of Asia." 3. Four brass guns. 4. A few houses, interspersed among palm trees,

* We must except part of the gateway and a portion of the lower part of the adjoining wall at the arsenal.

cujaned (*i.e.*, roofed with the leaves of the palmyra palm) where the Fort now is. 5. A population of 10,000, mostly fugitives and vagabonds. 6. Renegade Jesuits who fomented rebellion and endangered our lives. 7. A new chapter in the physical history of man, consequent on the rulers "levelling" down and not levelling up. 8. Half a dozen ricketty forts, such as we see to-day the remains of on Tanna creek. They crowned the knolls of Mahim, Reeva, Worlee, Sion, Sewree, and Mazagon. 9. A colonial Government from Europe, but without the law, the police, or the edûcation of Europe. 10. 40,000 acres of the best land partially submerged by the sea, and growing nothing but samphire.* 11. A few fishermen's huts on Dongaree Hill, and the villages of Parell, Mahim, Worlee, and Mazagon. 12. The ruins of an old stone causeway between Parell and Sion, a veritable "Bridge of Sighs," built as the annalist hath it "out of penances." 13. A climate three-fourths of the

---

* Half way downe,
Hangs one that gathers samphire; dreadful trade.
Shakespeare.

The samphire of Fryer and the flats, as also that of Suakim on the Red Sea, which is turned to profitable account, must be a different species from Shakespeare's samphire, which is saxifragoous, fleshy in the leaf, and makes an admirable pickle. It is still found on some of the most precipitous rocks on the sea coast of Scotland.

virulence of which was owing to the inability of the settlers themselves to comprehend the first principles of sanitary science; a climate which literally devoured every man and woman from England, and sacrificed some of the noblest lives that ever came to Western India. 14. A huge quantity of fish and fishbones. "They gathered them together in heaps and the land stank." This expressive sentence is taken from the unrevised Old Testament, and describes the condition of the Land of Egypt after the great plague of frogs. Such was the Bombay portion of the dowery of Catherine of Braganza.

Having now taken the gilt off the bridescake we fear that few of our readers will be able to recognise in this picture what Bombay has since become, the brightest jewel in the diadem of the Empress of India.

It was in 1675 that Dr. Fryer, a member of the Royal Society, suggested that out of all this scum there might arise another Carthage. He was a far-seeing man, for among the long bead-roll of illustrious names on the page of Bombay history, or books of travels, not one among them all ventures to forecast the greatness of the city or even hazard a conjecture thereon. Xavier,* Heber, Wilson ?

> I do not ask to see
> The distant scene, one step enough for me.

And it was ever thus. Not Aungier, not Wellesley, not Elphinstone, nor the eagle eye of Mackintosh which scans the destiny of nations, vouchsafes a single glance to revive the flagging courage of the plodding servant of Government, or animate the hopes of the merchant or the missionary, who had cast his lot on the dreary shores of old Bombaim. To him Bombay is "the most obscure corner of India."

But from first to last it was all the same ; we sowed the seed and awaited patiently the harvest. In spite of the blundering and villainy of Cooke, the rebellion of Keigwin, and a climate that mowed us down before the reaper's sickle, we held our ground by sending out fresh men to repair disaster. In the dullest and most dis-

---

* Xavier sailed three times from Goa via Chaul to Bassein, once in 1544 and twice in 1548. Most likely he sailed up our harbour and Tanna Creek ; but whichever way he came and went, this route or by the open sea, he was bound to see Malabar Hill and Colaba Point, by whatever names they went in his day. If he saw anything of Mombai, it could only be a stick and red flag on some peer's tomb fluttering in the breeze—

> Where shepherds once were housed in homely sheds,
> Now towers within the clouds advance their heads,
> They viewed the ground of Rome's litigious hall,
> Once oxen low'd where now the lawyers bawl.—*Virgil.*

couraging of times there was always some advance. Sometimes floundering but never despairing, our powers of endurance and administrative ability were tested to the very utmost. The work, however, killed seven Governors in one generation—we mean in thirty years. We may also tack on to this, one ambassador and one admiral. These were the days of darkness, when men's hearts failed them for fear, and when the tumults of the people were like the noise of the sea and the waves roaring. It was then we saw the sun set behind the Dutch fleet, which blocked up the view seawards and hung like a black thunder-cloud at the mouth of Back Bay. It was then that the Great Moghul, or the Seedee for him, was battering at the gates of Bombay Castle. Though the Dutch and the Moghul are now of little account, they were then about the strongest powers respectively in Europe and in Asia. The Dutch in the generation we speak of were the terror of the seas, had burned Sheerness and entered the Medway and the Thames ; and Aurungzebe had insulted the majesty of England by tying the hands of our envoys behind their backs and sending the Governor of Bombay about his business.

But we survived it all. There was a providence that watched over the infancy of Bombay, and well did she stand her baptism of fire. By and bye the great Augean stable was partially cleaned out and the Bombay climate became tolerable. Either good or bad, strong or weak as the party is that useth it; like the sword of Scanderbeg. She chased the pirates from the sea and the Pindarees from the land.* By opening up roads Bombay unlocked the granaries of Western India for her starving children, and by clearing the sea of desperadoes the Indian Ocean became the property of all the nations of the world. She did not wait for the trumpet blast of the Anti-Corn Law League, but quietly on her own account inaugurated Free Trade in 1812 during the Baroda Famine.†

In terms of her first proclamation she became an asylum for all: many men came from the West with the seeds of religion and civilisation, the

* The last of the Pindarees was killed near Asserghur, 1819. Chetoo was wandering about in the neighbourhood seeking rest, and finding none. Determined, if possible, during the negotiations with Jeshwunt Rao, to destroy this last and most determined of the Pindarees, Malcolm sent out eight or nine detachments in pursuit of him. Flying from one, the wretched man well nigh fell into the hands of another; and at last, driven to the jungles, was attacked by a more remorseless enemy than the British. We found his horse and his sword, his bones and his bloody garments. A tiger had fallen upon and devoured the last of the Pindarees.—*Sir John Kaye's Life of Malcolm*, 1856.

† *Basil Hall's Fragments.*

blessings of which are now apparent. They were welcome. Not one of them was injured. During the long period we have held this island —and it is a blessed fact to be able to record— no man has suffered death for his religion. So perfect was the security of life and property that many of the settlers slept with open doors and windows*. At length walls were found to be no longer necessary. They were a hundred years in building, and were demolished not by the hands of an enemy, for no enemy was ever seen within her gates. The same men (or their descendants) who erected them levelled them to the earth, and let him that rebuildeth them beware of the curse of Hiel the Bethelite. Little by little, as from the slime and miasma of some geologic era, an island city rose slowly from the bosom of the sea, fair to look upon, green with the verdure of an eternal summer, beautiful as Tyre and more populous than either ancient Carthage or Alexandria—crowned not only with the monuments of human industry, but with buildings to teach men the art of being industrious ; with a Government India had never

* Many had mistaken views of India, and thought it was not a safe land to travel or reside in. He could tell them from a long life of experience that life and property were more secure than in England. (Laughter and applause.)—*Lord Magdala after Dinner, 10th July, 1876.*

known before, that protects the weak from the oppression of the strong, and measures out equal law to every one irrespective of his colour or his creed.

> Clear innocence her shield ; her breastplate prayers,
> Armour of trustier proof than aught the warrior wears.

WESTERN INDIA IN 1583.

CHAPTER II.

WESTERN INDIA IN 1583.

It requires no very intimate acquaintance with contemporary foreign opinion to recognize the abiding truth of De Tocqueville's remark that the conquest and government of India are really the achievements which give England her place in the opinion of the world.—*Sir Henry Sumner Maine*, 1872.

For a long time we were a very weakly power in Western India, and our Bombay dominion for a hundred years was limited to such an extent that a good pedestrian in a single day might even walk over it. As for Surat, we were for more than a century merely tenants-at-will of the Great Moghul. When we agreed with his Nawab, all went on well: when we disagreed with him, he put us in iron. But frail and limited as this dominion was, we can now in 1881 aver that we have held it absolutely for a longer term than any of the former rulers of Western India. The oldest native of Bombay, even by tradition from his great-grandfather, knows of no other power than the power of England. It has outlived all the Soobadars of the Deccan. We have been longer here than the Peshwas were in Poona or the Nizams in Hyderabad, and our authority dates to a time when even the names of Holkar, Scindia, and Gaekwar were unknown. We forget the Hubshee of Junjeera, who, strange to say, with his semi-African genealogy, has outlived the wreck of nations, and, like Monaco in Europe, may protest against the Republic. It is true we are an alien race. But will you point to us in the history of India a race of sovereigns who were bound to the soil by community of birth, religion, and language? Who was Timoor the Tartar and his house, which for generation after generation from the Peacock Throne lorded it over India? From Tartary, from Room, from Georgia, from Khorasan, from regions beyond the Sutlej, Tartars, Arab mercenaries, and slaves who were themselves bought and sold, built up crown and kingdom from Mount Everest to Malacca. Our vanity is rebuked, however, when we begin to realize that there was a time when the face of an Englishman had not been seen on the shores of Bombay, nor its name on the map of India;

and yet there was such a time. When Shakespear was alive, when Elizabeth reigned, when Mary Queen of Scots was imprisoned, when Knox thundered in St. Giles, when Drake and Raleigh ventured their ships to compete with the galleons of Spain into unknown seas, no man of woman born had yet used English speech within our island. The first English bungalow had not been built, for the first Englishmen had not yet jumped ashore amid huzzas. The first bargain had not been struck, and consequently the grave of the first Englishman had not been dug. The grass on Malabar-hill was a cover for the hare, and a shelf on the cliff a nest for the sea-eagle.

We have been led to these reflections by the perusal of Jean Hugues of Linchotten's great work "Histoire de la Navigation." The author came out to India in 1583 with the Archbishop of Goa, and the copy of his book now before us, the third edition, was published at Amsterdam in 1638. It is in old French, through which we stumble with difficulty, and is full of engravings of scenes and costumes in Western India, taken with the accuracy and executed with the art which distinguished the Dutch in those days, for in these things they were then far ahead of us. It is a large folio in which the author, a Hollander, seems to give an impartial account of the countries through which he passed, and where the pictures become doubly valuable, as they represent the condition of things before the Englishman had put in an appearance on this side of India.

The Portuguese, our readers are aware, had taken possession of our island in 1532, but fifty years after, when our author was at Goa, it seems to have been of no account. He gives a full account of Goa in many pages and half-page descriptions of Cambay, Ormuz, Diu, Damaun, Bassein, Chaul, Dabul, and Onore, commercial emporiums of some note; but Bombay, or *Mombai* as we may then call it, had not even made itself so far known that an intelligent European coming to Goa and describing Western India should take any notice of it. A stranger on the *bourse* at Amsterdam might as well ask for Oorun or Trombay. That it was an outpost in which a few Portuguese from Bassein were stationed, round whom had clustered the cujan huts of Koli or Dongar, we believe. But no indication of such a site is given, and as ecclesiastical annals and Xavier's letters are equally silent on the subject of even a missionary being sent to us, we have come to the conclusion that our infant metropolis had at that time such a small nucleus, that it was not even worth looking after, and was nothing in comparison of, say, Bandora or Mahim,—a sufficient rebuke to our vanity or pride of place, if we have any. There is ample evidence, we think, that the shrine of Walkeshwur is of great antiquity, as on our very first contact with those shores, in 1662, it was a place of pilgrimage, and had doubtless been resorted to for ages by the natives along the coast. Of the harbour itself I am reminded that from remote times it has been a place whence the products of this region found an outlet, and at the same time an inlet for the produce and handiwork of other countries,—a commerce manipulated by the merchants of Tanna, and previously by Kallyan, before Bombay comes before us on the page of history; and though there is no evidence on the subject, it is highly probable that for the protection of that commerce a beacon fire was kept burning on Colaba point at night.*

* "To-day I went to Colaba. On the southern extremity of this island stands a light-house, where fire is kept during the night as a signal to ships which come into the Bombay harbour."—*Dr. Hove*, 1787.

But let us see something of Goa by the help of Linschotten's pictures.

THE MAN ABOUT TOWN.

It was during the time when Akbar reigned in Delhi, in 1583, that I entered the city of Goa, which was then in the acme of its glory. The Portuguese had been here 73 years, and being an idle man, I was resolved to have a look at it. The name *griffin* is not yet invented, so I am nicknamed *reynole*. But I do not mind this, and plunge at once into the heart of the city, feeling rather hotter than in Antwerp. All the races of Asia, even the Chinaman, are here bargaining with, or cheating, or amusing each other. Amid bags of pepper, bales of silk, and boxes of opium I take my stand, and see what I have come to see. The first thing I observe is that the Portuguese are our masters, and that every man among them is armed, riding, walking, sailing, or palanquinborne, and every retainer is armed, down to the veriest *chokra*. It seems to me that this does not imply much security of life or property. It is now early in the morning, and there is a great fair every day between 7 and 9, a kind of *bourse*, where men from all parts of the world make their market. The tongues are of Babel, and the noise deafening. Nobles or Hidalgoes swagger, with ostrich-feather stuck at one side of their wide-awakes. Here negro slaves, Arab horses, and dead men's effects are sold by auction. Men die here, even the Viceroy, and if he dies, his bed is sold from under him at once, and the amount credited to his executors; the rights of creditors, widows, and orphans must be respected. I observe that the Deccany men who have come in are all sandalled: other natives, except beggars, wear shoes. We stand for a moment at a marriage procession. The musicians and their native instruments are familiar to us. And there at her curtained windows, by the lattice-work appears in all her glory and debasement *Inda meretryx saltando et canendo, victim queretans.* She hath cast down many wounded, yea, many strong men have been slain by her. A Lusitanian swell is hovering about; and we are told the reason why these gentry are so well clothed is that they have one suit only among three, and that when the lucky turn comes for one to go on promenade, the other two go to bed, or rejoice in nether garments suitable for indoors in hot climates. Equestrians are numerous, and the horses are gaily caparisoned in kincob and velvet.

The harness, saddle, and horse-cloth are fringed with small bells, which make a mighty jingling and savour of Lyons or Paris. The inevitable man with the whisk follows suit. To see the ladies I have to go to church and stand an amazing amount of incense. One now emerges from her closed palanquin like a bride from her curtained couch. She has downcast eyes, and her hair brushed back from her forehead *à la mode*. A rosary is in her hand, and a jewelled crosslet on her bosom. A maid stands expectant with a book, another with a fan, a third with a cushion, and a fourth with a Persian carpet rolled up. She alights, steadies herself on *terra firma*, for there is a mystery about her feet, which is only explained by cork pattens six inches high, on which she has to move gingerly enough. Two *cavalieri serventi*, one on each side, support this angel of the church to her seat. The locomotion up the aisle takes her ten minutes.* I find that this is a terrible country for jealousy, and that the ladies, married or single, are guarded by a gang of slaves. I call at the house of a rich Portuguese

* What appeared to be wooden boxes, where the feet of the ladies ought to be, were a perfect enigma to me. The explanation, however, is given by Mr. Fonseca in his *City of Goa*.

and as soon as my name is announced I hear a clapping of hands, and I know that this is a sign in Turkey for the women to fly to the dim recesses of the harem. When a man comes into your bungalow, offer him at once a seat as good as you have yourself, hear what he has got to say, and bow him politely out. If a man comes into church, rise and salute him at once. Otherwise, if you do not attend to these maxims, you may, when out unwittingly on a stroll, get a bamboo on your back, or have a fillet filled with sand swung mercilessly on your head by some ruffian hired for the purpose.

The gentlemen wear peaked beards and moustachios turned up at the ends. The ladies float along *en boddice* on ornamented open palanquins; and over the head, half seen, rises an Elizabethan canopy (this is the age of Elizabeth), the green folds of which fall gracefully, supported on each side by a tassel as much for ornament as for use. The palanquin here is not a wooden box, nor a tonjon, but exhibits the harmony of form to perfection, and the bearers themselves are Portuguese, nearly as well clothed, to all appearance, as their masters. Ladies, indoors, wear shoes without stockings. Nunneries have not yet been established. There will be plenty of them by-and-bye.

The *entourage* of the European bungalows differs little from our own. A native climbing a toddy-tree with knife in his waistband, a woman drawing water, a parrot in a cage, and a pet monkey hanging on to the verandah by its hind legs, with a church in the distance, constitute an amusing and suggestive picture.

KING OF BALLAGAT.

I hear the sound of horns: there is a sudden rush of the crowd, and aloft in awful state borne upon a palanquin comes an ambassador from one of the Deccany kings. I know these sturdy bearers from beyond the mountains, as they pass into the city at a swinging trot, and now near the end of their journey, take their "canter up the avenue" or a last spurt as they breast the hill. A sombrero-wallah has enough to do to keep the sun from the dusky countenance of His Excellency, who stolidly contemplates the strange manners and costumes of the *Feringhi* which they have brought in their caravels, across the *kala-panee* from the other side of the world. His retainers are armed with bow and arrow, with spear and javelin, and shield of rhinoceros-hide from Africa; dusty and wayworn from some far off city in the Deccan—Beder, or Bejapore, or Golconda and its diamonds. Bejapore was now in all its glory, its citadel a crown of joy and rejoicing to it, and the architect of the big dome of Mahmood Shah busy at his work.* He frowns with contempt upon the Lusitanian and his works of *Sheitan*. Even his ships, are they not the works of the devil? A land of monks and monasteries, where their men are women, and their women children. Kaffirs every one of them.

THE MASTER-MARINER.

Before the Portuguese conquered the land here, they had to conquer the sea on the way to it. Hence these were the great days for the Master-Mariner. To be the captain of a ship was next door to being a prince. To round the Cape of Storms, to wrestle with the spirit of the storm like Da Gama in the Lusiad, to wield dominion of the seas like Cabral, was to be a king of men and crowned with acclaim by your fellows. Your name was written in letters of gold and colours

---

* *The biggest dome in the world.*—Pantheon, diameter 142 feet, height 143 feet; Duomo Florence, diameter 139 feet, height 310 feet; St. Peter's, diameter 139 feet, height 330 feet; St. Sophia, diameter 115 feet, height 201 feet; St. Paul's, diameter 112 feet, height 215 feet; Bejapore, diameter 124 feet, height 198 feet.

on the portals of the Viceroy's Palace, where the wondering stranger beholds with awe and pride the name of every ship and the date of its departure from Lisbon, with the date of its arrival, the New Jerusalem of the storm-tost sailor.* Henceforth your ship was among the immortals more famous than any one in the long catalogue of Homer's fleet. High over the rest shone the mighty name of Albuquerque, date 1510, for though he was not *primus in Indis,* no man until his time had ever heard the flapping of European sails in the waters of Goa, for

> "He was the first that ever burst
> Into that silent sea"

that lies beside the island of the thousand-and-one palm-trees.

DECLINE AND FALL.

It is interesting to note that the causes which un-made Goa and made Bombay are apparent at a very early stage of their existence. It would be unfair to contrast the colonial policy of Portugal in 1580 with that of any European nation in 1680, but we are fairly entitled to place it side by side with the attitude assumed by our own first settlers towards the surrounding peoples in

* Vessels were then few and far between.

Western India, after making allowance for such progress as had been made in the century between 1580 and 1680 in the art of colonisation and the doctrine of toleration. Goa and Bombay are islands of about the same size; they both have magnificent harbours. Upon the one the Portuguese sat down to exploit, and on the other the British. But the Portuguese were first in the race, they were stronger than we, by virtue of military conquest, and they had a wider area on which to exploit. The Colonial Empire of Portugal in the sixteenth century was a great empire, quite as great to the then known world as the Colonial Empire of England is in the nineteenth century. Their enemies were fewer in number, and less formidable by sea and land. They had the Dutch to oppose them. So had we. And what were the Mahomedan kings who had then established themselves in the Deccan compared to the daring of Seevajee or the might of Aurungzebe?

When we sat down to our work of government, the same difficulties that confronted them confronted us. There was a community made up of the same materials, a number of people drawn together of the different races, languages, and religions of Asia. Taking our stand, we appear both going to the same destination; but the point is a kind of reversing station, for though we set off together, the means which each takes to accomplish his government drives us in different directions. We both mean to govern, and we both do it in a different way. The evil that was bound up in the existence of the Portugal of these days was Church and State, not the one without the other, but the one *with* the other. If you accept my jurisdiction, you must accept my religious belief.

Hence pagodas, tanks, mosques, synagogues, and a whole jungle of unbeliefs from their point of view were cleared out of the cities of Western India, which presented the appearance of a compact form of Christianized communities with one aim and serving one master; but it was merely in appearance. The device was a hollow sham and makebelief, as every traveller who visited these cities in the 16th century testifies. Their own Camoens says:—"This land is the mother of great villains, and the stepmother of honourable men." The outer framework and policy of it was a sham. Human nature will not stand this sort of thing; so one day a priest is shot outside of Bassein, another day a monk is poisoned in a buggalow, and on a third news comes that four missionaries are massacred at Cuncolim. They are claimed as martyrs by the church, but they are martyrs to the stupidity and misgovernment of mankind.

We have touched in the previous chapter on the policy which was inaugurated by the English founders of Bombay, that all religions should have fair play. A later chapter will show how Aungier dealt with the Banias, and that he induced them to settle here by allowing them their religious rites, marriage processions, and burning of their dead. It was only after our occupation that the first Tower of Silence was erected on Malabar-hill; synagogue, mosque, and fire-temple, all make their appearance afterwards. We began by proclaiming Bombay an asylum for all, and this was the corollary. The silk weavers came in a body from Chaul, and we had to build houses for them. Then came the Parsees, who could build their own houses, and ships as well, one of which fought at the battle of Navarino, and on board another was written "The Star-spangled Banner." But whether it was the Banias of Diu or the Bhatias of Cutch, all were welcome. We hailed also the Jews from the river of Babylon. And this is the reason why

Bombay now contains 777,000 inhabitants, and is not, like Goa, a huge grassy tomb. We were not, and it is as well to remember this, *Societa propaganda Fide*, but the United Company of Merchants of England trading in the East Indies.

We need not, however, lay the flattering unction to our souls that we brought this doctrine of toleration to Asia. We found it here when we came, and wisdom will not die with us. For centuries, aye to the most remote times, there had been a most extensive commercial intercourse carried on by various nationalities along the sea board of Western India, so it had become pretty generally understood that if you wished to trade with a man, it was not necessary to knock him down, if he differed from you in religious belief. So the question had been very much solved in the maritime towns. For example, Seymour was very near Bombay. The site of it is still disputed. There were 10,000 Muslims in it.* The Hindus could not have been very intolerant here. Then at one time there were seen in the harbour of Ormuz 400 Chinese junks.† There must have been toleration there for the disciples of Confucius.

Seevajee neither burned mosque nor pagoda, and

* Aboulfeda par Reinaud.

† W. S. Lindsay's Merchant Shipping, 1875.

allowed dissent in his army, for there were many Muslims in it, and they had their own butcher.* And when Aungier took in hand the mongrel community of 10,000 vagabonds who swarmed round the Castle of Bombay, he found the punchayet ready to his hand†,—an institution native to India, which gave to every caste the elements of self-government, or, as Elphinstone ingeniously hath it, gave to the people justice when they could not get it elsewhere.

THE INQUISITION.

We learn from Mr. Fonseca's History of Goa that the horrors of the Inquisition have been much overrated. It is pleasing to think that it was a mild and beneficent institution, and that the dreams of childhood from Foxe's Book of Martyrs and Willie Lithgow's travels‡ are a delusion. We may now die happy, so far as the Inquisition is concerned. It was a great enemy of rich men, for their property was confiscated. But for a poor man? Why, he had a cell of his own, and, if an European, bread and meat to his dinner twice a week, with a bed and coverlet to protect him from the night dews. Not that the place was open

* Fryer.
† Bruce's Annals.
‡ In Spain, but nearly of the same date as Linschotten.

—only the cells had windows and doors. There was a great air of peace and tranquillity about the place, which arose from the fact that the warders in the galleries, who saw everything, would allow no noise. And they were right, for noise and tranquillity are strange bed-fellows. It must have been something of this kind that fascinated Ralph Fitch, an English merchant, who at Ormuz was kindly offered a free passage to Goa to explain matters, and is now here in free quarters in this year of grace 1583. If we remember rightly, he—like Baron Trenck elsewhere—found the place so comfortable, he wouldn't come out. "If I only once got to England, how happy should I be to come out again. Oh, gentlemen of England who live at home at ease, you little know the comforts of the Inquisition."

I read further that the ailments of the inmates are carefully attended to, that the Inquisitor with his secretary and interpreter—how considerate!—comes twice a month specially to inquire about them. I marvel at the ventilation of the cells. The doors are kept wide open to every breeze that blows every morning from 6 to 11. Sanitation is a perfect model. The etceteras are cleared out once in four days. Remember this is 1583. The eating hours are far in advance of any other town in India. Breakfast at 6 a.m., dinner at 11 a.m., and supper at 4 p.m. No wonder people who have been in the civil jails prefer the inquisition. Then *autos da fé* are not numerous; sometimes one did not occur for several years. Besides, there was no reason for your being burned alive. The alternative was always open to you, to confess Christianity, in which case you were only strangled, justifying the old saw, "confess and be hanged." The business afterwards was merely secondary and a matter of form, perfectly painless, and required no display of fortitude, for fire or water is all the same to a dead man; and it did not matter if your shin-bones, carried by a lot of guys in wooden boxes, rattled at the tail of processions for a century to come. I know Dellon tells differently to all this, but he lived a century later, and I do not believe Dellon in many things.

To speak seriously. At the trial there was no exhibition of the rude instruments and coarse enginery of persecution to harrow the poor soul. Some fools in Scotland in the seventeenth century tried this, but it only turned out, to use their own language, "an indulgence to tender consciences." You remember *Old Mortality* and the never-to-be-forgotten scene when Hugh Macbriar, *alias*

Mackail, stood before the judges in the High Court of Commission. A crimson curtain was withdrawn and revealed the grim manipulator at an oaken table, laid out with the horrible apparatus of torture, rack, boots, and thumbscrew, and that, as Sir Walter tells us, though a touch of nature brought the blood to Macbriar's cheek, he gazed at the apparition with composure. So clumsy were these old workmen, Lauderdale and Mackenzie, in dealing with heretics. They had not learned their lessons at this school. Here we act differently. We draw aside a green taffeta curtain and reveal—the cross. It leans against the tapestry on the walls, looms big, and stretches away up to the groined roof.* It is a black cross. Yes, under this holy emblem the work is done. The High Court of Commission and the Inquisition are nearly convertible terms. But Portugal or Scotland, it is all the same, no matter under what sky the deed is done; the palm-tree groweth here, and "the broom with its tassels on the lea" yonder, but it does not alter the eternal nature of things. Soon or

* According to a tradition current among the inhabitants of Goa, every individual charged with witchcraft or any offence against the Catholic religion was placed before the crucifix, when all of a sudden a thrill appeared to pass through his whole frame. He trembled from head to foot, and at last dropped senseless on the ground, incapable of fixing his eyes on it anymore.—Fonseca's *City of Goa*, 1878.

syne the end of these things is death—death not only to the victim, but death to the political system which first caught him, then incarcerated him, now tries him, and will burn him. No Government, be it Catholic or Protestant, be it Muslim or Brahmin, can engage in this warfare with impunity. To rid herself of it was the salvation of Scotland, to continue in it was the doom of Portugal.

On the yesterday of 1583 Portugal was a first-class power, and might have stood against the world; now none so poor as do her reverence.

MISCELLANEA.

Linschotten tells us that the non-Christian inhabitants of Goa had to leave the town every evening at sound of tattoo, and dare not practise their *superstitions diaboliques* under pain of death. He argues bad consequences to the country that every man serving under Lisbon, from the Viceroy downwards, has a tenure of only three years of office, and hastens to make the most of it.

The Goojuratis and Banians are the most subtile merchants in the whole of India. The climate and coast thirty miles north and south of Chaul (which embraces Bombay) are more salubrious than elsewhere. He states that the labourers and peasants who have made profession of Christianity are little better than the pagans, and that they practise pagan rites by connivance of the Inquisitors.

In 1583 concubinage and bastardy had already done their work, for the offspring of Portuguese fathers and native mothers are named *mestici*, and that of Indian fathers and Portuguese mothers *castici*.

On the cultivation and trade in opium he states that while much of it comes from Aden and the Red Sea, the greater part comes from Cambaia and the Deccan, meaning no doubt from the Malwa districts through the Deccan.* He is silent, as far as we can gather, on its export to China, or of its being used by the Chinese.

The following sentence, written in 1583, may have significance for Scotsmen on the eve of St. Andrew's Day, for we have seen the antiquity of tartan gravely disputed. Describing some cloths he says they are "bigarrez et semblable aux draps d'Ecosse;" so the Tartan beats them yet, and we shout *Doch in Dorus!*

ARCHÆOLOGICAL NOTE ON LINSCHOTTEN.

The binding and about 100 pages of letter-press, with the engravings, are in good preservation, but our "mortual enemies," the white-ants, have made fearful havoc of the *Cartes Geographiques* at the

* Duarte Barbosa, 1501-17 gives opium as one of the products of India.

end of the volume. The book boards at first sight look in capital order, but a narrower inspection discloses the fact that in the end one, two dozen holes have been bored, as if with a gimlet, through the book board, which is one-eighth of an inch in thickness. Once through this outer work, they have literally run riot, and round holes deftly cut out, the size of a sixpence, are perforated through the maps and a hundred pages of letter-press. The *incisiori*, if there is such a word, have apparently burrowed and littered here for a century ;* their final achievement being a chasm about two inches in diameter and half an inch deep. In a print about two feet long, representing a morning scene of the Goa Crawford Market of these days, they have spared neither age nor sex, and performed decapitations on hidalgos and their wives which would have astonished the Inquisition. So fragile and tindery was this portion of the work, that we dare not touch it. But the advent of the chief of the Archæological Department, Dr. Burgess, who is much accustomed to deal with ruins in their last stage of decomposition, relieved us of this responsibility, and he boldly disintegrated the shattered sheets which had been so riddled by the shot of the enemy. When the great map was spread out by the Indian anti-

* Since this was written we learn that the mischief was all done in six months.

quary, it looked like the flag of Drumclog, or let us say, as it is the work of a Hollander, like the English ensigns taken by Van Tromp, which are hung up in Rotterdam Cathedral. Our zeal was rewarded. There on the faded and battered surface lay the name of our dear old *Bombaim,* not itself dim or tarnished, but strong in the vigour of perpetual youth, her castellated battlements looking out on the Arabian Sea. With half the kingdom of Bisnagar eaten up, this was something to be thankful for. There is no confirmation here of the Portuguese name of *Buon-Bahia* ever having been given to our city. The date is 1594 on the margin of this map, which describes the geographical knowledge of 1583, and is the earliest record of the city we are aware of. The towns along this coast are Damaom, Danixno, Bacaim, Maim, Bombaim, Chaul, Danda, Quelecim, Dabul, R de Vitere, Zanguizara, Debetele, Cintapore, which we leave our readers to identify. Broach and Cambaia are north of Delhi, but it does not matter.

In the pictures we may add that while there are many Europeans and Natives consuming strong drinks, there is not a single trace of *tobacco* or other smoking indulgencies,—confirmation, if any were needed, that Raleigh's discovery came afterwards, and found its way from America.

BOMBAY BEGINNINGS.

CHAPTER III.

BOMBAY BEGINNINGS.

There was one man in Bombay in 1674 who read the account of the barbaric splendour of Seevajee's coronation, and had time to turn a philosophic eye on the infant colony—"The people who live here are a mixture of most of the neighbouring countries most of them fugitives and vagabonds"——And then he adds, as with the blast of a prophetic trumpet—"licensed out of policy as the old Numidians to build up the greatest empire in the world."* Who knew what would become of Bombay? Where are now the rich towns of Dacca, Malacca, or Macao? It is true that it was given to us, and that no man can cast in our teeth that we took this part of India. But everything was against it, and when we got it, it was not worth the having. Charles II. soon

* Fryer.

found out that it was a white elephant and handed it over to the East India Company, in free and common soccage at ten pounds per annum in gold. From the 8th January, 1665, when Humphrey Cooke took "the earth and stones" of Bombay, from Fonseca, Notary Public of Bassein, by public document, and for the next thirty years, it was surrounded by a blazing conflagration, the whole neighbouring continent being in a ferment. How it came out of its troubles is a perfect mystery. Our readers will recollect that its rise was contemporaneous with that of Seevajee, and that he held every stronghold on the coast for four degrees of latitude except Goa, Junjeera, Chaul, and Bombay. Then there was the Moghul of Delhi with whom we were often at war, the Dutch, the French, the Portuguese, and last, though not least, the Seedee from Junjeera," that damned train the scum of Africa inhabited by straggling runagates." There was mutiny, famine, and pestilence.

The mutineers held Bombay for one year; the Seedee held Bombay, except the Fort, for one year, and twice (in 1691 and 1702) the plague appeared and reduced the English garrison to seventy-six men. Once the standard of rebellion was hoisted among the Jesuits of Salsette, Cooke, the first Governor, becoming the first rebel. Once the Dutch appeared at the mouth of the harbour, and Seevajee's fleet once entered Back Bay. Bombay was at the mercy of the Seedee for those great necessaries, beef, mutton, grain and firewood, and he could, by a *hookum,* put the city on fish diet. Once it depended upon the island of Kenery for its supply of firewood; with the society of a *very* few English ladies, without gas, without firewood, without ice or tramways, with the certainty of not receiving a reply to their letters for two years from England, with their houses glazed with oyster-shells, and the Apollo, or *Pulla* Bunder (not our one), nearly impassable with mud, we need not wonder if during the dark days of the monsoon the citizens took to drink and divination. When would a ship arrive with news? Ah, that was an important question which necromancers (and Time) alone could answer, and wonderfully correct answers they gave, from the fate of a Governor down to that of the first *spin* who jumped ashore in hoop and farthingale. Then there was the dread of being poisoned. As an antidote they drank out of a cup made out of the horn of a rhinoceros, and wore as a jewel the marvellous snake-stone to shield them from the deadly bite of the cobra. Unfortunately, as we should say, drink remained. To a people who had no clocks and who measured time by the dropping of water, drink was convenient. There was first beer, and the *sack* that killed Tom Coryat on the banks of the Taptee. Then there was Bombay punch, a mixture of brandy, rose-water, and lime-juice, "that accursed Bombay punch, to the shame, scandal and ruin of religion;"* there was jagree arrack, distilled from sugar, mixed with water and the bark of the babul tree as hot as brandy; there was fool rack made from the blubber or carvel of the sea, and so called from its making fools of all who drank of it. Everything came "ready as the handle of a pintstoup." In their "gay humours" they quaffed a glass of *datura* and water, which had hitherto been only used for the killing of infants in Kattywar. *Bhang* and *hashish* did the rest. After drinking toddy rapidly, they took a disease called *barbieri* or *berri berri* in which a man tottered in his gait like a dying sheep or span round like a teetotum. On fish diet, and amid stinking fish, in constant alarms and drunken debauches, it was no wonder that the Angel of Death descended and the plague held Bombay in its grip, reducing its English population from 800 to 80. After

* Governor Aungier.

this there was a goodly show of tombstones at Mendham's Point, which the sailors caught sight of on entering Bombay harbour.* Verily "two monsoons were" more than "the life of man" in those days.

There was no daily newspaper in Bombay, or it might have had fine sensation placards :—

"*Plague Bulletin.*—Only three Civil Servants now alive, 1692. Angediva. 381 English soldiers dead out of 500."

"The Seedee lands at Sewree with 20,000 men."

"Bartholomew Harris and the whole factory at Surat put in prison."

"Vaux, Governor of Bombay, found in traitorous correspondence with the French."

"Sir John Child, Captain-General and Admiral of all the forces by sea and land in Northern India, bones the Building Fund of the Cathedral, Rs. 50,000."

"The brother-in-law of Child, one Ward, tampers with Seevajee to effect a landing on the island."

"Child sends a Banyan to Surat to poison one of his Council."

Another Member of Council flies and dies among the Sanganian pirates. "Dead and gone to the devil," wrote Child pathetically.

* This was the first English burying-ground. The tombs were all demolished when Sonapore was opened in 1760.

A man is hanged on Tuesday, and on the following Friday the judge summons him to appear! Not at that bar I ween. The judge forgot all about it, but the Recording Angel doubtless took a note of it. The hour in which the judge awaited that dead man's appearance must have been the darkest hour in the history of Bombay. But it is one consolation to know or believe that when these wicked men were in power the voice of flattery was unknown. "He that sayeth to the wicked, thou art righteous, him shall the people curse, nations shall abhor him," so the wretched race, if it ever existed, of panders and parasites, have been consigned to oblivion, while their masters have been "hung in chains" for the benefit of posterity.

The question may now be asked, why was Bombay not snuffed out like the settlements of Angengo, Onore, or Gombroon?* Why does the traveller not now seek out its ruins like those of Ormus, Chaul, Goa, or Bassein, overgrown with

* The *Bulldog of Onore.*—An English factory subordinate to Tellicherry. In 1670 the chief of the English factory got a fine English bulldog from the captain of a ship. After the ship was gone, the factory consisting of eighteen persons, were going a hunt and carried the bulldog with them, and passing through the town the dog seized a cow devoted to the pagoda and killed her. Upon which the priests raised a mob, who murdered the whole factory. But some natives who were friends to the English made a large grave and buried them all in it. The chief of Carwar sent a stone to be put on the grave with an incription "That this is the burial-place of John Best with seventeen other Englishmen who were sacrificed to the fury of a mad priesthood and an enraged mob."—*Hamilton's New Account*, 1720.

sacred Banian or religious fig? It was clearly the will of God that Bombay was not to perish, and to this end, he gave to the men who founded it noble resolutions mauger many defections which we have not failed to enumerate. For we shall observe that amid all this dissolution of morals, never more conspicuous than in the end of the seventeenth century, there were among the English (and we use the word in the generic sense) who first colonised Bombay, men who knew the right and did it, men who kept alive the spirit of just acts, the spirit of forbearance and toleration, and above all the spirit of liberty and ancient freedom inherited from their ancestors.* We have given a sentence from Aungier. It is brief, but reveals the noble character of the man. England gave her best blood in the foundation of Bombay, for when the sword, famine, and pestilence had done their work, fresh supplies were forthcoming, to carry commerce and civilization into distant regions and to subjugate by their influence the beastly and barbarous habits of swarthy races of men, and to show by their example that the principle of free inquiry and private judgment was a surer title to

* Even the mutineers we have alluded to handed over to the East India Company the treasure they captured in the Fort to the last rupee.—*Hamilton's East India Gazetteer.*

dominion than the sword of Philip or the Inquisition of Torquemada.

Hence men of every nation, as they still do, flocked under the standard of Bombay Castle, and the population rapidly increased from 10,000 to 50,000. Even her enemies did not hesitate to entrust their lives and property to her protection. To many people these may seem wild assertions, but we can give a reason for the faith that is in us, and here it is. Khafi Khan, to whom we owe the best history of these times, was in the service of Aurungzebe, was a bigoted Muslim, and a hater of the English. He came on a visit to Bombay in 1694 after the first great plague. He came from Surat, where the English Governor had been put in irons for months by Aurungzebe. English pirates had just seized the richest pilgrim ship from Mocha with fifty-two lakhs under circumstances of horrible barbarity, two events calculated to produce great exasperation on both sides. He did not come as a diplomatist, simply as a merchant carrying piece-goods to the value of two lakhs to Raighur, that hot-bed of political discontent. He might have well paused on the frontier, and the Portuguese advised him against coming. But he says :—"I, however, put my trust in God and went to the Englishman." He was right: we did not burn either mosque or pagoda. The Governor of Bombay gave him a public reception, a kind of Durbar. There were 7,000 soldiers, Native and European, youths and gray-haired men, and some fair-haired children with blue caps with pearl and tassel, the men and women of the next generation. Khafi Khan was not a coward; on the contrary, he was decidedly cheeky and told the Governor some most unpleasant things, true and untrue; told him he was a rebel for coining money in the name of his impure King (he could only have heard of Charles II.), denounced the seizure of the big ship by Englishmen, and gently reminded him of the cruel fates of the Kings of Bejapore and Hyderabad and the ghastly sight at Toolapore, where the son of Seevajee was executed. The lesson intended was that what Aurungzebe had done he might do again. The Governor listened patiently. It was dignity and impudence, *a la Landseer* with dogs converted into human beings. We give his own words, "On hearing this the Governor laughed loudly." And Mashallah! after a few words in season Khafi Khan was allowed to depart in peace, with his oxen and his sackcloth* and his inner man no doubt replenished with *kabob* and *pilau*. As he walked out of the fort gate he felt that his head was on his shoulders.

The English laughed. Long may they do so. It was the laugh of conscious strength, of men made great by hardship. Mere levity to Monk and Muslim! But every reader of these dismal times will thank God for such noble courage and right good cheer amid unparalleled disasters, and re-echo the prayer of Burns appropriate to every age and every islander—

> "Then, however crowns and coronets be rent,
> A virtuous populace may rise the while
> And stand a wall of fire around our much-loved isle."

MORTUARY RETURNS.

Humphrey Cooke, Sir Gervase Lucas, Sir George Oxenden, Gerald Aungier, Henry Oxenden, Sir John Child, and Bartholomew Harris, are the names of the Governors of Bombay (either independent or subordinate to Surat) during the first thirty years of its existence, say from 1665 to about the end of the century.

They all died here or in Surat. Our Admiral, Sir Edward Shipman, died at Angediva, and our Ambassador, Sir William Norris, died on his way

* All English cloth then so called.

home. Vaux, who acted *pro tem.*, was drowned with his wife in the Tapti. Gray, who was to have succeeded Aungier, died. Of their immediate successors, one, Sir John Gayer, was imprisoned by the Moghul, and another, Sir Nicolas Waite, was dismissed by the English.

They did not find Bombay an *Eldorado*, for the days had evidently not yet arrived when men amassed fortunes quickly and returned to spend them in England.

We mention these names to show who were the men to whom we are indebted for laying the foundations of Bombay in tempestuous times, and organising the basis of the polity on which the government of this Island was afterwards conducted. We say *Island*,* for our interest in Western India for ninety years was concentrated within that sixteen square miles which lies between Sion Fort and Colaba Point. Among these giants of early Bombay times, we shall meet with all varieties and shades of character. Cooke was a most wretched man. He was not a *pucka* Governor. He made himself Governor,

* ACQUISITIONS.—Bombay 1665; Bankotc 1756; Salsette, Trombay, Elephanta, Butchers Island, Karanja, and Hog Island 1775; Kolaba, Angria's Territory, 1810.

and a most *cutcha* one he was.* He purloined the revenues, he accepted bribes, he manufactured title-deeds, he became a rebel against the Government he had sworn to defend, and worst of all, when poor old Shipman died, leaving £4,420 after his three years' service, Cooke, who had been his secretary, charged his widow fifteen per cent. on the estate. Child, the brother of the Chairman of the East India Company, while in Bombay was Governor-General of India, and while his character has been defamed by his enemies, it has been lauded by the Company, by whom he was presented on one occasion with one thousand guineas. Aungier, without title or distinction of any kind, seems to us to have been the greatest of them all. He saved Surat and Bombay, not only from capture and disgrace, but from utter destruction. Without Aungier we are safe in saying that Bombay would have been lost to the English nation. It would have fallen a prey to the Seedee or Seevajee, or the Dutch, or some other nation, European or Asiatic; and for the fact that it did not to do so we have to thank Aungier.

There is something touching in the old man's

* Cooke's having taken over Bombay without its dependencies involved us in fearful trouble for more than a century.

request to resign and go home, and then—the inevitable.

"There is a tomb in Surat," says Mr. Campbell in the *Gazetteer*, "without an inscription, supposed to be that of Aungier." He does not need it. *Si monumentum quœris circumspice.* We may well pause and drop a tear on the grave of Aungier—

> "No sculptured marble here, no pompous lay,
> No storied urn, nor animated bust,"

for, no martyr, who ever died by stake or faggot, has a left fairer name or a more unsullied reputation than Gerald Aungier. Why do we recall these facts to the memory of the reader? Why do we bring forth forgotton lore from dusty recesses? To keep alive the memories of our great men—precious nowhere else, if not in Bombay.

These were the early Governors, but we must remember that a Governor then was Commander-in-Chief, Chief Justice, Port Trust, including the Fortifications, Chamber of Commerce and Municipal Corporation all rolled into one. He was liable to great temptations. This was the age when the King of England sold his country to France and French mistresses. If the master is not a model of virtue, we need not look for much in the servant at one of the outposts of civilization. Some men seem to begrudge them their very tombstones* as if they had enriched themselves at the expense of the nation, when, in truth, it was they who enriched England. The Americans are wise in their generation, and do not dive too deeply into Paul Jones, who first unfurled the flag of their freedom on the Atlantic Ocean.† Let us follow their example. The men who built up the fabric of Bombay's greatness on Rs. 200 per mensem‡ may well be excused when they occupied their leisure hours in making out invoices of pepper and cardamoms, or in looking over account sales of Golconda diamonds. At all events the voice of calumny may be hushed for ever by the verdict, "*Died at their post.*"

EXCHANGE

Is a tough subject, but is easier to deal with in the past than in the future. We may presume that *hoondies* or inland bills were in circulation

* Eastwick in "Murray's Guide," Ed. 1857.

† "Our First Century" Devens, Ontario, 1878.

‡ £300 per annum at exchange of 2s. 6*d*. Even making allowance for the difference in the value of money in these times and adding all perquisites, this sum is a small salary for such an office.

in India as bank-notes were in China centuries before we touched these shores.

> " Blest paper credit ! last and best supply
> That lends corruption lighter wings to fly.
> Gold imp'd by thee can compass hardest things
> Can pocket states, can fetch and carry Kings."

Tom Coryat in 1616 valued his rupee at 2*s*. 6*d*., and in 1664 Bernier wrote " a rupee is about twenty-nine pence." Gilchrist in his *Vade Mecum*, 1825 : " There have been instances of some firms declining to offer 2*s*. 6*d*. for a Sicca rupee, bills being payable at six months after sight in Europe, while others whose stability appeared equally solid offered 2*s*. 9*d*. for the same accommodation." Our belief is that there were no exchange banks in Bombay, until the Oriental Bank Corporation opened in 1842.

It would thus appear that exchange during the seventeenth, eighteenth, and first quarter of the nineteenth centuries ranged from 2*s*. 6*d*. to 2*s*. 9*d*. We have seen even 3*s*. mentioned. It is not, however, all gold that glitters, and remitters need not envy those times.

The Sicca rupee, which was the current medium until 1835, had eight per cent. more silver in it than the Company's rupee, and a thirty days' sight bill in 1694 really meant a bill at thirteen months' date. Ships then took twelve months, and, in 1825, four to six months to make the passage to England. Besides money in Bombay was then worth twenty per cent.

PROFITS OF TRADE.

Civilians at this time, after paying natives 20 per cent., made large profits, trading with China and other places. The two following extracts show what profits were common. They are from the Company's Records :—

1675.—Pepper was 7*d.* per lb. in England, and here 2½*d.* They write that unless 30 per cent. profit can be made "the Indian trade would become unproductive."

Now for diamonds. The period had not yet, if it ever, arrived, described by Pope, when

> "Asleep and naked as an Indian lay
> An honest factor stole a gem away."

But the demand for diamonds was very large in Europe at this time. Our readers will recollect that this was the showy age of Charles II. and Louis XIV., when worthless women in a blaze of diamonds flaunted on the glacé floors of Versailles and Hampton Court, and when nothing was esteemed

> "More precious than Golconda's gems
> Or star in angel's diadems."

The Court write in 1680 : "If the profit on

diamonds sold in England should exceed £60 per cent. (including interest and insurance) such excess was to be equally divided, one moiety to belong to the Company, and the other to the President Agents and Councils by whom the diamonds had been obtained, in equal proportions, *but not to be paid till their return to England.*" Cautious Court !

THE COTTON TRADE.

There seems to have been a forecast of a cotton export. The Company in 1684 sent out the first cotton screw, but the earliest notice we meet with in the East India Records is dated 1693, when instructions are sent to Sir John Gayer "always to have in readiness a large quantity of pepper and *cotton-wool,* to meet the arrival of the shipping."

These are the initial letters of the Bombay cotton trade, which has grown into an export of one million bales. It had been an export from Tanna in Marco Polo's time.

THE IMPORTS.

In the first years were greatly in timber, iron and iron work for the fortifications, and cotton cloths or sack cloth as it was called. Amongst the earliest imports is beer, which always accompanies the Englishman. The story is told that a wealthy Indian expressed his surprise at the opening of a bottle of beer. "It is not," he said, "the sight of the drink flying out of the bottle, but how such liquor could ever be put in." We observe that there is no notice of the now favourite drink in Bombay, whiskey, for the substantial reason that it was not known in Scotland until 1745, claret having been the safer drink of the Caledonian previous to this time.*

Having exhausted our commercial circular we turn to

FREIGHTS,

and regret that we have only one morsel to communicate under this important branch. Mr. Aungier took the King's ship, Leopard, down to the Viceroy of Goa in 1662, and offered her at the rate of £21 3*s*. 6*d*. per ton. The Portuguese merchants offered £8 per ton. The transaction, therefore, was "broken off." Mr. Aungier was otherwise a most estimable man, and in an evil hour had undertaken the duty of being his

* We think that Burns' testimony on this point will be held all sufficient. In "Tam O'Shanter" it is "ale." In "Dr. Horbook" it is "ale." In the "Whistle," or great Bacchanalian contest, 1789, at which Burns was a spectator among the landocracy, it is wine.

"To finish the fight turn'd ower in one bumper a bottle of *red*,
And swore 'twas the way that their ancestors did."

own broker, to which may be attributed the non-success of the negotiations.

JOVIAL TIMES.

Dr. Fryer is our great authority on this head. He was a member of the Royal Society, recently instituted, and was a Royal Drinker. He says with an evident relish : " The Dutch at Vingorla treated us with dancing wenches* and good soops of brandy and Delf's beer till it was late enough." We can still see from his portrait that Fryer had a "jolly nose," fruit of imbibing much liquor. At those long nautches, where there is so much weariness of the flesh to Europeans, he felt woe-begone. At a Mahomedan entertainment the *sherbet* palled upon him, and he relates with much satisfaction that he obtained the necessary stimulus from the flask he had no doubt quite accidentally brought in his pocket. This exhibits great presence of mind, and when he reached home, so far as the flask was concerned, or we give him too much credit for his sobriety, he would no doubt

" Whistle ower the lave o't." †

He was asked on a medical mission to the

* Nautches.

† *Free translation :* Whistle over the leavings of it.

monks of Bandora—foreign territory—and they were very kind to him.

> "The monks of Melrose made gude kail
> On Friday when they fasted."

So did those, whilom of Bandora ; and Fryer, no doubt, challenged them in the spirit of the quaint old ditty :—

> "I cannot eat, I'll have no meat, my stomach
> is not good ;
> But I do think, that I can drink, with him who
> hath a hood."

He recrossed the frontier in a boat in perfect safety. The great drinkers of this period were the Dutch, and, we believe, that when their "Sweet William" in 1688 went over at the Revolution to govern England, one-half of them in India got very merry. They are the only nation except the Scotch who ever carried their drink into the church-yard, and the Scotch have done this very rarely, and then only in their own country, when a legacy was left to drink to the "pious memory" of the deceased. "In Surat cemetery there was the tomb of a great Dutch drinker, a relation of the aforesaid Prince of Orange. At the top was a great cup of stone, and another at each corner. Opposite each cup was the figure of a sugar-loaf. Dutch drinking parties used to frequent this tomb, brewing their punch in the large stone basins; remembering their departed companion they sometimes forgot themselves."*

This may be a delusion, as there is no such thing in the Surat cemetery nowadays. The Dutch went there for quietness no doubt, and to carry out the solemn, but absurd, injunctions of the defunct toper.

The reader will not thank us, if after bringing him so far, we do not take a saunter into

BOMBAY GREEN.

But before doing so, we may as well ask him to take a map of Bombay in 1880, and wipe out with a brush nineteenth-twentieths of all the streets and buildings thereon. Clear away the whole palatial structures on the Esplanade, and substitute cocoanut forest, such as you see on the road to Mahim, a stray panther depicted here as in old maps sprawling over the paper, will lend an interest to the scene. Knock down Forbes and Medows Streets, leaving untouched the old Portuguese country church (now Convent School) standing alone among coco trees. "Take away the bauble" fountain that spouteth water to the memory of the Duke of Wellington and

* Ovington, 1688.

place a few English graves near the Cooperage. Make one conspicuous by rude lettering. *This is the grave of Thomas Mendham, the first Englishman who died in Bombay.* It will look well under one of the big banian trees. Sprinkle a few tombs in the earliest style of Sonapore, evidently copied after Mahomedan originals. Place here Mendham's Point, and on the ground hereabouts "fill in" with old wells, pit falls and stone heaps, and in lieu of Colaba Causeway re-open a tideway* rushing violently into Back Bay or *vice versa,* separating you, except by boat, from the "Old Woman's Island" which runs like a spit into the sea and is well stocked with antelopes and other "beasts of delight." Serve imaginary warrants of ejectment on Rampart and Hornby Row, and pull the whole blessed mass to pieces. Have no respect for antiquity. Place a tank on the site of the old Secretariat, where Jonathan Duncan died, and a *free coup* full of dead dogs and cats on the sea-beach where the Mint now stands. We fear also that the Town Hall and St. Andrew's Kirk with all the build-

* There is a story told of a French corvette having been enticed into Back Bay by a Bombay buggalow by the deep water channel which runs alongside of Malabar Point. The corvette gave chase into this Colaba channel, from whence the buggalow escaped into Bombay harbour, but the corvette is said to have stuck fast in the mud somewhere near the present position of the Bombay Tramway stables.

ings between them will require to go by the board. People Moody Khana Street on the sea face with crimps, land-sharks, budmashes, pirates, and bunder gangs. Demolish all the Parsee and Hindoo five-storey architecture which came in with such force after the English occupation. It is no doubt very picturesque; but never mind. Don't even think of the Fort walls of your early days with their Apollo, Bazaar, and Church Gates. You will find them fifty years later. Dot here and there, amid the green mass of jungle, a few Portuguese-built houses, such as we will describe farther on, and high above them all "paint in" the frowning bastions of Bombay Castle, mounting 100 guns, and leave a wide open space covering fifteen acres (in or about the centre of which now stands Elphinstone Circle) for the grand old Bombay Green, which for one hundred and fifty years was the scene of so many balls, reviews, and theatrical displays to the generations which have passed away.

This work of demolition will prepare the way for an imaginary inspection in which we shall see a little of the internal economy of the place. A pleasing picture of the Bombay of this period might be constructed, but we cannot do it. The dirt and stench are too great; and over all, an overpowering odour of fish and fish-oil. Bumaloes here, there, everywhere.

"All flesh is fish" here with a vengeance.* You leave Bombay. It's no use, merely getting "out of the pot into the fire," for Bandora Mahim and Tanna are fishy, fishier, fishiest, a region of blue-bottle flies where the land is manured and the trees also with fish, and where pomphlet, seer fish, and pulla, take their place at dinner in one eternal round. The eggs and milk taste abominably of fish, and the tea as if a red herring were boiled in it. The Mazagon mangoes are suspicious. We are sorry to say this of a fruit that was devoured with relish probably under the peacock throne of Delhi by Shah Jehan. Still the people here are not quite so bad as those in Hydramaut on the opposite coast of Arabia genuine fishyophagists, who fed their horses and cattle on fish. On the contrary, they gave their horses a meal of sheep's head. We suppose minus the trotters.†

---

* Hugh Miller's "My Schools and Schoolmasters."

† Another strange thing is that they feed their horses with boiled rice and boiled meat.—*Marco Polo.* Rice is frequently given by the natives to their horses, and a sheep's head occasionally to strengthen them.—*Note by Dr. Caldwell.* The sheep's head is peculiar to the Deccan. It is told of Sir John Malcolm that at an English table where he was present, a brother officer had ventured to speak of the sheep-head custom to an unbelieving audience. He appealed to Sir John, who only shook his head deprecatingly. After dinner the unfortunate story-teller remonstrated, but Sir John's answer was only "My dear fellow, they took you for one Munchausen; they would only have taken me for another."—*Colonel Yule's Marco Polo.*

A town of 20,000 inhabitants, consisting mostly of Gentoos (a horrible word, which even Burns makes use of) with a street about a mile long, stretching from the Castle to Dungree Fort of small houses surrounded with gardens. You may see a representative of this style of Bombay houses, not now with oyster shells instead of panes of glass, in Cowasjee Patel Street, still standing in line with the Cathedral High School at the back of the Hongkong and Shanghai Banking Corporation Building.

The huts in which the servants lived were thatched with palmyra leaves, but so was the old Colaba Church until very lately. A curtain and one or two bastions of the Fort may still be seen on the way to Bombay Castle. Comparatively, and to *us*, these "auntient ruines" are quite as interesting as the Tower of David is to Jerusalem or the old walls to the City of Chester, and these words may be written on them

NEVER TAKEN,

which cannot be said of Jerusalem or Chester. Some of the Seedee's shot lies embeded in the walls. But let us walk into "the Green," and first of all inspect the Cathedral walls. They still stand unfinished, fifteen feet high, as they have done for the last dozen years. Some wicked person has chalked upon them in large letters, "My house shall be called a house of prayer"—you know the rest. It is a feeble inuendo which explains the ragged and unfinished condition* of the building. Half-decayed plaster and stones have always a lowering effect on the spirits, so we instinctively enter a victualling house, where some commanders of the East India Company's ships have gone before us and are lounging about. They are very fine men, and their dress contrasts with the "hodden gray" of the new-comer—blue coats, black velvet lappets with gold embroidery, deep buff waistcoats and breeches, cocked hat and side arms and gilt buttons. Their talk is of dogs, bull-dogs, sleuth hounds and gray dogs. A coursing match was being made up for Malabar Hill, where the long grass afforded ample cover for the hare,* but some griffins had run the greyhounds at midday, and the sun, which respects neither man nor beast, had destroyed several of them.† There is much uproar in this

* On our return from Malabar Hill we started a hare as large as an European one.—*Dr. Hove*, 1787.

† Greyhounds and hounds if they chance to hunt with them about noon, the ambient air mixing with the natural, when it is fermented and chafed, commonly proves too strong for their constitutions.—*Ovington*, 1688.

hostelrie and some heavy jokes at which "the landlord's laugh is ready chorus." But we are not going to be deprived of our drink, so we call for what we believe to be the orthodox refresher of the time,

A SNEAKER OF BOMBAY PUNCH,

and showing at the same time that we are quite *au fait* at the manufacture, we ask for a quart of the best Goa arrack, half a pound of sugar, and half a pint of good lime water, and compound the liquor forthwith. As things go it is a long drink and a satisfactory drink, and we carry it discreetly. We may remind you that this is 1694, not 1880.

On handing the publican the reckoning, half a rupee (it does not seem much) one of the aforesaid commanders snatches the wooden bowl from our hands and examines it minutely. And then, as if he had been a Chinaman taking a great oath, he dashes it in pieces on the ground. We ask a reason for this strange conduct, and are informed that an order of the Bombay Government, dated 13th August, 1694, has just been promulgated, "that if the clerk of the Market's seal is not on any bowle, it may be broken and payment of the Punch lawfully refused!" "Drink, weary traveller, drink *and pay*," so we hand Boniface a rupee, and doffing our *topi* to the naval men make our exit. We can aver that there is a wall here and a gate, for we pass the sentries, who are busily grabbing a fourth fish (You see that it is still fish) from each basket for the Fort Adjutant's lucrative perquisite. We peer out of the gate and beyond it. The Mahim coco-palms and toddy trees come right down to the very walls, a clearance for the Maidan not having been effected for many years. A pelting shower, our reader will be glad, drives us home, and ends the day, so far as our stroll is concerned.

A HOME IN BOMBAY IN 1694.

At our domicile we close the day by a stroll on the house top, from which we can observe the Mody Parsee Tower of Silence, the smoke of burning bodies, and two or three well known citizens in wig and breeches taking their three miles' walk on the sands of Back Bay. All night long, varied by the beating of tom-toms and the unearthly yells of jackals, we hear at intervals above the eerie sough of the Indian Ocean and the rustling of dry palm leaves, the watchmen calling to each other, the night watches and the morning hours, while from our charpoy we can descry fires blazing away on Thull, Caranja, Henery, and Funnel Hill showing us that the Seedee is abroad. In the grey of the morning or false dawn, and long before other people are awake, a sound comes faintly on the ear, women grinding at the mill, a sound as old as Ur of the Chaldees, and the lilt or music which accompanies it may be older still. The women ply their task, and the prayer of millions, "uttered or unexpressed," continues the same from age to age, "Give us this day our daily bread." The day ends

> "So when the sun in bed
> Curtain'd in cloudy red
> Pillows his chin upon the western wave,"

we bethink ourselves of home, hie to the Dungree Killa, resign ourselves to sleep, hearing familiar voices from the fatherland, "low and sweet," like the voice of Annie Laurie,

> "Perhaps Dundee's wild warbling measures rise
> Or plaintive Martyrs worthy of the name,
> Or noble Elgin beets the heavenward flame."

Perhaps.*

---

* Burn's "Cottars' Saturday Night."—This is no wild fancy. A Scotch minister, Mr. Stirling, was in Bombay, which argues a following of "Brither Scots" in the last quarter of the seventeenth century. All Scotsmen did not "leave their religion at the Cape," and those who were then here, were less likely to do so as they came from the brunt and fire of the "killing times" of Charles the Second.

GERALD AUNGIER, GOVERNOR OF BOMBAY.

CHAPTER IV.

GERALD AUNGIER, GOVERNOR OF BOMBAY.

WHO HE WAS.

His first appearance in Bombay was on the 18th September, 1662, when, deputed by the Surat Government, he stood side by side with the Earl of Marlborough to claim this island for the King of England. He thus saw the first of us in this quarter. By his name we take it that he came from Angers in France,* and that he was a Huguenot whose forefathers had fled to England after the religious massacres in that place (1562-72). He was of good family. His shield of arms, blazoned on the chalice in the Bombay Cathedral, shows a demi-griffin and a boar *passant*. No likeness or description of him that we are aware of has been preserved, and we know the man only by his acts. On the death of Sir Geo. Oxendon, 14th July 1669, he suc-

* There is no such name as Aungier in the Paris Directory, but several of the name of Angers. Almost all French names, since the Norman conquest, have been slightly altered on their introduction into England. We observe also that Mr. Campbell, in the Gazetteer, spells it *Angier*.

ceeded him as President of Surat and Governor of Bombay, to which he paid a short visit early in 1670. He came again to Bombay in May 1672, and resided here until 1675, dying in June, 1677. "General Oxenden was the first Governor under the Company's rule, but he never resided for any length of time in Bombay. Under President Aungier Bombay became the established seat of the Company's rule, and the rest of the factories in Western India, including Surat, were placed in subjection to it."

During these sixteen years Aungier was the contemporary of Seevajee. They eyed each other across the narrow boundary of English and Mahratta dominion, and though sometimes in conflict were never mortal enemies, never bosom-friends.

WHAT HE DID.

1. He it was who first among the English people, and long before the name of Calcutta was ever heard of, was confronted with the problem of how to govern an assembly of Moslems, Hindoos, and Parsees. He found the element within themselves, and never refusing the good from whatever quarter it came, which he quickly saw in the *Punchayet* or representative five men from each section, worked it up into the fabric of

self-government, and made this institution responsible for the good behaviour of their respective communities,—something, he says, like what is known in history as English incorporations.*

2. The fortifications engaged much of his time : bastion, hornwork, curtain, and embrasure, attempted, continued, or finished. A dock was made. A town laid out on the site of a few fishermen's huts. A judge was settled. A court-house was established in the most frequented part of the bazaar, convenient for all litigants, "*char derwaza kolah*" (four doors open).† The Militia was embodied, 600 in number; police was established ; and, finally, a Mint was authorized to commence operations.‡

3. He was called in 1674 to quell a mutiny among the English soldiers, and the first execution by martial-law, or any law as far as we can learn, in Bombay as an English settlement, was

* The *Punchayet* or five men is an essential part of the village system in India. Mountstuart Elphinstone, who does not mention Aungier in his "History of India," has this significant note. Writing in 1820 on the *Punchayet,* he says : "The Government, although it did little to obtain justice for the people, left them the means of procuring it for themselves."

† My room is a thoroughfare from morning to night ; no moonshis, dewans, dubashes, or even chobdars, but *char derwazah kolah,* that the inhabitants of these countries may learn what our principles are at the fountain head."—*Sir John Malcolm.*

‡ In 1670 was established a Mint in Bombay, which was confirmed by Letters Patent in 1676. Mr. Smith arrived in 1681 as Assay Master and Mint Master at a salary of £60 per annum. In 1672-3, some bright genius recommended the coinage in Bombay to be as follows :—Gold *Carolinas ;* silver *Angelinas ;* copper *Coppcroons ;* and tin *Tinnies.—Bruce's Annals.*

ordered by him. That execution took place on the 21st October, 1674, when Corporal Fake was shot. The first man who suffered death by the law under English administration was a white man,—evidence surely enough of the unswerving impartiality of the English Government, when we offered up one of ourselves on the altar of Law and Justice.

4. Our right to Colaba is founded on a deed which he, this same year, wrested from the Portuguese, and his far-seeing eye pointed it out as specially adapted for a military cantonment (a judgment which has since been endorsed by Lord Magdala), so that not one inch of it, for a century, was alienated by Government.

5. It was in his day that Bombay was declared an asylum to all merchants and manufacturers. Whoever you are that are oppressed by Moghul or Pathan, Seevajee, Seedee, or Portuguese, come here and enjoy the fruits of your labour. This is a city of refuge; your lives and property will be protected; our arms are wide enough to embrace you all. The judgment of the Indian Council at Surat on his death, might have been appropriately inscribed on his tomb: "Amid a succession of difficulties he preserved the English trade for sixteen years."

6. The population which he found in Bombay consisted of vagabonds and fugitives, for the most part, and he waged war with their excesses in every form. He had been bred in the school of Cromwell, and not in the soft and silken manners of Charles the Second. Hence he was the declared enemy of Sabbath profanation, drunkenness, duelling, gambling, and prostitution. He saw that native concubines and mixed marriages with the Portuguese would drive the colony to destruction, and he sent home for English wives for the factors and others.

7. On the 3rd of October 1670, Seevajee invaded and pillaged Surat of immense treasure, but Aungier secured the lives and the property of the Company. He was asked, when at Surat, to lower the flag of the Company to that of the French fleet, and he did not do it. The Dutch fleet (with whom we were at war) hovered over Bombay with 6,000 men, but was filled with terror by his army of *Bandoreens,* those fierce fellows who tap the toddy-trees, whom he armed with clubs and bill-hooks.* When the Dutch saw

* Spenser must have had something like a vision of these Bandoreens, from his fine description of the men of our coasts.

"And on his head a roll of linnen plight
Like to the Moores of Malabar he wore,
With which his locks, as black as pitchy night,
Were bound about and voided from before.
And in his hand a mighty iron club he bore."

The Faery Queene.

them they quickly sailed away. Orme says that on this occasion Aungier "exerted himself with the calmness of a philosopher and the courage of a centurion." Manuel de Saldanha, the Portuguese General at Bassein, made a vow that unless we complied with his conditions he would invade Bombay and take it by force. He was actually on the march, but when he saw the attitude of Aungier he beat a retreat, and the English laughed.

8. But he was more than stubborn,—he was wise. The English at this time never could have held together by mere courage without brains. To "temporize" and return evasive answers, in these days, was the highest wisdom. His constant reply to Moghul and Mahratta, Seevajee and Seedee, was: we are merchants; we can take neither one side nor another. Hence we find him one day sheltering in the harbour, and another day refusing to admit, the Moghul fleet. Thrice he sent envoys and made treaties with Seevajee, on the third occasion sending ambassadors to be present at his coronation; and you may be sure that his "weather-eye" was constantly open to every movement of Alumgir, "the Lord of the world."

9. The glory of Aungier, however, was that of an administrator, and exhibits him in the light

of one of the most far-seeing, and one of the most liberal-hearted men of his age, making us believe, without any other evidence, that he was bred in the school, if he did not actually sit at the feet of John Milton. If so, the disciple is above his master.* We are sure our Aryan brethren will rejoice in the man who first in India, ages before Queen's Proclamations, recognised the equality of all religions before the law, and first granted to them the precious boon of toleration. What follows, though it refers specially to the Banias, may be held to apply to all sects. In the engagement with the Banias of Diu (when this flourishing caste first made their appearance in Bombay history) the Company stipulated that they were to enjoy the free exercise of their religion without molestation, to be allowed to burn their dead, and to perform all their ceremonies in peace. "Lastly, it was engaged that none who profess their religion, of whatever age, sex, or condition he might be, should be compelled to embrace Christianity."† The date of this is the 22nd March, 1677. These are marvellous words, and they were not idle words. The Banias, from that day to this, have burned their dead on the

* Of course on the question of toleration.
† Anderson's "Western India, 1851."

edge of Back Bay, and have performed their ceremonies without let or hinderance. It was reserved for the natives of this island to enjoy privileges, which were then, owing to the violence of party, denied to many of our own countrymen in the land of their birth. We may well, therefore, claim for Aungier the character of a statesman, though he was the Governor of an island only sixteen square miles in extent.

TRAITS.

You ask me if he was a religious man ? Yes, severely religious—a puritan. But it is a curious fact that your religious men very often, when emergencies occur in national affairs, come to the front. He *phrased* religiously, and the man was not ashamed. So when the plague was raging and men were dying like flies, he wrote :—" It hath pleased God to let us see what we are by the frequent mortalities that have happened among us." On handing over the business of Surat to his successor he gave him this parting salute : " We recommend to you the pious order observed in our family, to wit, morning and evening prayer."

In these dim old times of how many a ship it might have been said—

> " On India's long expected shores
> Their sails were never furled ; "

so when a vessel was signalled at Walkeshwur or Dewa Dandi there is a *Laus Deo,* "Thanks be to Almighty God." On the death of his chief surveyor, Colonel Bake, and just three months before his own decease, he wrote: "We desire Almighty God to prepare us all for our last change." We are not going, as some men have done, to carp, cavil, or make light of all this. Read Carlyle's Cromwell aright, and you will not quarrel with Aungier.

HIS SILVER CHALICE.

Two years before his death he presented to the Christian community of Bombay a silver chalice. This was in 1675. The Cathedral was not opened until 1718, the congregation having previously met in a room within the castle-walls. There is now lying in the Cathedral this oldest tangible memorial of our existence as an English settlement. Deeply indented, in somewhat rude lettering, but as clear as if it had been cut yesterday, is the compact inscription:—

HUNC CALICEM
EUCHARISTÆ SACRUM ESSE
VOLUIT
HONORABILIS GERALDUS
AUNGIERUS, INSULÆ BOMBAIÆ
GUBERNATOR, AC PRO REBUS HONORABILIS
ANGLORUM SOCIETATIS INDIJS
ORIENTALIBUS MERCATORUM AGENTIUM PRÆSES,
ILLUSTRII.
ÆRÆ CHRISTIANÆ.
ANNO 1675.

It redounds greatly to the credit of the ecclesiastical authorities in this city that this priceless heirloom, amid all our vicissitudes and fluctuations of population, has been handed down to us from age to age. There is no harm, however, in the gentle reminder specially in the last clause: "Rust doth corrupt, and thieves break through and steal." If Bombay were Venice, it would appear in the Reliquary of St. Marks, with candles burning before it night and day. It weighs 137 tolas, so it can never "be sold for much." Nevertheless such a memorial as this in Bombay history should be placed beyond the reach of all accidents whatever.

WHERE HE LIVED.

Few of our readers have been in the Bombay arsenal, but more, we daresay, would go if they knew what it contained. It is a step from the Cathedral, but people do not go there. Somehow the Mint and Townhall seem to block up the avenues to it and debar all progress; and yet the sentries ask you no questions. You pass under a lofty gate, which was built before "the well of English" either defiled or "undefiled" was poured forth in this quarter; in other words, before the English occupied Bombay. The two figures which look down upon you are manifestly Portuguese soldiers, in their trunk-hose, the knickerbockers of those days. Each bears aloft the great globe itself, significant emblem of an inflated idea of dominion by sea and land. The folding-gates are of massive teak, scarred and blackened with round holes made by the Seedees' shot, smooth and glistering with countless coats of tar, and the hands of generations of men passing in and out, and sorely wizened and weather-beaten by two hundred monsoons. You now ask, where is Bombay Castle? You are already in it—a fact which the soldiers, who mount guard day and night, know to their cost and the place where you now stand is that delectable garden, "voiced" with so many pleasantries, which you have often read of, belonging to the Portuguese, and which the English soon filled with "bold ramparts."

On one of these grows a brab or palmyra tree, shooting up seventy or eighty feet high, the last of a family-group which once stood together, and are laid down in the oldest charts of Bombay harbour, and which of yore gladdened the hearts of our sea-sick progenitors. They used to be the landmarks first seen by the sailor making Bombay harbour, but time and the cyclone of 1854 have reduced their number to *one*; and the new clock-tower, or the tower where the clock should be, is now the highest point seen from a distance. We never knew what *towers* Heber referred to in the lines,

> " Bombay, they say, thy towers gleam fair
> Across the dark-blue sea."

" They say," It is reality now. There are some big banian trees here. Do trees make a garden ? At all events Milton did not think the Garden of Eden perfect without planting a fine banian tree in the midst of it. Wherever he got it, from Strabo or Pliny, we claim it as one of ourselves.

> " The fig tree, not that kind for fruit renowned,
> But such as at this day to Indians known,
> In Malabar or Deccan spreads her arms."

You see this is a quiet shady place, suited for reflection.

> " These auntient ruines we never set our foot upon them,
> But we tread upon some reverend historie."

There are guns lying about of all sizes and ages, 1679, 1681, some of them with beautiful ornamentation, from small six-pounders—regular " spit fires—" up to the great gun weighing seven tons, captured by the Duke of Wellington in 1803 at Ahmednugger. You now understand from all these munitions of war, that though the date of Bombay Castle in the *Government Gazette* is a fiction, the Castle itself is no more a fiction than the Castle of Otranto.

HIS HOUSE.

This section is archæological, and may be skipped by the uninterested. As soon as we enter the gate, we see, right before us, in the middle of the open space, a four-square house with the words, "Pattern Room," printed on it. If this is the house you are in search of, it verily is an example of the *res angusta domi.* One or two extracts may help to clear up matters. *Ovington* was here in 1689, and his book was published in 1696.

"In this Fort one of the Company's Factors always resides, who is appointed Governor."

Hamilton was here in 1690. "Cooke built a fort round an old *square house,* which served the Portuguese as a place of retreat."

Fryer was here in 1673. "Cooke found a pretty well situated, but ill-fortified *house.*"

Ovington gives us, "*A delineation of his Majesty's Citadel and Fort of Bombay, taken* 2*nd April,* 1668." It is partly perspective, and shows us exactly how the place stood in Gerald Aungier's time. There is a sea-view and a land-view. It is a picture of great value, where you may even now easily identify some of the lines of circumvallation. The artist has taken his view from the land side of the large tank opposite the Mint, now on the road from Elphinstone Circle to the Prince's Dock. In his view the tank appears as a pond with ducks swimming in it: no doubt the tank has been stone-faced later on. Taking our position to-day on the artist's view-point, looking across the tank, and obliterating the low tile-roofed houses, dykes, and trees which have cropped up since 1668, we easily catch in the perspective our slightly transmogrified friend, the "Bombay Citadel," *alias* "Pattern Room," and the truthfulness of the artist's view bursts upon us. It is a strong building, still in use, and not what Burns calls

"A houlet-haunted biggin"
Or kirk deserted by the riggin."

That the walls of this "house" in the picture slip right into the sea goes for nothing, for Bruce in his "Annals" tells us distinctly that the bastions "towards the sea" were not built in 1668, which by the way, must have been our very first "Reclamation."*

The lower storey of this house is vaulted and

---

* "But towards the sea, batteries only were erected, as *bastions* would be the work of *the subsequent years.—Bruce's Annals, vol. 2, page* 288, 1670-71.

bomb-proof; the upper storey, modern. We are told by those who have seen them, that the stones in the jambs of the door are strongly clamped with iron.* We have collated such passages in history as bear upon the subject, and personally inspected the building, but though the strongest evidence we can now avail ourselves of is in the affirmative, we prefer for obvious reasons (with the usual caution of our countrymen) to assume the position of a querist.

Is this the house in which Aungier resided, and several of his successors—the Government House, in fact, of Bombay in those early times, the "*house*" we took over from the Portuguese,—our citadel, ark, *Balla Killa,* or Acropolis if you please; and, if so, the cradle from which emerges our Bombay history as an English settlement? We have initiated the question which may be left for others to answer.

CONCLUSION.

The first great work which Bombay had to accomplish was to fortify herself, so that like a

* Lord Edward Fitz Clarence's body was laid out in this Pattern Room on its way to England. He died at Porendhur and like his brother (the Earl of Munster) was full-brother of Lady Falkland, the wisest and wittiest woman of her day (Bombay 1848 to 1853), children of the Duke of Clarence, afterwards William IV., by the celebrated actress, Mrs. Jerdan.

strong man girt in armour, she could look her enemies boldly in the face.

"The Mahrattas are upon thee," was the first cry; but as time wore on the English settlers found that they had more formidable enemies to cope with even than the Mahrattas. They came by sea, and they came by land —not alone from the narrow boundaries of Western India, but from far off countries in Europe, with one of whom England was at war—threatening to swallow up this little outpost of commerce in the Indian seas; and though the cry was "still they come" from great nations—Holland, France, and Portugal—Aungier, with "the soul of a stubborn old Roman" in him, bared his arm on those bastions which he threw up between Bombay Castle and the sea, and defied them all. It is to men such as these that we owe almost everything we have and are. The reply, of course, is, that if we had not had the luck to get Aungier we would have obtained men quite as good. Did Onore or Angengo, places of importance in those days, have as good men? If we are to believe the stubborn facts of history, were they not nearly annihilated as trading stations, the one by the ignorance and the other by the folly of the man who conducted its affairs ?*

Providence, as a rule, does not raise up men like Aungier twice in a generation. When we had "the luck" to lose Aungier did we find such another ? We are safe in saying that England was never so low before or since, in this island or in India, as she was at the close of Sir John Child's administration, when the Emperor of Delhi raised the siege of Bombay on condition of Child's expulsion from India. It was a new thing in English annals to have our envoys' hands tied behind their backs and laid prostrate before Indian Royalty.† But so it was. "He did the disgrace," and we had to lick the dust. It is by comparisons such as these that the figure of Aungier stands out in bold relief on the page of history—the first man in India who taught us the art of self-government and the wisdom of dealing with our neighbours—sage in counsel and

* At the close of the seventeenth century the English chief of Angengo *insisted* on paying the queen of this country a personal visit to pay his dues or taxes, against all remonstrances. The chief and factors were murdered.

† "Mr. Child, who did the disgrace, be turned out and expelled. This order is irreversible."—*Last words of Aurungzebe's Firman, dated 27th February*, 1690. Harris and the other factors were released from prison on the 4th of April, 1690 ; but the Seedee, who had remained more than a year in Bombay, did not withdraw his army until the 22nd of June, when the property captured by the English had been restored and the fine paid to the Moghul. He then departed, having first set fire to the Fort of Mazagon, and the same day William and Mary were proclaimed in Bombay King and Queen of England.—*Anderson.*

bold in action—the Moses, if you like, of our English exodus whose last words were,—" be strong and of good courage." *

Alexander Hamilton, the sea-captain, sailed and traded in the Indian seas for thirty-five years, 1688 to 1723. He was an " interloper," but the shrewdest of them all. This was the judgment of the late Dr. Wilson, and that of the *Bombay Quarterly Review.* Forty six years *after* the death of Aungier he penned these words: " *The name of Mr. Aungier is much revered by the ancient people of Surat and Bombay unto this day.*" Remarkable words when we consider that they were written by an avowed enemy of the Company, and by a Scotchman, of an Englishman, in the year 1723.

Of how many Bombay men, during the last two hundred years, could such words have been written, where reputations have sprung into existence, like Jonah's gourd, in a night, and withered in a day ? We erect statues to our heroes—to Aungier we give a nameless grave.

* " And no man knoweth of his sepulchre unto this day."

SEEVAJEE.

CHAPTER V.

SEEVAJEE.

No plunder no pay.—SEEVAJEE'S MAXIM.

THE statement will surprise many people, that the history of Western India is more abundant in details than that of some parts of the British Isles. Take the case of the Wigtown martyrs. Two women were drowned for non-conformity in the reign of Charles the Second, and though Macaulay devoted a page or two to the narrative in his History of England, and though Europe and America were ransacked from one end to the other, not one scrap or letter, printed or written, bearing upon it about the same date as the judicial murder could be discovered, and the souls of righteous men were vexed from day to day at the revilings of Mark Napier who consigned the event to the region of ecclesiastical myth and legend. It was proved independently of written testimony, but not until an old Session Book was discovered in the Wigtown Manse was scepticism silenced. Now, had any event of a kindred nature taken place in Western India about this period, we would have every particular connected therewith duly chronicled *at the time*. Had Seevajee tied Mr. Sterling, the Scotch clergyman in Bombay of his time, to one of the fishing stakes which then dotted the harbour and left him to be devoured by the waves and the sharks, we should never have heard the end of it. Every man and woman would have sat down and written long accounts to their friends at home, which would no doubt have been preserved for our edification, and so nothing would have been left to tradition. In the same way, in the sack of Surat in 1664 we make little doubt that an industrious bookworm could make a complete inventory of every pot and pan taken out of it by Seevajee. In the History of Western India, there is nothing more apalling than the amount of *materiel*, in English, French, Portugese, Italian, Dutch, Persian, and Arabic, even Chinese is laid under contribution.

These remarks apply in part to Seevajee, the

greatest man in Mahratta history. Though many people have vague notions about him, the books letters and journals in several languages from which the story of his life may be gathered are so full and minute in every particular, that a work like Lord Hailes' Annals of Scotland, though it was praised by Dr. Johnson, becomes in comparison dry annal or mere conjecture.

The obvious defects of this sketch are therefore not due to want of materials.

HIS COUNTRY.

It has been said by geologists that the Ghauts were the great seawall against which an ancient Ocean hurled its remorseless waves and that Matheran and Mahableshwur were islands. Were those black bluff headlands we now call Chowk or Sidney Points once fragrant with samphire and sea pink? Did the waves fret and eddy round the knob of Parbhul or One Tree Hill, or mould these cone-like masses we now see rising from the Konkan plain, or

> "Boil in endless torture"

in tumbling abysses under the very nose of that Sphynx-like projection on Louisa Point? Were the Funnel Hill (Kurnala) and Lingana Ghur fashioned into their present form by the action of the waves; grinding, rounding, and polishing, as if by the hands of a cunning artificer, these mighty outlying bulwarks or skerries of a primæval sea? We cannot answer these questions. Our business is with the Deccan of history and of Seevajee.

The highest bit of earth in the Deccan is Kulsabhai, 5,409 feet over sea level.* But the land bristles with hundreds of mountains from 2,000 to 5,000 feet in height, with steep scarps of volcanic trap crowned with forts and bastions, with almost everyone of which is indelibly associated the name of Seevajee. This mountainous region seems to bid defiance to the foot of man and horse. Khafi Khan, who was much about Raighur Seevajee's principal residence,† says:—"The country around may be considered a specimen of hell, for it is hilly and stony and water is very scarce." Let the strongest pedestrian in this year of grace 1880, as a piece of holiday exercise, travel to and ascend, say twelve, out of the five and forty hill forts captured by Seevajee. Let him furnish himself before starting with "Galton's Art of Travel," Crosse and Blackwell's tinned meats and the best Deccany tattoo he can lay hands on, and

* On your right as you go to Nassick.
† About ten miles from Dasgaum.

every appliance and comfort of modern times, and we will be bound to say that his thews and sinews and " poor feet " will come out of the expedition much the worse of the wear. As for his boots and shoes he may throw them to the dogs, cast himself on the first *charpoy* he can get, and hum himself asleep to a long season of repose with the tune of

" I'll gang nae mair to yon town." *

He will, however, have learned a lesson of the marvellous toughness and endurance of the Mahratta, and more than this be filled with admiration at what were once heroic virtues—walking, running, and climbing. " The best runner," said Seevajee," makes the best soldier."

HIS BIRTH.

Some of the kings of the East have had a very humble origin. The first Nabob of Oude was a petty merchant, the first Peshwa a village accountant, Hyder Ali's father was a belted peon and commenced life as a groom, the ancestors of Holkar were goat herds, and those of Sindhia slaves, the first of this family who became so powerful was slipper bearer to the Peshwa, and nearer our own time Mahomed Ali of Egypt

* *Free translation* : I will never go again to those places.

was the son of a tobacconist in Cavallo in Macedonia.

Seevajee's origin was a contrast to all these. He did not rise from the ranks, but came from an ancient line of Rajas, the Bhonslas, men in the position of the great barons of England when they were powerful enough to defy alike sovereign and people. Both by father and mother's side his ancestors had won distinction in the field as vassals of the Kings of Ahmednugger and Bejapore. His mother was a Rajput, and her name of *Jadow* was as old as the first Mahometan invasion of India in the thirteenth century, when *Devgiri* was the name of Dowlatabad, and ere ditch and scarp had made that renowned fortress unscaleable except to the ant or the lizard. His great grandfather was patel of Verole, Ellora thus becoming

"The mother of a race of kings,"

an addition to its other wonderful attractions. Both his father and grandfather were two of the most powerful men in the Mahratta dominions, the first in command of 5,000 horse. Seevajee was born in the Fort of Jooneer or Sewneer* in 1627. Some one says, "he was born in a fort and died in a fort."

* About twenty-four miles from Poona.

HIS PERSON AND CHARACTER.

Here is a good etching of him taken by an European.* *Scene* Surat, *aétat* 37. Neither Grant Duff nor Elphinstone seem to have been aware of it.

" His person is described by them whoe have seen him to bee of meane stature, lower somewhat than I am erect, and of an excellent proportion. Actual in exercise, and whenever hee speaks seemes to smile, a quicke and peercing eye, and whiter than any of his people. He is distrustfull, seacret, subtile, cruell, perfidious, insulting over whomsoever he getts into his power. Absolute in his commands, and in his punishments more than severe, death or dismemberment being the punishment of every offence if necessity require, venterous and desperate in execution of his resolves."

This is by a contemporary on the spot, and there is nothing left to us but a feeble attempt to fill in the blank spaces between the lines. And first of all, he was superstitious to a degree, and we may be sure, that the cry of a hare, the howl of a wolf, or the scream of a sarus distract-

* Escalliot to Sir Thomas Browne, author of *Religio Medici*, 1664.

ed him, and schemes of the greatest moment were suspended, if the augurs were against him.

When the English Ambassador in 1674 went down to Raighur to "assist" at his coronation, he found Seevajee had gone on a pilgrimage to Purtabghur to a pagoda of the goddess Bowanee and Oxenden and his companions were detained *a month* in the Fort, until his idle ceremonies at Raighur were accomplished. He was mightily imbued with his religious rites and ceremonies and would do anything to carry them through. Witness his landing at Malabar Point, at midnight and at the hazard of his life, to pass through the stone of Regeneration. He was most attached to his mother and exercised filial obedience until death divided them, and he was kind to his dependants and relations. It is said that his manners were remarkably pleasing and his address winning. This refers to men, but it is not so well known that he had a wonderfully fascinating power over women. We do not prove this by the fact that he had three wives and married a fourth two days after his coronation in the 47th year of his age.

But a story which Mackintosh heard at Hyderabad seventy years ago has come down to us. It appears that when a prisoner at Delhi he exercised this *glamourgift* so effectually, that one of the Princesses of the House of Timur, a daughter of Aurungzebe, was devoured by love for him. No doubt, a glance from behind the *purdah* did it all. However, it lasted her for life. Seevajee was told by "the cruel parient," and *she* also, no doubt, that the marriage could not come off unless he became a Muslim. This could not be, and it is an affecting instance of the power and endurance of youthful affection that *Moti Bowreah*, such was her pet name, never married and in extreme old age long* after Seevajee was dead and burned tended his grandson and carefully watched his up-bringing. Some of Aurungzebe's daughters were most accomplished, full of music poetry and all that sort of thing, which Seevajee loved so well that he would go a long way out of his beat to attend a *kutha* or meeting of bards and singers. A tomb of white marble was erected to her memory—and she well deserved it—which may still be seen near Bejapore, an oasis in the desert.

HIS ACCOMPLISHMENTS.

He was a good horseman, swordsman, and marksman. He had sprung from a race of

* Twenty-seven years after.

mighty hunters and athletes. His father died an old man from a heavy fall he had from his horse in the hunting field. His spare wiry form and small stature admirably adapted him for climbing and his training from boyhood put him on a par with the best climbers in the Deccan. Every corrie, gulch, and Jacob's ladder was better known to him than the *tulsi* plant at his own door. He not only loved climbing for its own sake, but admired and rewarded it in others. When he had finished the fortifications of Raighur he one day called an assembly of the people and held out a bag of gold and a bracelet worth Rs. 500 as a reward to any man who accomplished the ascent in any way except through the gate he had constructed, and without rope or ladder. A *Mhar* ascended, planted the flag, then quickly descended and made his obeisance to Seevajee. The man received the rewards in presence of the assembly and was set at liberty. We need not add that the way by which he ascended was closed.

His power of endurance is a perfect mystery. Take his flight from Delhi.* All the way to Allahabad was his son with him, a lad nine years of age, at first mounted "ride and tie" on the same Deccany tattoo, then on foot disguised as

* Escaped in a hamper.

a fakir, his face rubbed with ashes, swimming rivers with his *kupra* on his head to keep it dry, outrunning the swiftest trained couriers of the Great Moghul, and this during the monsoon through a thickly wooded country from Allahabad to Benares, from Benares to Gaya, from Gaya to Cuttack, from Cuttack to Hyderabad.

Or his night raid into Poona in 1663. He left Singhur *after dark*, entered the gate as part of a marriage procession, attacked the Mahomedan Viceroy's palace, slashed off two of his fingers as he descended from a window, killed his son and most of his attendants. It seemed the work of a moment; and *that same night* he ascended Singhur amid a blaze of torches visible from every part of the Moghul camp.*

Seevajee was weighed against gold and turned the scales at 112 lbs. This was good riding weight; though a small man he had infinite pluck. A weasel has been known to fly at the throat of a man on horseback, and Seevajee had a fierce will and intensity of purpose, and was full of resolve.

> " Come on Resolve and lead the van
> Thou stalk of carlehemp in man."

* Let the reader take a note of heights and distances, and " the roads before they were made " on his first *picnic* to Karackwasla. It was on this road that Colonel Mignon lost his life crossing a torrent during the monsoon.

The most distinguished Mahratta, awkward and sturdy at the best, was ungainly side by side with Seevajee.

He never could sign his own name. He had, however, a Persian writer and a keeper of his seal which was put to all documents. This, however, need not be held as a crime against him. Our readers will recollect the words put into the mouth of Archibald Bell-the-Cat in Scott's Marmion. He is speaking of Gawain Douglas, Bishop of Dunkeld, the translator of Virgil,

> "Thanks to Saint Botham, son of mine,
> Save Gawain ne'er could pen a line."

Though his face was white his *shendee* was as black as the raven's wing.

> "Spare and swarthy
> Cruel and crafty."

PART SECOND.

> Happy for him if he had lived to see
> His country beggar'd of the last rupee.
>
> SIR PHILIP FRANCIS.

I have searched for Seevajee's motto in vain. His war cry and that of his Mawulees was *Hur Hur Mahadeo*. I have come to the conclusion that his motto was the one engraven on the heart tablet of all cattle lifters and man lifters, and which the great Scotch Reiver Cranston of Cranston had the honesty to carve on the architrave of his castle gate—

"Whoever wants I'll no want."

TRAITS BAD AND GOOD.

He had a weakness for cutting off hands. Meadows Taylor makes one of his characters shudder in the shadow of a dark passage, as his eye suddenly caught sight of a human hand swimming in a bason of blood.

When James Forbes was at Dubhoy, a hundred years afterwards, his party were much tormented by a reiver in the jungle. At breakfast one morning his Bheels entered with a tray on which was something covered with a cloth. Present of a peacock or a haunch of venison? The Bheels with a grin of delight lifted the coverlet, when lo and behold the head of the wild man of the woods. I fancy Seevajee's morning meal was (not) disturbed occasionally by a similar incident.

"I have found thee, O! mine enemy," after which, digestion would go on with accelerated pace, like a dram in the morning to a confirmed toper.

He had a news intelligencer whose duty it was no doubt to poise himself in naked majesty for hours on some outlying bastion or "coigne of vantage," look at the sun without winking, mew his mighty youth and preen himself,* scanning with falcon eye the great plains from Wassota to Purundhur, or worm secrets from some spy or straggler, and report the same to Seevajee *or* his mother who lay huddled up like a bundle of clothes, chewing betelnut in some corner of the "Palace." This man was Seevajee's "Press Commissioner," but wrote nothing, his business being "word o'mouth," for Seevajee disliked writing and writing men, like Lord Lake,

> "Damn your writing
> Mind your fighting."

In size, in physique, in soldier-like qualities, and in powers of endurance, the nearest likeness to him in our day, making allowance for the difference of the times was Sir Charles Napier, and, for a certain impetuosity and ubiquity, Seevajee comes nearer to "the bearded vision of Sind" than any other man we know of.

In this last quality Seevajee was a perfect *Sheitan ka bhaee.* This from Napier's diary will do well enough for Seevajee.

"In 1845 I rode a camel seventy-two miles

* We all know what that means in India.

without a halt one night which is said to equal in fatigue one hundred and forty. I was once on horseback without being knocked up twenty-two hours. Napier, on the scene of Afzul Khan's murder on his way to Mahableshwur, is a piece of quiet writing and curious in its way.

"The scene of Seevajee's honest conduct!! He and his *wagnuck*, it is their way; Seevajee, the founder of the Mahratta power, met Afzul Khan, the Bijapore General, at an arranged conference, pretending to embrace him, and having previously armed his own hands with steel claws—the *wagnuck*—tore him open."

That he had some good qualities is undeniable. His discipline, his practice of the toleration of religion, his respect and treatment of women are vouched for by his most inveterate enemies and are beyond all praise. A Muslim writer of his day says—

"His orders were to do no harm to the mosques, the Book of God, or the women of any one."

At a well which he built near Raighur, there was a seat.

"Here Seevajee would sit down and when the women of the traders and poor people came to draw water he would give the children fruit and talk to the women as to his mother and sisters."

All honour to him for a course of conduct which was entirely reversed by that "unlicked cub," his son and heir Sumbajee.

When the army was on the move Seevajee would not allow a woman in it, and it is said when thus occupied that he would rather hear the neighing of his enemies' horses than the sound of a woman's voice.

HIS TWO GREAT CRIMES.

As the gates of Mahratta history are thrown wide open to us, we see depicted thereon like the bas reliefs of Ghiberti two great crimes. They are crimes of such conspicuous magnitude that in modern times they have only been equalled by Mahomed Ali's massacre of the Mamelukes and Napoleon's murder of prisoners at Jaffa. They are the same in kind, but different in degree. The end was the same. They were the first great strokes of Seevajee's policy and the blood then shed cemented the foundation of the Mahratta Empire.

The Purtabghur tragedy is so well known that we merely name it. The murder of the Raja of Jowly is less known. He was owner of all the hilly country south of Poona from the Ghauts inclusive to the sources of the Krishna, and had remained strictly neutral during Seevajee's progress to power.

Seevajee sent a Brahmin to open negotiations for his own marriage to the daughter of the Raja of Jowly. *With his knowledge and approval,* the Brahmin assassinated the Raja, which Seevajee followed up by taking possession of his country, towns, villages, and forts.

HIS MASTER PASSION

Was the love of money. All other passions were subordinate to this. The power of the sword is great—the power of money, " the sinews of war," is greater. It booted little that Seevajee was a good swordsman, marksman, a fit soldier in his shirt of mail *cap a pie,* if he had no money. He early in life recognised this truth, plundering peaceful *kafilas,* and carrying the proceeds to Torna. The cunning fellow when he took possession of this fort, dug up the treasure as if by accident—a miracle of the goddess *Bhowanee.*

In every step of his onward progress, his necessities became the greater until he had a mint of his own at Raighur.

" His desire of money is soe great that he

spares noe barbours cruelty to extort confessions from his prisoners at least cutts off one hand, sometimes both. . . . There were then about four heads and twenty-four hands cutt off."* If for nothing else than bribery he required money. It was bribery first opened the gates of Torna and Singhur. More potent than the sword of Bhowanee† (for when all else failed), it struck down the supple courtiers of Delhi and Bejapore.

He bribed the Viceroy of the Deccan. Without bribery he never could have escaped from Delhi, and without bribery he never had been able to assassinate Jowly or Afzul Khan. But to carry on the business of a great State, to equip, say 30,000 horse and 40,000 infantry as in the expedition to the Carnatic in 1676, required large funds, and the national robbery—we can call it nothing else which he perpetrated on a great scale—supplied him with the means of doing so. Hence the annals of Seevajee are just a long series of burglaries and piracies. There was first the royal convoy at Kallian, then followed the sack of Jooneer, and the plunder of ships to the Red Sea and Mecca, the booty from Rajapur and

---

* Escalliot to Brown.

† The Genoa blade presented to the Prince of Wales in 1875 during his visit to India by the Raja of Kolapore and now in the Indian Museum.

Dabul; Surat, which he sarcastically called his "*Treasury*," was twice sacked by him and yielded enormous loot.

Barcelore, 130 miles below Goa, and other rich mercantile towns on the coast, incredible plunder from Hoobli and Jaulna, and forced contributions from Karwar to Golconda. Revenue with him meant war and war meant plunder.* "No plunder no pay" was his maxim. "I rob you to reward my soldiers" was the salvo he laid to his breast. So early as 1665 at the Treaty of Purundhur, so anxious was he for a settlement with the Moghul that he engaged to pay forty lakhs of pagodas or two crores of rupees, and we do not wonder at it. He was quite good for five times the amount.

He was often gorged with plunder. Of goods, for example, he had often more than he knew what to do with, and as much perplexed as a merchant whose warehouses are overstocked. He wanted *money*, not goods. An Agra merchant came to him when he was at Surat thinking to propitiate him with 40 oxen loads of cotton goods. Seevajee said, "where is your money?" The man

---

* "When the Mahrattas proceeded beyond their boundaries, to collect revenue and make war were synonymous."—*Grant Duff*.

replied, "I have had no time to sell my goods." The man's right hand was immediately cut off, and his goods burned before his face: Yes, that man ought to have had money.

Every year added to the pile at his great robbers' den of Raighur. There is one night during the Dewali when the Hindoo brings out all his treasure and worships it. Seevajee's god, *pour l' exposition*, must have been overpowering, gold, silver, diamonds and rubies, with cloth of gold and the richest vestments of Asia, "garments rolled in blood," a heap worthy of Tyre or Babylon. When he died he must have had several millions in specie at Raighur, rupees, Spanish dollars, gold mohurs of Hindustan and Surat, pagodas of the Carnatic, Venetian sequins, and Sycee silver.

He loved diamonds and pearls much, for they are easily carried. On his flight from Delhi, a phoujdar recognised him, and a diamond and ruby worth a lakh of rupees saved his life, the phoujdar wisely concluding that they were more valuable to him than the head of Seevajee. Even then he had gold mohurs and pagodas in walking-sticks, jewels in old slippers, rubies encased in wax and concealed in the dress, and some jewels in the mouths of his followers. Seevajee's period was the great diamond time when Tavernier found 60,000 people working at a single mine thirty miles from Golconda. It was the gleam of a diamond ring that made his eye sparkle even on the coronation throne.

"The English made their obeisance at a distance and Narien Sinai held up the diamond ring" (value Rs. 125) "that was to be presented to him. *He presently took notice of it, and ordered their coming* nearer even to the foot of the throne." Noble king! Gracious Sovereign! *Hur Hur, Mahadeo!* It was a monsoon morning and the sun was spear high. Did the English Ambassador throw his buckled slippers at the king for luck and elbow his way barefoot amid the unblessed and unbreeched multitude to the foot of the august presence? History informs us not, but we give as much as we can gather from the Ambassador's report.

Behold, then, this piece of dumb show on the barren rock of Rairee.

SEEVAJEE'S CORONATION.

See him on his golden throne like a waxen image at Madame Tussaud's. On one side of him two heads of colossal fish with enormous teeth all of solid gold, and on the other side horses' tails on the ends of lances, Tartar emblems, no doubt, of dominion by sea and land.

A pair of scales were suspended from the top of a gigantic lance—a mockery—cruelty and injustice having long since turned the beam and sent up to Heaven the cry of an injured people,—a people whose homes were desolate, whose land was untilled and unmanured, for whoever sowed the seed Seevajee reaped the fruit—a people who could scarcely keep body and soul together, who built their houses with doors low enough that a man could not enter on horseback, whose koonbies were objects of commiseration even to Bombay coolies, whose Brahmins and merchants were tortured with pincers until they told where their money lay, and whose land, Deccan and Konkan, in twenty years was reduced to the condition of a desert.* We come to

HIS DEATH.

In the midst of "these combustions" in 1680 died Seevajee. Returns to Raighur after a long and bloody raid to Jalna, swelled knee joint, spitting

* In 1674 an English traveller near Kallian, with several villages in sight, had great difficulty in procuring even a hen for his breakfast.—*Fryer.*

Bombay, that was one of the pleasantest places in India, was brought to be one of the dismallest of deserts.—*Hamilton*, 1688.

"And was nothing done for Justice, Bulwunt? Was Justice dead in that country? Justice! echoed Bulwunt Rao. Justice, ah meah, what can the poor do for Justice?"—*Tara.*

of blood and all that sort of warning before death. Goes to " where the wicked cease from troubling and the weary are at rest." Here we leave him. Not so his Muslim historian Khafi Khan who pursues him with relentless fury to the other world. " The date of his death is found in the words, *Kaffir bajahannim rafl*, the infidel went to hell, which was discovered by the writer of these pages."

Here Napier's Sukkur address comes pat enough.

" Gentlemen and beggars may ride to the devil, but neither gentlemen nor beggars have the right to send other people there."

His place in history may be gathered from these words of Aurungzebe, Emperor of Delhi, his greatest enemy who spent twenty years in the Deccan in the vain endeavour to subdue him and those who came after him.

" He was a great captain and the only one who has had the magnanimity to raise a new kingdom while I have been endeavouring to destroy the ancient sovereignties of India.

" My armies have been employed against him for nineteen years and nevertheless his State has always been increasing."

Seevajee *may* be compared with Sir William

Wallace. Both were well born. Both began life with guerilla warfare. Both dwelt in a land bristling with mountains, forts, and castles, and both created out of chaos the seeds of a Nation's Life and Character by dealing heavy blows on the invader of their country. A Mahratta might carry it farther, but here the likeness ends. The judgment of well educated men in every land will, we think, be in accordance with what we believe to be the dictates of eternal justice that while Seevajee was an aggressor on the liberty of man, Wallace was the saviour of his country and the hero of Scottish independence.

KANOJEE ANGRIA AND THE PIRATES OF WESTERN INDIA.

CHAPTER VI.

KANOJEE ANGRIA AND THE PIRATES OF WESTERN INDIA.

I fear thee, ancient Mariner,
I fear thy skinny hand ;
And thou art long, and lank, and brown,
As is the ribbed sea-sand.
I fear thee and thy glittering eye,
And thy skinny hand so brown.—*Coleridge.*

EARLY NAVIGATION.

WAS the Arab or the Hindoo first in the race of navigation? Which was the main agent in placing India *en rapport* with Europe? Arabia has no timber: the architecture of the houses and the building of the ships on the Red Sea coasts, are clearly of Indian origin,* and yet the earliest notices which have come down to us are

* Schweinfurth, 1873.

of Arab sailors. Nay more, the names of every spar or piece of gear, rope, or tackle in an Indian craft, from the dhow to the bandar-boat, are all Arabic.* Both have certainly had a hand in it. Though the Hindoo hates the *kala panee*, or black water, India doubtless contributed the timber, iron, and sails for the first vessels that navigated the Indian Ocean. The Arabs, settled from time immemorial on the coasts of Western India, may have built and manned the ships; but we must not forget the lascar and the place he still holds, or the fact that it was a native of Gogo† who piloted Vasco da Gama into Calicut, and that a Hindoo pirate directed the point of attack made by Albuquerque on the city of Goa. At all events, the subject of this sketch was a Hindoo.

The native craft on these coasts have remained very much the same for centuries, perhaps for thousands of years. W. S. Lindsay, who navigated a small vessel down the Persian Gulf, noticed that everything nautical was as in the days of Nearchus ;‡ and if you look into Mariette's Museum at

* Anthony Vaz, Marine Interpreter, 1879.

† Gogo at this time was almost a Mussulman town.—*Bombay Gazetteer*.

‡ W. S. Lindsay, *History of Shipping*, 1875.

Boulak, you will see that the silver models of ancient Egypt are the counterparts of the buggalows which now sail on the Red Sea,* or of those in Bombay Harbour. The Indian Ocean, as far as we know, has never been without ships, and apparently never without pirates, for the dawn of history no sooner opens upon us than we meet with them on the coasts of Western India. Almost every traveller, both before and after the Christian era, notices them. The greatest of them all in either ancient or modern times was the lord of

ANGRIA'S KOLABA,

Called Kanojee, who had his dwelling place twenty miles from Bombay, and was born at Angarwadee, from which he took his name. The period embraced by the history of the Angrias, from the first notice of the family in 1690 to the year 1840, when for want of a legitimate descendant their territory lapsed to the British Government, is one hundred and fifty years. They once held a great slice of land in our immediate neighbourhood,—at their *acmé* 150 miles in length by 30 to 60 miles in breadth. Before the close of their existence their revenue had dwindled

* See also *Laborde*, 1836.

down to three lakhs of rupees. They have a very respectable genealogical tree, counting about ten rulers, and mustering seven generations, full of Kanojees, Manajees, and Raghojees.* There is no obscurity whatever about their origin or their disappearance from the page of history. The first man of the name was Tookajee, who served in the

FLEET OF SEEVAJEE.

It was a great mercy that Seevajee was not a seaman, otherwise he might have swept the sea, as he did the land, with the besom of destruction. Even as it was he was very nearly doing it. He liked the sea, but the sea did not like him. So strong was his love of the salt-sea wave that when a young man he took up his abode at Mhar, on the Bankote Creek, and resided there four years; and farther down the coast, at Malwun, he is said to have worked with his own hands at

---

* Here they are, with dates as far as known to us:—

Tookajee	1689
Kanojee	1689 to 1728
Sakojee	1728 to 1734
Sambhajee	1734 to 1735
Manajee I.	1735 to 1759
Raghojee	1759 to 1793
Baburao	1799 to 1813
Manajee II.	1813 to 1817
Raghojee	1817 to 1838
Kanhojee, a few months old, died	1839

the fortifications of Sindoodroog. His foot-prints are still shown here, not on "the sands of time," but in the solid rock; and the "erring brother," meaning no harm, worships him as an avatar;—silver mask for every day; gold mask for *burra din* or big days.* Poor Seevajee, who is now worshipped as a god, was sea-sick like ordinary mortals; and though he arrayed himself in red fez with jewelled tassel, a big green wave off the *Chaul Kudur* would have no mercy on him, but bowl him over, hubble-hubble and all, into the lee-scuppers; and then—bilge-water and *mal de mer*.

> "The victor overthrown;
> The arbiter of others' fates
> A suppliant for his own."

On the land Seevajee was a robber; on the sea and sea coast he was a pirate, and his achievements in this last department were by no means contemptible. Here are his chief maritime exploits in historical order. He got Dabul and its dependencies from Aurungzebe; occupied several neglected forts on the coast for purposes of piracy; opened batteries against Jingeera; built Rairee, Malwun, Severndroog, and Vizadroog, and prepared vessels at all those places;

* Nairn's *Konkan*, 1875.

made Kolaba, twenty miles from Bombay, his principal arsenal, from which he effected considerable captures; commanded, once only, his fleet of 85 frigates (30 to 150 tons) and 3 great ships (3-masted vessels). This was when he sacked Barcelore; and six years afterwards, when his fleet had grown into 160 ships, by way of naval demonstration and "show off," he brought it round to the mouth of Back Bay to let us see what stuff he was made of. He captured a large Portuguese ship off Damaun; he took Carwar; refused our ambassadors at his coronation to treat on the question of wrecks; and finally, the year before he died, fortified Kenery, so that from it, like another Tenedos, he might watch the Bombay shipping before it entered our Hellespont. We give these details to show the hereditary training of the Angrias. It was the sea that made them, and without the sea they never would have been heard of in history.

THE COMMERCE ASSAILED BY THE PIRATES

In the beginning of the eighteenth century was important. We must not suppose that the Indian trade was a small trade in those days. For bulk and value the commerce that now floats on Indian waters is beyond all precedent, but we suspect from all we can learn that India then monopolised as large a proportion of the gross trade of the world as she does at present. There were ships in those days. Alexander Hamilton says, "My ship drew 21 feet of water. I saw a dhow at Mocha: her mast was one piece as large as the mainmast of a 74."

There were merchants also, and money then had thrice the purchasing power it has at present. Vorge Vora, of Surat, was "reputed the richest merchant in the world: estate worth 80 laks."* "I was acquainted with Abdul Gafour," says Hamilton: "he drove a trade equal to the East India Company. When he died the Court had a fling at his heirs, and got about a million sterling from his estate."† "The honest factors of the Company, who wore wigs and breeches, feared God and worshipped star-pagodas."‡ Child left his widow £100,000, and the Oxendens founded the baronetcy of Brome, in the county of Kent, which survives to this day.§ The words of Adam

* Escalliott's letter to Sir Thomas Browne, 1664.

† A. Hamilton in Pinkerton's Travels.

‡ Wheeler.

§ Anderson, 1857.

Smith, in 1776, are worthy of a passing thought: "The East Indies offer a market both for the manufactures of Europe and for the gold and silver as well as for the other productions of America, greater and more extensive than both Europe and America put together."* Some of the merchants in India hoarded their savings, and others spent them with ostentation. Of the Banian brokers of Surat it was observed, "They are each worth 15 to 30 lakhs, and spend Rs. 3,000 to Rs. 4,000 per annum †; and on the other hand, the Emperor Jehangeer told Sir Thomas Roe, our ambassador in 1615, after he had delivered his gifts from the King of England, "Your presents have been inferior to those a merchant you have seen here has brought."‡

WHAT HE COST US.

Our readers would not thank us for a history of Kanojee Angria's exploits. Each of the three great European nations in Indian waters had a shy at him and his family, and each came off second best. Though he died in 1728, his piratical instincts were faithfully transmitted to his posterity. Between 1724 and 1754, the English lost 2 ships of war, French 1, Dutch 3.

---

* *Wealth of Nations.* † Ovington, 1689. ‡ Roe's Embassy.

We sometimes joined hands with the Portuguese, then we tried company with the Mahrattas, and again with the Seedee to batter down his forts, the ramparts of which still frown from the great sea walls of Western India. We hammered away at Gheria, and our cannon-balls might as well have been made up of cotton-wool or saw-dust for all the execution they did. We had to keep a special fleet to act against him, which cost us £50,000 a year. When Angria took the Success it involved us in a war with his family that lasted 38 years. It was then that he wrote impudent, but clever letters to the Governor of Bombay, for he could write, and was not like Seevajee in this respect. In 1739 the merchants of Bombay dug a ditch round the town, in case he should come and measure his strength with us at our own doors. And it was no uncommon thing long afterwards for our merchants, on the arrival of the fleet from China, or elsewhere, to present the commander of the ship of war which acted as convoy with a purse of 500 sovereigns.

HIS CROWNING ACHIEVEMENT.

But the most startling feat of Angria was his march to, and capture of, the fort of Loghur, when he took the Peshwa prisoner, and prepared to advance on Sattara, in 1713.

Passing Narel on your way to Poona, you may see on your left a fort, conical in shape, twelve miles away, Kotlighur, a small Dowlatabad in appearance, and having also a spiral passage like it, cut inside and *through* the rock, and some old guns lying about it.* Further on, beyond Kurjut, as you enter the Khundala Ghat, and still on your left, across the gloomy ravine of the Oolas, towers aloft Rajmachee, the Royal Terrace, from which this sea-eagle looked down and scanned the Konkan plains. Still further on, but now on your right at Lanowlee, is Loghur, the killidar of which, Dundoo Punt, was asked by the Duke of Wellington in 1803 to " come down." He had not been down in the plain for thirty years. It appears that Angria held Kotlighur and Rajmachee for twenty-one years, from 1713 to 1734, when he presented these forts to the Peshwa. They commanded the highway to Poona. Sattara was in a state of great trepidation, and sent Ballajee Wishwanath, the ablest man she had, with an army against Angria.

* We are indebted for these facts to Mr. Cousins, of the Archæological Survey, also that it is called by the natives *Kolli Killa*, and lies twelve miles N. E. of Kurjut.

Wishwanath turned his cheek to the smiter, and the smiter extorted good terms on releasing the Peshwa, being guaranteed in the possession of ten forts and sixteen fortified places. And now, lo and behold, Kanojee Angria is made *Sarkheil* or Admiral of the Fleet, for the Rajah of Sattara; and Wishwanath, who made the treaty on behalf of the Bhonslas, was for his services on this important occasion created Peshwa, and became founder of the dynasty of which, in our own day, Bajee Rao was the last descendant. We thus see that Angria was not altogether a sea-monster. Seevajee at sea and Angria on land forsook their native element. Angria's country was, of course, the pirate coast where every *chokra*, as soon as he could float a mimic fleet of sedge and bulrush, or paddle his own tony in his native creek, kept a sharp-look out for "flotsum and jetsum." His revenue was the "cotton of the sea," the "chouth of the sea," and the grist rolled on his rock-bound coast by white and stormy waves. But he could penetrate far inland, and take forts as well as ships. He was a great land-shark, or *mugger*, if you will, who came up out of the water and strode across the land, eating every green thing for his mere diversion, "Behold

Behemoth, he eateth grass as an ox."* The Angrias were not, however, to have it all their own way. "The mills of the gods grind slowly, but they grind exceeding small;" so the

VENGEANCE

which seemed to sleep for forty years came upon them at last. The British Government, which had been always anxious to root out the nests of piracy which lay along the Mahratta coasts, in 1755 commissioned Commodore James to do the work; and he did it effectually at Severndroog,† a few miles south of the Bankote river, taking the four forts of which it consisted without the loss of a single man. For its day, or any day, this was a great naval success, and the Commodore was made a baronet.

On Shooter's Hill, London, there is a monument, erected to his memory by his widow from

---

* We cannot remember any instances of pirates carrying on their depredations on land, except Paul Jones' on the Earl of Selkirk's silver plate. We notice it to observe that it was faithfully returned to his lordship in due form. We may here tack on the first verse of an old ballad :—

"You have heard o' Paul Jones,
Have you not? Have you not?
And you've heard o' Paul Jones,
Have you not?
He came to Selkirk Ha,
Did he not? did he not?
&c., &c.

† Droog, a fortified hill or rock.

the booty, which recounts this exploit. As its elevation is 140 feet higher than Saint Paul's, it is seen from afar, and still retains the name of Lady James' Monument. So much for Severndroog. In 1756 Admiral Watson and Lieut.-Colonel Clive, whose great name appears in this history, captured Gheria, or Viziadroog, 170 miles south of Bombay, and seized Toolajee Angria with his wife and family, and all the plunder, amounting to ten lakhs of rupees, which he had taken from the East India Company.* A curious incident lately occurred at Gheria, when some English visitors, including, we believe, a late Governor of Bombay, were confronted by a venerable native, who gravely averred that he himself was a spectator of this great action. This throws Washington's nurse completely into the shade.

We come now to speak of a painful subject,

THE ENGLISH PIRATE.

The English Government in Bombay had to deal with all kinds of pirates—Somalee, Seedee, and Sanganian; but worse than any of these, she had to bring down her right arm on those of her own

* *Low's Indian Navy*, 1877.

flesh and blood who desecrated the name and the honour of England on the Indian Ocean. The Mahratta pirate was bad, the English worse, for he had learned more and profited a great deal less. The trade was new to the one and hereditary to the other. Kidd and Evory and Green are the names of some of these ruffians, who committed robbery and murder on the high seas, and the scope and duration of their crimes far exceeded those of any individual attack on life and property on land. Their sweep was wide as the Indian Peninsula and adjacent seas, and imperilled the existence of every Englishman and woman thereon, as well as the condition of future generations. Quick work, therefore, was made of their authors and abettors. Kidd, who was never in Bombay, but not far from it, was hung in chains at Tilbury, and his goods confiscated to Greenwich Hospital.

Green, "afterwards hanged in Scotland," says Hamilton, noticing that he came on board his ship "very much overtaken with drink." Evory fled to Barbadoes, and five of his accomplices were hanged. A Persian scholar* of this period, whose works have been recently translated,

* Khafi Khan.

lifts the veil from the horrors which accompanied his capture of the big pilgrim ship Gunjee-suwaee. This mildest manner'd man who ever scuttled ship or cut a throat was, of course, sent to Gehenna by the Moslem, and to the hell of heated and burning copper, one of the twenty-seven hells of the Hindoos. The English pirate rarely reached home with his ill-gotten plunder. Allan Ramsay writes in 1722 :—

> "Much dawted by the gods is he
> Who to the Indian Main
> Successful ploughs the wally sea,
> And safe returns again."

Not much fondled by gods or men was the pirate in his native *gaum*. The finger was pointed at him as the man who had sold his soul to the devil for as much gold as filled his boot. * The English pirate was the principal cause of Child's war, which cost £440,000. Aurungzebe would not see in those piratical acts anything but the action of our accredited agents. Hence he told Sir William Norris, our ambassador, if the plunder was not redeemed, he knew the way he came, and might go "back again."

England did not rest satisfied until she had hunted out the last of her degenerate children

* Skipper's boots, specially those of pirates in those days, were large.

and amply redeemed their follies by the great part she took in

THE POLICE OF THE INDIAN SEAS.

There is not one fact in Bombay history of which we may feel more justly proud than the imperishable services of the Indian Navy, from the day that Hawkins stood before the Emperor Jehangier at Agra in 1609 to the abolition of the service in 1863, when its flag was hauled down and it ceased to exist.

It is true that what we attempted we did not always succeed in, but we ultimately attained the object we had in view, which was no less than giving a safe throughgate to the vessels of all nations by making peaceable men of these wild marauders of the sea. The suppression of piracy and slavery on the coasts of Arabia, the Persian Gulf, and Kattywar is a history by itself, and that history belongs to the Indian Navy. Why is it to-day that the Indian Ocean is as safe for the vessels of every flag as the Solent or the Medway? We may well enquire the reason why. And why do men sleep on the way from Aden to Bombay, for they did not always do so? It was that the course initiated by the Government of Bombay against the Mahratta pirates, by Oxenden and his successors, was followed up by the brilliant exploits of James, of Watson, and of Clive against the Angrias until the pirates were driven out for ever, and the entire sea left clear and uninterrupted to all who chose to enter it. Without this, of what use would be your steam navigation, your Suez Canal, and electric telegraph? With the pirates, Waghorn and the overland route would have been an idle dream. Security was the first element; speed the second.

THEIR CRUELTIES.

What men suffered and endured at the hands of the pirates it were vain to enumerate. Much is known, much more is unknown, and it is, perhaps, as well it should be so for the credit of our human nature. It is a blood-stained Book of Martyrs at the best.—Sawbridge and his crew tortured and put on shore at Aden to die of thirst;* Petit, a member of Council, leaping from the burning ship which he defended to the last, only to be carried off to Goojurat, where he died a miserable death;† Rasalghur, near Mahableshwur, was the prison-house of an English officer who was captured by Anandrao

* 1696. † 1684.

while carrying despatches to the Court of Directors.*

We need not, however, ransack the pages of history. Our own time furnishes us with an example. It seems but yesterday that a man who bore on his body, like a "crusader's badge"† the marks of the pirates was alive. Captain Grant, of Barholm, Kirkcudbright, commanded in 1820 the naval force of the Guikwar to put down piracy, and on his way inland from Diu Head was captured and imprisoned. He lay for two months and seventeen days on the top of a mountain in the Geer jungles. From a letter, dated April, 1871, to General Sir George Le Grand Jacob, we take the following :—"My sufferings during confinement were almost beyond endurance, and I used to pray in the evening that I might never see the morning. I had my boots on my feet for the first month, not being able to get them off for the wet. Severe fever, with ague and inflammation of the liver, came on, and with exposure to the open air drove me delirious; so when let go, I was found wandering in the fields, covered with vermin from head to foot. I can never forget the foregoing incidents,

* 1780. † Died 1871.

though it is now upwards of fifty years since they occurred."

THE LAST OF THE ANGRIAS.

Meanwhile the Angrias at Gheria and Kolaba, all these years, ate and drank, married wives, and begat sons and daughters. "Very much married," as Artemus Ward would say; the last of them, in 1838, left five widows. Some of their wives were of good mettle, and one of them, about 1798, Sakoovurbaee, the wife of Jeysing, performed a feat which for one hundred years had defied all the power and ingenuity of the Bombay Government. She took Kenery, and the island would not have been wrested from her, except by the foulest treachery. The commander of Sindia's forces at Gwalior came down and offered to relieve her husband from prison if she give up the fort. She did so, and Jeysing was killed, and this heroine and her family put in prison.

Then there was Anundubaee, who was like Jael, the wife of Heber the Kenite; the women of these days fighting much better than the men. She was the widow of Raghojee, "the beloved," and besieged Kolaba and imprisoned her stepson, Jeysing, and executed his chief adviser;

fought bloody battles in person at Khundala and Heerakot ; and at length in 1796, on hearing of the destruction of her army, died of a broken heart.

Such were some of the strong minded and strong bodied women among the Angrias. The family seem to have been a very quarrelsome set among themselves, literally picking each other's eyes out. The dull monotony of their daily existence on shore, for they never absolutely bartered away their piratical instincts for the gifts of civilisation, was varied by sewing up their relations in sacks, or hurling obstinate members of the family to their last resting place down the steep cliffs of Sagurghur. The reign of the last man, Raghojee, 1817 to 1838, was called *Angrak*, which, we understand, means Mars, an evil star for man and beast in Hindostan. A posthumous child born to him died in 1839, when the possessions of Angria lapsed into the Kolaba Collectorate.

Alibagh is a fine name, the "Garden of God," and placed amid a waste of salt marshes, with its flowers, fruits, and aromatic herbs, ought to justify the title. Opposite to it—you can almost walk over at low tide—is the island rock of Kolaba. The only pleasing episode we can recollect in its history is the visit in 1771 of James Forbes to the then ruler, Raghojee Angria (1759 to 1793). This man was very much beloved, and to him we owe the number of trees in the landscape. He was of a comely person and pleasing manners, which were friendly, almost obsequious to Englishmen. Forbes records that his palace, treasury, and public buildings were in Kolaba, and the gardens at Alibagh.

Like most seamen and descendants of seamen, he was fond of horses, and possessed a magnificent stud of Persian and Arab animals.*

THEIR OLD HAUNTS.

South of Bombay on the coast there were the "Golden Fort," the "Fort of Victory," the "Ocean Fort," and the "Garden of God." Their present state is described in the Ratnageeree volume of the *Bombay Gazetteer*. The sea-eagle builds its nest in a banian tree overhanging the sea-wall of the picturesque old island of Severndroog. Gheria, or Viziadroog, has twenty-seven bastions, which "over their whole length are ruined by trees and evergreens." The cannon which we captured in 1756 appear to be still lying there—250 rusty and unserviceable

* Oriental Memoirs.

pieces. Angria's dock is choked with mud. Sindoodroog, or Malwun, is a mere shell. Thirty-two flags used to wave triumphantly over as many bastions, where now a hoary and solitary *Adansonia digitata* rules supreme. The once great arsenal of Kolaba is unapproachable from the sea owing to outlying rocks. To the north of Bombay the temple of Somnath (for the pirates took possession of the holiest of places) is now "desecrated and defiled, and scarcely distinguishable from the mass of ruins which surround it." Pirim, at the mouth of the Gulf of Cambay, where seamen still make an offering to the great local pirate, now reflects a diopteric light; Kenery, that erst, and almost within the memory of man, was the abode of Angria, the enemy of legitimate commerce, has been converted into its friend, and now points the way to the mariner across the midnight waste of the *kala panee.*

Man in these parts goeth forth to his labour in the morning, but not now for purposes of piracy.

CONCLUSION.

The Angrias were a stiff-necked race, born and begotten of the sea, and full of its wild and restless energy. They were rocked to and fro by its waves into hardihood and indomitable pluck.

No memorable scene in this history rewards the patience of the reader. We seem to hear for ever the flapping of the great lateen sail, and toil on from wreck to wreck amid floating masses of burning ships and sinking men. Not one ray of family affection comes from these embittered households; and a century of their history does not offer one instance of filial devotion to the living, such as that of Seevajee,* or the veneration for the dead that was exhibited at Wye and Panwell by the widow of Nana Furnavese.† In the dull and weary annals of the Peshwas there is the great Poona Durbar of 1790, when in the magnificent Gunesh room of the Shunwar or Saturday Palace a hundred dancing girls came forth amid fountains and fragrant flowers to welcome our ambassador, Sir Charles Malet ‡. In Seevajee's history there is the barbaric splendour of his coronation. Angria conducted his affairs by ruder methods. He was never crowned, so he sits on a throne built

* Meadows Taylor works this well up in *Tara*.
† The Duke, Lord Valentia, and Lady Falkland all paid her a visit.
‡ Daniell's Great Picture.

up of plunder and sea-wrack. The story of the Angria family goes a long way back, and comes down to our own times.

The first man of the name that we meet with, was a tindal in one of the gallivats of Seevajee. The widow of the last ruler—her name is Yashodee—still (1880) lives at Alibagh.

SUPPLEMENTARY NOTE.

The issue of the tenth volume of the *Bombay Gazetteer* is opportune to us, for the bulk of it is devoted to this subject. When the British in 1818 took possession of Rutnageeree—the country from Bankote to Vingorla, 160 miles in length, and stretching 30 to 40 miles inland—it was in a miserable condition. It was like the prophet's "valley of vision," full of dry bones, the vultures of previous times having left us only the skeleton of a country. During the previous one hundred and fifty years various birds of prey had been sucking its blood. The Peshwa had done his work, and Angria had done his work, and that black eagle of the desert—Seevajee! It was a country without roads. That means nothing comparatively. It was a country without money, which means a good deal when none of it passes between man and man, and where a rupee in the hands of a tenant is a rare sight. It was a country where a man wearing a decent turban, or ever so coarse a dress, was an object of attraction. It had reached that last stage in a people's degeneracy when industry ceases to be a virtue—when the bonds of society, or whatever you like to call it, are broken up, and men take to the open country to feed on the roots of the earth and leaves of trees, or wage war for existence. When Fletcher of Salton, amid the gloom of "bondage days" and hereditary jurisdiction, was asked what was to be done with the 100,000 beggars who then roamed over his country, he replied :—" Sell them as slaves." But what are you to do with a people where this has been already accomplished? The deed was done, in a kind of way, for without bargain or sale the Khote and the Koonbee had created between them a personal servitude for the latter where " the only limit was the absolute necessities of nature."

" An impoverished, a dispirited, and a degraded people," " little better than abject slaves." These are the words of the Government officials of the day, and it is no wonder that they added that the prospect was "almost hopeless." Bajee Rao in his last days seems to have begun to realize the disagreeable truth that taxation had exceeded burden-bearing limits. The ass lay down, and to get it on its legs again the wiseacres of that day suggested that £50,000 a year should be doled out to the miserable wretches, so that peradventure the beast of burden might be cobbled into tax-giving capability. When this experiment was going on we arrived. We then took stock, and made an inventory of the legacy that accrued to us. It consisted of a teak forest sown by Kanojee Angria on the borders of the Bankote river; Angria's dock, silted up, at Gheria; an old Mahratta bridge at Rajapore; and 365 crazy forts—there was one for every day in the year—through the loopholes of which we were staring into utter vacancy, when lo and behold, the Khote controversy was added to the list, and soon worried out the lives of two generations of civilians! With such rotten materials did we commence the work of regeneration. The battle, however, had to be fought and the victory won, and the history of political economy in the restoration of moribund States can scarcely furnish a greater triumph than is exhibited in the present condition of that country we now call Rutnageeree, the scene of the Angrias' exploits.

We began by covering the country with a net

work of 507 miles of roads. We opened up the passes in the Sahyadree Hills for cart traffic. We encouraged steam navigation, and as the coast was rocky, we planted four light-houses on the most dangerous points. We abolished the labour cess, by which the Khote could exact, *nolens volens,* one day in eight of personal servitude. We encouraged enlistment, until in 1879 we had in the army 5,579 men, while 7,009 more were receiving pensions amounting in the year to £45,452. We sent out on their rounds 743 native policemen with a single European superintendent. The office latterly has been nearly a sinecure, for in 1878 of £2,659 *alleged* to have been robbed, £1,583 was recovered. The population in 60 years has risen from 462,651 to 1,019,136 until it literally overflows. They don't object to leave the country; 100,000 to 150,000 souls every year after the rice reaping finding their way to Bombay, and returning before the rains. Our cotton mills are full of them. The acuteness and astuteness of the Konkanee Brahmins have become a proverb. In Bombay they affect everything—law, police, medicine, Sanscrit, mathematics. They are the Highlanders of the Bombay Presidency, and every year this Highland host so leavens our population that every seventh man, woman, and child we meet is a Rutnageerian. When we came there was little or no trade. Between December, 1876, and December, 1877, 150,000 tons of food-grains left Bombay for Southern Mahratta ports, and the sea trade of Rutnageeree has increased from £104,484 in 1818 to £1,841,411 in 1878. The revenue in 1832 was £117,829, in 1878 £230,470. The wages of labour are enhanced. A labourer before 1860 received 1 to 2 annas a day, now 3 to 4; and masons and carpenters, then getting 3 to 6, are now paid 8 annas a day. In such a hilly country the amount of arable land, or rather land under tillage, is absolutely marvellous. Of its entire superficies of 2,424,960 acres, 1,020,836 are under tillage. Add to this, that there is a great air of comfort everywhere, and that the villages on the coast in cleanliness compare favourably with any in India. The men now wear sewed waistcoats, shoulder cloths, shoes in dry and sandals in wet weather, and deck themselves in turbans, while the women are very neat in their dress and style of wearing the hair. You recollect that Sir James Mackintosh travelled in 1805 over 1,000 miles of the Deccan without seeing an unwalled village or a detached bungalow. Here there are no walled villages. The people are neither frightened of us nor of each other.

Thus has the pirate coast been reduced to order by a systematized government, and its race of spies and buccaneers been replaced by a frugal and an industrious people.

> "Where briers grew midst barren wilds,
> Shall firs and myrtles spring.
> And nature through its utmost bounds
> Eternal praises sing."

BOMBAY, 1750.

CHAPTER VII.

BOMBAY, 1750.*

GROSE'S ACCOUNT.

[This book is the property of Mr. Tyrrell Leith, barrister-at-law, and it is by his courtesy that we have been enabled to present this meagre *rechauffé* of the Bombay portion of it to the public, as well as a copy of Grose's Map of the City to some of our Bombay Institutions. The book is so rare that we have seldom seen it quoted, or referred to in any publication heretofore. Mr. Leith's collection of books on the history of Western India, we make bold to say, is the best selected of any that exists in the Presidency at the present time, and certainly neither Mackintosh nor Elphinstone had anything approaching to it.]

Now by the powers o' verse and prose !
Thou art a dainty chiel, O Grose !

Burns on Captain Grose.

It may be as well at the outset to state that the hero of this article is not the Captain Grose

---

* *A Voyage to the East Indies.* By M. Grose, London, 1772.

of Burns. He has, however, some strong affinities to him. The lines

> "He's ta'en the Antiquarian trade.
> I think they call it,"

And

> "A chiel's amang ye takin notes,
> And, faith, he'll prent it"

fairly apply to him in Bombay. Our Grose was a writer and covenanted servant of the East India Company, a close observer and a man of much intelligence; and we think we will be able to show that he has left on record the best account that exists of Bombay as it was in the middle of the last century.

WHEN GROSE LANDED

in Bombay, Poona had just become the capital of the Mahrattas. Our territorial acquisitions in Western India were no bigger than they were in 1665, when we took over the island from the Portuguese, unless indeed we add to this a few square miles of earth at Tellicherry. We were still on the tenterhooks of uncertainty, for our position was quite as precarious and critical as it was in the end of the seventeenth century, when Aurungzebe and Seevajee laid waste the Deccan and Konkan plains. Those twin giants, the Gog and

Magog of our early Governors, had disappeared, and were now no longer a menace to us; but the existence of Bombay as an English settlement was still a matter of doubt in the future. For that dominant power which Seevajee had quickened into life was now in full swing at Poona, Sattara, and Raighur. The right arm of the Mahratta nation was as yet unbroken by the defeat of Panipat—their Flodden field, where the Afghans drove them from the north of India, and inflicted a blow upon them from which they never recovered.

We had enemies in all quarters—north, south, and east, and even in the west; the sea, our ancient and natural ally, whence alone we could draw men and munitions of war, was covered by the fleets of Angria, who had wrapped up in the folds of his piratical dominion a wide extent of country stretching away south from the mouth of Bombay harbour. Moreover, the fall of Bassein in 1739 was an event of sinister import to us, and added new dangers to our political situation, for we were now hemmed in as we had never been before. Bad as the Portuguese were in Salsette, they were better neighbours for us than the Mahrattas, who now, after sweeping over the island, confronted us with their outposts on the hill of Bandora. And this may be said,—that weak as Portugal was, so long as she held Salsette it acted as a barrier between us and the enemy, and broke the force of the mass that was pressing down upon us from the Deccan hills.

Our readers will see that the outlook from the bastions of Bombay Castle was at this time altogether a dreary one ; for though the sun rose then as it does now, there was this important difference,—that there was not a peak or valley in the wide panorama which it lighted up but what was in the hands of the enemy. Kolaba, Thull, Oorun, Caranja, Kurnala, Prabhul, Matheran, Bhowmalang, with the Khundala range ending in Rajmachee, with all the intervening country and ten times as much beyond it, with the islands of Henery, Kenery, Elephanta, and Trombay, were governed or misgoverned by the enemies of England.

The truth seems to be—and it was well understood by those who then lived in Bombay, and by those who lived out of it, who had studied the subject—that we could not afford to quarrel, just at this particular time, with either the Peshwa or his great henchman Angria ; and though we did not turn our cheeks to the smiter, we had from motives of expediency to allow their gibes and jeers, and scoffs and taunts, to pass apparently unnoticed. When we made a ditch round the fort, they told us that they would soon fill it up in a single night with their slippers. When they seized a supply of our swords, they sent word to us that they would not cut butter. Once we went so far as to negotiate with Angria, and try and buy him off, by an annual subsidy, an attitude which looks like temporising. He asked for twelve lakhs of rupees or £150,000 per annum. That was what he estimated the worth of his predatory commerce. But this policy had one good effect,—that it enabled us to gain time, bide our time, recruit our marine, and strengthen our fortification, which before this time was, between the bastions, of the nature of a garden-wall. The destruction of Angria and the defeat of Panipat came afterwards ; and it is not too much to say that it was almost a miracle that Bombay was not now swallowed up in the Mahratta dominion of Western India—

> A living prey
> Unto their teeth,
> And bloody cruelty.

Such was the political situation of Bombay when our author landed here in the autumn of the year of our Lord 1750.

He came out in the Lord Anson, East Indiaman, and had a voyage of five months, which was considered a good one. There is no doubt, we think, that he landed at our present Custom House bunder, and if so he would be most conveniently placed for paying his respects to the Governor. So at six in the evening he hied him to Government House, as in duty bound. It was quite near, and you may still see the framework of it within the Arsenal. The Governor was affable and courteous, and *sans ceremonie*

ASKED MR. GROSE TO SUPPER

that very evening. His name was William Wake, and he was now completing the eighth year of his reign, to be succeeded by a man better known in history as the Honourable Richard Bourchier, Esq. And here it may be as well to observe that the hours of business at this time in Bombay were from sunrise to 1 p.m., when its cares and troubles were laid aside and our breeched and wigged citizens, and our patched dames and demoiselles, spent their time, like the little children in France, in eating, drinking, and sleeping. If the *mauvais quart d'heure* was about 12, the time of universal satisfaction was 1 p.m., when dinner was served. After this came the hookah, the gurgling noise of which, sooth to say, had a wonderfully soothing effect, and sent the guests asleep. It is averred that the siesta was invigorating, and that they rose like giants refreshed, and sallied out to walk, ride, or drive on such oxen-drawn vehicles as were then available in the neighbourood of Bombay Green. Fortified with the fresh sea-breeze along the Back Bay sands, or a lounge on Mendham's point, our diners of 1 o'clock returned at 8 with renewed appetite to attack the ghost of the feast, to which there were added some piquant dishes with which the cooks of those days no doubt found it their interest to titillate the jaded palate. And if they could not eat, they could drink. For Niebuhr tells us they were nothing loth to grapple with the strong wines of Portugal, the consumption of which, he avers, contributed to swell the mortuary returns. In addition to these, Grose tells us of three drinks which now burst upon the bibulous world of Bombay with astonishing effect. The three viands which now divided public attention were the spirit of Deer, the spirit of Mutton, and the spirit of Goat, to such marvellous ingenuity are men driven to invent new names for liquors to quench their thirst. These drinks were in great vogue, and the way they got their names was this :—A haunch of venison, a joint of mutton, or a quarter of goat was thrown into the vat when the arrack was being distilled, and while correcting its fiery nature, imparted a new flavour which was considered mighty fine. The blend of each of these spirits was different ; every man had his favourite, some the one, some the other, the deer, no doubt from its wild *gout*, outrunning the other animal spirits in the chase. We ourselves should rather object to any one of them, but as matter of history this explains the consumption of arrack, of which it is said the English were the best customers of the best brands from Goa. There could be at this supper only

A FEW LADIES,

as in 1739 there were only eight unmarried ladies in the Bombay Presidency, twenty married ladies, four to eight widows, and "never more" than seven children. This last Malthusian statement, even though seven is the complete number, seems to us preposterous, and throws discredit upon the entire statement. It is quite true that Niebuhr was here for six months in 1764, and tells us that during the whole time he was here neither marriage nor baptism took place.

But even this statement does not warrant us, on the vital statistics of Bombay at any period, uttering the cry of Poe's raven—"*Never more!*"

But we are now on safer ground. All the ladies wore patches. At least Mrs. King, the Chief's wife, of Angengo, did, and Angengo, if we recollect rightly, was then a more lucrative post than Bombay. Here it was that Orme the historian was born, and Eliza Draper; so we imitate Sterne in asking pardon of the reader for the "digression." But to the patches. Grose records that at a reception some leading natives condoled with Mr. King on his wife's distemper, and hoped that there would be no more breaking out of boils and blains! At this supper party there could be no lack of

SUBJECTS OF CONVERSATION.

The Scotch Rebellion was already an extinct volcano, and Grose does not notice the Scotch unless to call attention to the fact that the Deccany tat resembles those shaggy brutes that are reared on the mountains of Scotland. The peace of Aix-la-Chapelle is not once named. People do not talk statecraft after dinner, much less after supper; so Grose amuses us with the way he dodged the sea-sickness by going on board the Lord Anson with an empty stomach. No doubt everybody having supped, resolved to try the same on going home, the sea moaning bodefully all the time on the black rocks outside the big dining-room. Grose was told of two fearful bugbears to new comers, the Berbiers and the Mordechino, but was consoled by the fact that the doctors of Bombay were now a very different lot from the rusty razors of past times. The health of the city was greatly improved, for which we had very much to thank the doctors.

To have good doctors you must pay them well. This is an axiom that cannot be disputed, so Grose avers that the small allowances granted to surgeons in the early days of Bombay was a principal reason why its mortality had become a byeword in Europe, where Bombay was termed the grave of Englishmen. He tells us that Governor Phipps (1720 to 1728), anxious to curry favour with his masters at home inaugurated a number of reductions, and among others in the Bombay Marine. On examining a schedule of salaries, he observed the surgeon's salary put down at Rs. 42 per mensem. "O ho! there must be some mistake here; the figures are transposed." And sure enough, he altered them to Rs. 24.*

Grose gives us the particulars of a race of pigmies in the Carnatic. Two specimens had been sent by one Vencajee trading in those parts to Robert Horne, Governor (1734-39), and Captain Boag was commissioned to bring them up to Bombay. The creatures were two feet high, were without hair, sallow white in colour, and walked erect. They were melancholy, had a rational sense of their captivity, and many human actions. They made their own beds, and the joints of their legs were not re-entering like monkeys, but salient like those of men. The sea air did not

---

* Shortly before this period there was considerable grumbling among the writers of the Company, and in 1739 they sent home a representation that their income was insufficient to defray their expenses accompanied by the following schedule to show that their living could not be "done for less."

Calculation of Monthly Bombay Expenses.

	Rs.	qrs.
One fowl per diem at 1 qr. 6 p. each	9	3
One chicken or fish and rice 14 p. each	5	1
Flour, pepper, mustard, &c.	0	2
Greens	0	3
3 rolls per diem, 2 p. each	2	1
Wine and Punch, Rs. 2 each	15	0
Ghee	0	3
Oil and Candles	4	0
Wood 1,200 billets Rs. 2-2 per mille	3	0
Tea half cally	1	2
Sugar or sugar-candy	2	2
Milk	0	3
Butter, 2 lbs., Re. 1 per lb.	2	0
Water-bearer	0	2
Rs.	48	2

The drink and oil bill mean late hours, for though the bill is small, those items form a large proportion of the gross expenditure.

agree with them: the female sickened and died, and the male became inconsolable and died also. Boag buried them at sea. Horne, like many men, was fond of specimens, and asked the captain why he did not preserve them in spirits, who replied bluntly that he never thought of it. So this new race perished on their way to Bombay; for though Governor Horne wrote to Vencajee to get another pair, the pigmies would not be coaxed out of their lair, but remain impenetrably fixed in their native jungles.

THE GOVERNMENT HOUSE,*

where Grose took his supper, is still to the fore, and must be the oldest house in Bombay. It is marked "Governor's House" in his map of Bombay, and now faces you as you enter the gate of the Bombay Arsenal,

* When the English took possession of this island, they found, in that part of it which chiefly commands the harbour, an old fortified house, the residence of the Portuguese Governor, and though this house might have served for other valuable uses, they were tempted to make of it the centre house of the castle which they built round it. It is, however, impossible to conceive in every sense a more incommodious structure, and the same or perhaps less cost than the reparations and additions have stood in to the Company would have built a much better mansion new from the ground. For the false economy of preserving this old piece of building, which need only to have been demolished or thrown away, had such effect that it hindered the English not only from consulting a more commanding position to the harbour which is that of Mendham's point, but made them blind to the disadvantage of the Fort built round it, being overlooked by an eminence near it called Dungharee point, on which there is only a small untenable little fort of no defence which serves now for the town prison for debtors or criminals.—GROSE.

with a board upon it, on which is printed the prosaic inscription "Pattern Room." In the paper on Gerald Aungier, we hazarded the conjecture that the "four-square house" we took over from the Portuguese was still extant, though the moderns have piled an upper storey on its bomb-proof roof. The discovery of this map of Grose sets the question at rest. This venerable relic still exists, and can never cease to be of interest to every man who is proud of his city and curious of its early history. Here the first twenty Governors, from Aungier to Hornby, had their abode, Oxenden and Child in the seventeeth century, and such magnates as Boone, Bourchier, and Crommelin in the eighteenth. Not all wassail and wine, for here, no doubt, Cooke was disgraced, Child died, and here in 1734 Robert Cowan received his notice to quit the service of the East India Company, and not very far off within the four bastions and curtain of Bombay Castle, some of the most momentous scenes of Bombay history have taken place.

We are sure our fellow-citizens will join in the wish that such a venerable relic should be carefully preserved. It may, and it may not. The spirit of improvement is abroad; and not very far off.

So great is the rage for improvement now-a-days, that we think it is highly probable that some one full of bran-new ideas will remove it as an excrescence.

The Castle, as our readers are aware, is a quadrangle, and the bastion facing Mody Bay was called Tank Bastion. Not for the reason that it was near the big tank which faces the Mint, but because there is a tank of water within the bastion itself. Here is also one of the oldest sculptured works in Bombay. It may indeed be Portuguese and before our advent. This is

A COLOSSAL SUNDIAL,

ten feet high, with much grotesque carving, heads of men, monsters, and animals, intermingled with leaves, towering high above the dial-face. The visitor will observe that the disc looks out seaward. Indeed, as you stand on the bastion the face cannot be observed without a considerable craning of the neck, and the angle seems, exactly the same as that of the clock-face of the Arsenal observatory, to catch the eye of the mariner on entering the harbour. The gnomon is gone, but even if a new one were fixed in it, it could be of no use, for the roof of some buildings obstruct the view of it from the sea. The hours are now as distinctly marked as on the day that they were cut in the stone, and in the rim or border which surrounds it a seed of the peepul tree having found a matrix, projects a branch covered with big leaves, which wave to and fro in the breeze over the dial-plate, as if in mockery of time and the strongest efforts of man to measure it.

The time that we have spent with Grose in

THE BOMBAY OF 1750

leaves no doubt in our mind that it was a dirty, uncomfortable, exasperating kind of place. There is much to interest one, however, particularly a new arrival. We are shown the Breach, now the Vellard, and which has been long known as

HORNBY'S VELLARD.

[Dr. Buist seems to have been aware that the Vellard was built before Hornby's Governorship, for he tells us in an article on the Geology of Bombay which is published in the transactions of the Bombay Geographical Society Vol. X., 1852, that the embankment between Love Grove and Mahaluxmi was completed " about a hundred years before," *i.e.* 1752, which, it is said, has contributed much to the improved health of the place.] It has already cost £150,000. We had always understood that this was the special work of Governor Hornby, Governor 1771-84, and indeed that this was the last work he executed. But here it is in a book published in 1772, a second edition, and which was certainly written ere Hornby could have done anything to it as Governor. He may, however, have given the finishing touch to it. But let us look at

THE FORT.

The walls appear very much as they are laid down in Murray's Guide-book map of 1857, ere the levelling process had commenced. Barring Elphinstone Circle, the configuration of the business part of the town, its main streets and lines of communication, are very much in appearance what they are now in 1882. In a picture in this book taken from about the site of the Town Hall, we are glad to renew acquaintance with our old friend, the Cathedral. It is the same, and not the same. Being shorn of the upper portion of the tower where the clock is, it looks stunted in the picture, what Dr. Chalmers to an agricultural friend called "a church of the short-horned breed." It looks abashed and less crowded than it now is, and altogether in a lonely and noiseless neighbourhood.

We can aver that the same tree, a *ficus*, which still overshadows the fountain between the Circle and the Cathedral, where so many men and beasts slake their thirst and find a shelter from the noon-day sun, is there. On the site of Sassoon's Buildings (Kemp's) are two double-storeyed houses, the upper storey having a verandah the exact counterpart of that which you may still see in the old Secretariat, Apollo-street, and which may be accepted as the type of the houses which were being erected about this time. In this neighbourhood, and occupying as it were the rim of the Bombay Green, were the houses of the leading Government servants and merchants, but mostly one-storeyed bungalows, as the want of room had not begun to tell, the best proof of which is that on looking up Church Gate-street we can see that the great block now opposite Mrs. Lake's shop, extending for two or three hundred yards up our present Hornby-row, is covered with cocoanut-trees. That quarter within the Fort walls occupied by what Grose calls the black population—we mean what is embraced between Hornby-row and Mody Khan-street and the Circle, and the outlet to the north of Bazaar-street on your way to the Boree-bunder station, where the old Bazaar-gate stood—seems as densely peopled as now. The population of the island was then about 100,000. Not only so, but Apollo and Marine-streets, Church Gate-street, Hummum-street, Medows-street in all its integrity under another name which we do not know, as General Medows' Governorship was so late as 1788 to 1790, and even the lanes, such as Ash, Dean, Rope Walk, and others, debouching on our now Rampart-row, are extant; while the block on which the Oriental Bank now stands, and which some of our readers will remember as the site of Treacher's shop, stands out like a promontory parallel with the walls of the town. There is now a house, two-storeyed, and as the phrase goes, self-contained, at the end of Medows-street, nearly opposite the old *Bombay Gazette* office, which represents a style of this date (and another of a similar character may be seen next to the old Court House, in Apollo-street), and which a Glasgow reader would recognise as an exact copy of the buildings in Virginia-street, belonging to the same period. It must have been, we think, the residence of some European magnate who courted the sea-breeze on this outskirt of the Fort; and the walls of some portion of the Convent School and Chapel in the same street are so old that you need not be afraid to carry them back to a time anterior to the English occupation. As for Cowasjee Patel-street, Parsee Bazaar-street and Mody Khan-street, there are no doubt houses there, either inhabited or in ruins, as old as Bombay Castle.

There was scarcely at this time in all Colaba a single building except three tombs (one of which at all events remains) in the middle of the island, which were always kept whitewashed as a guide to vessels entering the harbour; and at the extreme end, on a small eminence, a look-out house (he does not say a light-house) for ships. The whole of Colaba, he tells us, was let in 1750 for grazing at £20 or Rs. 200 per annum. We are afraid we must bring Mendham's Burying-ground nearer the Fort walls than the Bandstand and Cooperage, the site usually assigned to it. The portico of St. Andrew's Kirk as it now stands (1882) would be, we estimate, about 200 feet from the gateway of Mendham's Burying-ground, which was a parallelogram apparently about 500 feet long and 250 broad, and so near the sea (you must make allowance for reclaimed land) that at high tide on walking along the beach you would, as in the case of Colaba churchyard, require to elbow your way round the corner between the sea and the cemetery walls. We know that Mendham's Burying-ground was cleared away in 1760, and Sonapore opened at the same time. Grose's map lays down Mendham, which is evidence in itself that it was drawn before 1760. The banian-trees near the Young Men's Christian Institute are no doubt exuberant for obvious reasons. We must not omit that in our *coup d'œil* past the Cathedral, we descry at the terminus of Church Gate-street the gate itself, turreted (near the Floral Fountain), and with perhaps a sleeping-room above, also a side door or "needle-eye" for late men who were on the *wandergang* and required the pass or word of the night during the small hours. At this period, and long before it, there must have been many residences, country-houses of rich Portuguese and others, at Mazagon. Of what may be termed the new Native Town, north of the Esplanade, the eastern part, say about the present Jumma Musjid, comprehending the Market, Mandvee, Oomerkharree and Bhooleshwar districts are much older than the western, *i.e.*, Dhobee-talao, Girgaum, Chowpattee and Khetwadee, which latter appear as a mass of cocoanut-gardens, so late as a map of 1806. It is astonishing how even now the cocoa-nut seems to swallow up all the buildings in this last-named district in a mass of greenery. For look at it from Cumbala Hill or the new road on Malabar Hill, in the month of May when every green herb without water is here withered up, and this is the case. Much more from the summit of the Clock Tower ; and Mr. Geary mentioned in the account of his balloon ascent, that at an altitude of several thousand feet, almost everything of Bombay disappeared except the docks and the coco trees, in fact, I think he hinted that our abode for this very reason might be called the "Green Isle." Speaking of

THE DOCK YARD

we may as well accompany Mr. Grose to it. He calls it the Marine Yard, and to-day we enter it by the same big gateway opposite the old Court House, the ground being still devoted to the same purpose as in 1750. A crowd of new buildings have since sprung up with which we do not at present concern ourselves. The original Dry Dock of Bombay still exists in all its integrity. It astonished not only Grose but Niebuhr, who notes that two ships could be repaired in it at one time. Though ship-building has much outgrown the dimensions of this dock, it can still accommodate two craft of considerable burthen at once, and to our hazy notions of hydraulic engineering, seems a splendid piece of mason work, as good to-day apparently as it was 150 years ago. The newer dock nearer the Sailors' Home, and lying in juxta position and parallel with this, does not at all events by way of contrast offer anything favourable. Outside of these, and we now approach the utmost limit in this direction of the Bombay fortification seawards, is a salient angle covered by a most venerable relic of antiquity, and which you ascend by stairs much the worse for the wear. This is no less than the Royal Bastion of Bombay, on which no doubt much bunting and gunpowder were expended in former generations. The ground sounds hollow under your feet, for lascars of sorts or marine men and women seem to have taken up their abode in Troglodyte fashion within the vaults beneath. On descending you observe an arch as old looking as the hills, which leads through a tunnel to the other and shore side of this bastion and great sea-wall. Here Grose no doubt heard the waves of the Indian Ocean dashing at his feet, and saw before him the melancholy main, with, in one direction, no land intervening between him and the coast of Africa. This bastion to a favoured few at 6 p.m. must have supplied in 1750 the place of the Apollo-bunder, and a more eligible spot for enjoying the sea-breeze and a view of the harbour we cannot imagine.

CARTOGRAPHY OF BOMBAY.

Dr. Fryer's map is the earliest, say, about 1675, though the book which bears his name was published later. Mahim woods and the fishing-stakes in the harbour are laid down precisely where they are at present (1882). "Only one Tower of Silence recently built." Ovington gives a plan of the citadel in 1668, the main lines of which may still be traced and identified. Baldaeus, a Dutch clergyman, has good plans and pictures of the castle about the same date. Grose's map is simply invaluable, though it is only of what is within the walls (Mendham excepted), for every street is laid down, and it is accompanied by a scale of feet. Niebuhr's map of the Island of Bombay (1764) has all the forts from Reeva and Sion to Mazagon and Dungaree, and the castle, on the tank bastion of which, he flies the flag of the English nation. We have inspected a hand-made map of 1806 (Mackintosh's time), a most elaborate performance : the Government House near the Cathedral, brilliantly coloured, and the new town, that is, near the Crawford Market, already covering a vast amount of space. Our readers have observed two promontories on looking out from the Vellard. They have tombs on them. The name of the left-hand one is Bawa Hajee ; the right Beebee Hajeen. Of maps, the worst is that which accompanies Murray's Hand-book, 1881, and which ought to be the best. We ask the reader to look at it. There are about three dozen names to illustrate 400 pages of letter-press, and the map is a miserable specimen of the engraver's art, and falls far behind the plan of Bombay published in the same book in the edition of 1857. The best map of the Island of Bombay, both for accuracy and execution, was printed in London in 1843, and represents the city and island in 1812-16, the population being then 243,000. This map of Thomas Dickenson is a perfect *chef d'euvre.* Major Jervis' signature is at the foot, with the picture of a tortoise as a tail-piece, and the motto *Paulatim.* No need for apology. Slow but sure, this is a perfect gem of the engraver's art, and can never be excelled. The largest map that we have seen, with all the docks and reclamations up to 1881, is in Messrs. W. and A. Graham's office, and was constructed for that firm. It covers a side of a large room, and resembles Colonel Laughton's great masterpieces of Revenue Survey in this, that spread out on the ground, it would require one to take off his shoes, and crawl, spider-like, over the surface for days and nights together, with occasional intervals for refreshment.

In 1750 we do not doubt that most of the houses and streets round Mombadevee and Pydhonee, *i.e.*, Copper-smiths' Bazaar, &c., were in existence. As for Malabar Hill and Breach Candy at this time, we may leave their bungalows as not either in *esse* or in *posse*, except the Parsee ones on the left, half way up Malabar Hill, and possibly one or two situated on the slope of the hill near the foot of the Seeree road, now cut away by the Back Bay Reclamation, and one of which was occupied by Arthur Wellesley in 1803. Belvedere, near the beach at Mazagon, was inhabited shortly after this time by Daniel Draper of "Eliza" celebrity; but so late as 1812

Colonel Dickinson gives only two bungalows on Breach Candy—the Beehive and the Retreat, the last of which under the name of the Wilderness, as we take it, has been known to our readers for a great many years. On Malabar Hill in 1812-16 there is not a single bungalow in Colonel Dickinson's map, and we believe that the one occupied by the Municipal Commissioner was the oldest, having been erected about 1830.

THE TOWERS OF SILENCE.

Niebuhr only mentions one in 1764, as Fryer does in 1675. Our author (1750) only mentions one, and gives a picture of it. He says it is 25 feet in diameter and 12 feet high. He was told that if anybody looked into it, he was sure to die. He went, nevertheless, but a Parsee told him to desist, otherwise he should not long survive his idle curiosity. Niebuhr tells us why the Towers of Silence are closed against strangers—

> "cet edifice est actuellement
> formé depuis qu a ce qu'on
> raconté une jeune et belle fille
> qui etait morte forte subitement
> et enterreé tout de suite, avait
> reçu encore une visite de son
> aimant dans ce lieu funebre."—*Arabie.*

FIRST PARSEE IN EUROPE.

Our readers will recollect that Briggs, in his book on the Parsees, states that Maniar, a Parsee, accompanied by Hurriman, a Hindu, visited England in 1781 as agents of Bajee Rao Peshwa of Poona. They were guests of Edmund Burke at Beaconsfield, and Briggs considers it the earliest visit of a Parsee to England on record. This book, published in 1772, records one still earlier. Grose's words are "Nowrojee Rustomjee, who was here in England, and whose family was of the greatest consideration among those people, deduced his descent from the Kings of Persia." No doubt; but it is his descent upon England we are noticing at present.

A PLUCKY WOMAN.

A Ranee, whose son had been killed in battle by the first Bajee Rao, and who was so powerful as to be able to raise 5,000 horse, sent him a challenge, which Bajee Rao declined in the following characteristic manner. The stake, he said, was not equal, for though she might gain immortal reputation by conquering Bajee Rao, he could not possibly gain any by conquering a woman.

ELEPHANTA.

He takes the condition of the caves as proof positive that no earthquakes of any consequence have visited this district within the historic period. He is not so happy in elucidating the meaning of the sculptured group, so familiar to us all, where Sheeva takes hold of the child. Where he sees the judgment of Solomon, Dr. Wilson descries a pourtrayal of the infanticide of India, that dark shadow of the saddest crime that ever afflicted humanity.

Here is

HIS PORTRAIT OF KANOJEE ANGRIA,

the founder of the family. He was a well-set, corpulent man, rather blacker than commonly the Deccanees are, full-faced, with a sparkling eye and stern countenance. He was very severe in his commands and exact in punishing; otherwise liberal to his officers and soldiers, with whom he effected a sort of military frankness, not to say familiarity. He was too, like the Mahrattas, not very careful of keeping faith, and excused the making any peace with him on which it was fore-known that no reliance could be had. His general appearance was thus quite the opposite of Seevajee, who was a fair, lean, and wiry man. Of

RAIGHUR

Grose heard fearful accounts. Caernarvon and Dunstaffnage were nothing to it. He asserts that it grew as much grain as the garrison required. There was a great mystery in those days about Raighur, and this was, no doubt, one of the inventions of the enemy to make Bombay shake in its shoes; for our readers are aware that the top of Raighur is a very narrow superficies comparatively, and was crowded with buildings. He relates a story of which we think Seevajee must be the hero. He says it was the Maharajah; but such stories, when they are good, are passed on from age to age. It appears that there was a sorceress on the hill, and he resolved to put her to death, but had the curiosity to see her first. The woman accordingly appeared. "She was about forty, very corpulent, and not of an ill presence." Why doesn't he say at once she was fair, fat, and forty? He asked her sternly if she knew why he had sent for her, to which she replied that she knew he s going to put her to death. "I hope," she said, "for your own sake you will allow me to give you a salutary warning." Curiosity, or a belief in witchcraft, induced him to comply, when she ordered a cock and a hen to be brought before her into the royal presence. "The cock was set down on the ground, full of life and spirit, then taking the hen, she desired the Raja, to mark the consequences. At these words she wrung the head of the hen off, when at the same time the cock, though untouched by any one, imitating all the convulsions and agonies of its death accompanied the hen in it." "This, Sir," said she to the Rajah determinately, "remember to be a type of your fate and mine." Henceforth he was bound up in the bundle of life with her, and it is needless to say the witch was provided for, had a pension ever afterwards, and a palanquin she could call her own.

BULLION AND EXCHANGE.

As for exchange it was 2s. 6d.; and Grose says "The East Indies is a bottomless pit for bullion, which can never circulate back to Europe, and when bullion fails trade must cease,"—which are nearly the very words that Bernier uttered a century before. In bills he records only one transaction, but as it is of an abnormal character, we are tempted to give it. A jogee came into Ajmere and presented a bill of exchange for Rs. 2,000 to the Governor drawn payable to the bearer by the god Ram. The Governor told him with a laugh that he was an impostor, and he went all round the town, but everybody received him with scoff, and said that it was a bad bill. At length a rich oilman devoutly accepted it, and paid the amount. The fakir immediately left the town, and fulminated a curse of leprosy upon all the inhabitants of Ajmere for twelve years, which immediately took effect. We need not add that the oilman was excepted from the ban, and that the fakir took the proceeds of the bill with him.

NATIVE CHARACTER.

We have on a former occasion alluded to the settlement of the Bania caste in Bombay under Gerald Aungier, a race which has contributed very much to its aggrandisement. But strange to say, almost every writer has described them as of surpassing greed. Dr. Fryer, otherwise a most impartial traveller, opens the vials of his wrath on their head, and says that the fleas and the Banias are the vermin of India, and that they are a mass of sordidness; that they are blood-suckers, horse-leeches, cheats, liars, and dissemblers. Grose has something to say which is worthy of note. He says that he has read all that has been said about them, and he thinks that their probity in Surat is equal to that of the European, and his belief is that the bad character given to them must be understood as only applicable to the petty under-dealers among them. An English captain would come ashore with the invoices, musters, and samples of his cargo, and after striking a bargain the cash—£20,000 or £30,000—would be paid down to him on the nail, with no further trouble to him. What he means to say is that the better classes are good business men and not addicted to sharp practice.

There are, however, occasional glimpses in which we may see character higher than this; how near it approaches generosity and beneficence, we leave each reader to determine for himself. The instance Grose cites we give in a foot-note.* The story in this conjunction, though the resemblance does not go further than that there was a European on the one side and a native on the other, must occur to the reader of Malcolm in his errant days. But the most memorable instance is that which is cited by Mountstuart Elphinstone. It apparently fell within his own knowledge, and as such illustrates a pleasing branch of Indian ethics which we would fain hope is not yet extinct.†

MALABAR HILL.

About the year 1735 there came to Bombay a preacher who made a prodigious sensation. He

* "Don Antonio de Sylva Figueroa, Vice-Admiral, on receiving an order from the Viceroy of Portugal to equip a squadron for sea, found himself utterly unable to furnish the requisite advances to which the duty of his post obliged him. This naturally made him uneasy, and melancholy, which being observed by his mistress, who with some difficulty wrung the cause of it from him, she left him abruptly, and in a manner that made him conclude she was, in the style of that sort of woman, going to add her desertion to that of fortune, and which would not have been the least of his afflictions; but he was soon surprised at her return with a casket of jewels and gold to the amount of near three thousand pounds, being more than he wanted, and which she, with very good grace, obliged him to take as a mark of her affection. This piece of generosity, from its being so uncommon, made the more noise, and reaching the ears of the late King John of Portugal, it affected him so that by the next ship he sent out letters of legitimation to the Admiral's son by that dancer."—*Grose.*

† "A perfectly authentic instance might be mentioned, of an English gentleman in a high station in Bengal, who was dismissed, and aftewards reduced to great temporary difficulties in his own country; a native of rank, to whom he had been kind, supplied him, when in these circumstances, with upwards of £10,000, of which he would not accept repayment, and for which he could expect no possible return. This generous friend was a Maharatta Brahmin, a race, of all others, who have least sympathy with people of other castes, and who are most hardened and corrupted by power."—*Elphinstone.*

In a view of Bombay a little after this period we find in

was a jogee or fakir, and had been to Tibet, China—yea, to Tartary. Far-away fowls have

---

Niebuhr, the father of the historian who was here in 1764, and to whose memory Palgrave dedicates his book on Arabia, what is wanting in Grose. Between the two we need not be at a loss. That the population was 140,000, and had doubled itself in twenty years; that the old Government House on the sea side was *un vieux chateaux de peu de consequence;* that there was the most abundant toleration are facts expatiated on by both these writers. Some of Niebuhr's small facts are interesting—that he met some Greeks settled in Bombay; that the English wear tight clothes; that the houses have tiled roofs; that European foreigners do not make much in commerce; that the highest military officer, who is also a member of Council, has only the title of Major; that there are many Polish, Swiss, Dutch, and German officers in our Indian Army; that there is only one clergyman for the whole of Western India, the minister of Bombay, who does duty at Surat, Angengo, and Tellicherry, and that when he dies, the faithful must wait until word is sent home and another comes out; that the Europeans in Bombay were a non-marrying race, for neither marriage nor baptism took place when he was in the island; that the Pope had sent out a Bishop of Bombay, but the Governor announced that there was no need of an ecclesiastic with such a high title; that the African slaves owned by Englishmen and others were all Roman Catholics, and that the church at Parel was already a magnificent *salle a manger* and dancing-room. From Grose we learn that the island was divided into three Roman Catholic parishes: Bombay, Mahim, Salvaçam, the churches of which are governed by any nation but the Portuguese. He also informs us that there was a public garden at Parel, and that there were European deserters in the fleet of Angria, and that—*mirabile dictu!*—some Englishmen chewed betel-nut, and finally—

> Il est permis a tous de faire
> commerce depuis le President d'un
> etablissement jusq'u au moindre clerc.

and

> Les Indiens sont bien la nation
> la plus tolerante de l' univers
> car dans quels pais de l' Europe
> permettoit on a gens d'une
> autre religion de precher
> ouvertement contre celle qui est
> la dominante dans le pais!

a bitter satire on the state of religious toleration in Europe in 1764.

Love-grove.—Maria Graham in 1814 tells us the romantic story of the two lovers. We have given their names. The name of Love-grove is, no doubt, due to this incident. We understand that Vellard is a Portuguese word for causeway. The lovers were Muslim, but both Muslim and Hindoo pay great veneration to these tombs.

bonnie feathers ; so the Bombay folks took to him amazingly. His raiment was scant, and his hair was long.

Mahmood Begurra of Ahmedabad, the Blue Beard of Indian history, could twist his moustaches over his head, or tie them under his chin. But this man's hair was so long that it reached down to his heels, and to prevent it trailing on the ground, he doubled it up again to the crown of his head. Here the force of nature could no further go, so it was wreathed in rolls, and rose in a russet spire, into which colour it had been sunburnt from its original black. He made a pile of earth on the shore between the Walkeshwur Pagoda and the sea. He surrounded the pile with faggots, and after setting them on fire, he stood up within the blazing circle and preached from the midst of the flames. The effect was marvellous, and a perfect *bursat* of rupees was the result.

The little brownish-yellow pagoda you descry from the Malabar Point grounds, on the sea-shore, is very picturesque and owes its existence to this fervid preacher. The ground hereabout seems to have a horrible fascination for devotees, for our readers will recollect that about a dozen years ago a fakir built himself up in a square piece of masonry, out of which nothing would tempt him to come.

Grose is enthusiastic on the scenery of Malabar Hill, and notices the trees on the way to the Point, with their branches twisted by the wind at right angles and all in one direction. They give one an idea, he says, of the temple-groves so often pictured by the ancients. We are glad to meet with these old friends in 1750.

It is Mackintosh, we think, who states that Gray, the author of the Elegy, was the first, or among the first, who in his letters expatiated with exquisite taste on the pleasure derivable from the contemplation of fine scenery. Mackintosh, we daresay, never saw this book. Had he done so, he would have seen described at his own doors a scene which evoked this earlier notice; and as it has more than a local interest, we give Grose's memorable words, which will receive commendation as long as there is an eye or a mind to appreciate the beautiful in nature :—" On the sea-side stands the Gentoo Pagoda. The other three sides are surrounded with trees that form an amphitheatre on the slopes of the hill towards it, than which no prospect that I ever saw or can conceive forms a more agreeably wild landscape." So say we all of us.

THE BOOK OF GOMBROON,

1752-53.

CHAPTER VIII.

THE BOOK OF GOMBROON, 1752-53.

A mirror wherein passed to and fro the images of the ancient days.—*Chaldee Manuscript.*

The Book of Gombroon has lain in Bombay for one hundred and twenty years; and it is almost in perfect condition and legible, thanks to the papermaker, the ink with which it is written, the large round hand of the scribe, and thanks also to the zealous interest of those who have kept it among their archives and transmitted it safely from generation to generation. If all the books in Bombay were printed or written on such paper, we would have no fear of their future condition. But, unfortunately, this is not the case. That which the locust hath left the caterpillar hath eaten, that which the caterpillar hath left the cankerworm hath eaten, and the palmerworm and white-ant will devour the residue. If things go on as they are, we are safe in saying that in the year 2000 every book now in Bombay will have crumbled into dust or leaf-mould, except the *Birds of Asia*, which may still maintain a feeble and fluttering existence on the tables of the Asiatic Society. We except also the holograph Wellington and Contemporary Despatches, in the Secretariat, which have been, as respects climate and insects, *carefully* bound in 8 vols. morocco, by a late Secretary to Government ; and no doubt, if well kept, they will defy the lapse of time and the fingering of visitors. Every reader in the public libraries of Bombay will bear us out that the leaves of many of the books are as brittle as tinder. You must take them up tenderly ; and woe betide the unlucky wight who, at the tenth hour, when deep sleep falleth upon men, foldeth down the corner of the leaf he is perusing, for when he next openeth the tome, the dog-ear will drop to the ground, a silent monitor to remind him not only of the ravages of the monsoon and the white-ants, but of his own stupid and unpardonable act. And as for newspapers, we question very much whether a perfect consecutive series exists for the last thirty years. If it does we have not been able to find it. This is much to be deplored, for a time will undoubtedly come in the progress of this city when everything connected with its history and the preservation of its public muniments will be regarded with more zeal and interest than at present. If our University and all those seats of learning that are rising around us mean anything, they mean that men will come forth from their walls who will ask the question how Bombay comes to hold the pre-eminent position it does as a city among the nations of the East, what were the means and who were the individuals who helped to accomplish this great end.

HISTORY NOT ANTIQUARIANISM.

Why should this species of knowledge be relegated to the domain of antiquarianism, as if the history which God has given us for our profit were a collection of tinpots, rusty pans, and old-wives' fables? History surely has nobler uses than this; and the English have nothing to hide in regard to the part they have played in the history of Western India. No injury can possibly accrue to the natives by a knowledge of the past. Let them know that their ancestors were plundered by the Peshwas almost within the memory of man, and their heads beaten with wooden mallets, and that they had never a pice they could call their own; that the land which now waves with rich harvests of grain and cotton was once overgrown with weeds; and that their masters were such tyrants and oppressors, that industry itself ceased to be a virtue, and men were driven to the open country, to fight for existence like the wild beasts of the earth. Those were the days in Bombay when there were no meetings of Town Council, nor in Poona drives in open carriages to Bamboorda. They will be all the better for this knowledge; the seeds of philanthropy and religion will then fall on a kindlier soil, and the men who are now suspicious of you will become your friends and allies, helpers in the great work of the regeneration of mankind. The natives of this country are not less sensible than we are to the lessons of history. They only need educating in it; and for them the history of Western India must surely be more interesting than, say, the Conquest of Peru, or even the Decline and Fall of the Roman Empire.

The text which has called forth this sermon is a small one, for it would be difficult to select a place less known, or less fitted to awaken an interest of any kind in the reader. You cannot get excited about Gombroon,* for the history of a small factory on the Persian Gulf, subordinate to Bombay, at a time when Bombay itself was not above the level of mediocrity, is certainly not attractive. And yet from 1621 to 1759 successive relays of Englishmen were sent to its inhospitable shores, to help to build up somehow, not even in India itself, the fabric of the Indian Empire. For the Englishmen of those days stuck at nothing. Persia was in anarchy: there was bad trade; there was nothing but disease; there was nothing but death. But still the procession up the Straits of Ormuz went on, of these belated victims, doomed to die.

MORTALITY BILLS.

The scene opens with Danvers Graves, President; Wood, Percival, and Wents, council. A few days pass, and the black camel which kneels at every man's door† comes for Graves. Graves mounts, obedient to the summons. Then it kneels for Percival; then for Wents. They all, at intervals, ride away to the silent land.

Emboldened by success, it came for Wood. Wood was tough; looked the grisly undertaker in

* Represented by Bunder Abbas.
† Turkish Proverb.

the face, and probably said with Wycliffe, "Go away! I shall not die, but live and declare the works of the Lord," or more probably he said, "I shall live, make money, and sell piece-goods." The brute this time does not kneel, merely makes a feint of doing so, curls the lip, snarls, groans, and passes on. Wood was saved by the skin of his teeth; in his own words, "through the mercy of God, who thought fit to prolong my life, for the enjoyment (I hope) of a more agreeable climate."

The fittest survive; sometimes they do. It is not a bad thing, however, in qualifying for this competition for existence to have a strong heart, stout lungs, and a steady pulse; in other words, to be sound in wind and limb. But Wood was so nearly dead that Dr. Forbes gave him up, and Brabazon Ellis in Bussorah, believing that he too had drunk of the promotion wine, becomes almost hilarious, and writes all imaginable compliments to his supposed successor, taking good care to warn the *locum tenens*, whoever he might be, black or white, not to break a seal or touch dead men's effects until a properly covenanted servant arrives. The scene changes. A fresh batch of Civil Servants from Bombay, consisting of Douglas, Sedgwicke, Secker, and Parsons, soon make good the deficiency, take their places at the Council Board, examine accounts, and sign their names in token of the correctness thereof. But still man is mortal. We observe a gap where the name of Sedgwicke ought to be—between the other signatures—left vacant for him by the considerate courtesy of his colleagues. Will he no come back again? Alas! not this journey. An entry, a few days farther on, tells us the reason, laconic enough, "Mr. William Sedgwicke departed this life of nervous fever and fits." So the gap still stares us in the face in 1881, a *memento mori*. In these days every epithet of deserved abuse was heaped on Gombroon. They may all, however, be summed up in the sailor's proverb:—"There is an inch deal between Gombroon and hell."

The wonder to us is that, under such circumstances, any books at all were kept; and yet here is a book of 160 pages closely written, of the same shape, but of course not so thick, as a merchant's ledger. When one man laid down the pen, another took it up. Every letter, inward and outward, is copied: what orders were received, what orders given, buying wool, selling drabs, recording visits, noting politics, repairing premises, fitting out ships, reforming drunkards, cash received; each item, disbursements likewise, month by month, details of servants' wages, stable and garden expenses, accounts examined, and attested by the holograph signatures of the survivors or survivor.

The year 1752 was *annus mirabilis*. It had only 354 days in it; and yet we have here over 200 entries, many of them pages in length neatly written under as many days.

Such are some of the prosaic details of which this volume consists; but it was by such methods the Englishman gained standing ground in the East. Not all the glory belongs to Clive and Wellington. By unknown men, and in places equally unknown, the battle was fought and the foundation laid of the Indian Empire. They had almost none of our advantages, though they helped to make them. They worked in obscurity and they died in obscurity, mute and inglorious if you will, but not unheroic as they laid themselves down to sleep on the deserts of Asia.

THE INKSTAND.

Amid these sombre shadows there is a gleam of human activity and misdirected energy. As often happens in an emergency or big disaster, some one is found busying himself with the veriest trifles. As in the catastrophe on the Bhore Ghaut, some years since, where poor Howard was killed, the gentleman next him, extricating himself (besmeared with blood) from the débris of the broken train, was confronted by his servant, weeping bitterly, and bearing in his hand the fragments of a cigar-box, the cause of all his loud lamentation. But we proceed. The new comers from Bombay take their respective seats at the Gombroon Council table, and resolutely proceed to overhaul the accounts. The fact gradually dawns upon them that from the property of the East India Company a silver inkstand is missing. We are left in doubt as to whether it was solid silver, German silver, or Britannia metal—two species of bi-metallism that gave the world much trouble in the eighteenth century. On this the depositions are silent. It *apparently* existed once, but not in the memory of man; but nevertheless year by year it stood in the annual balance of accounts a substantial asset of the factory. It could not walk away of itself. Mr. Wood does not aver that it was stolen. It could not wear away like napery; or old knives in India, reduced to attenuated shadows by grinding and attrition. What if Wood melted it down into bangles for his aunt, or domiciled it with his uncle. In any case is not this a crime of the first magnitude, to be punished by the judges ; fraud, culpable carelessness, breach of trust, falsification of accounts, and all that sort of thing?

We know not whose lynx eyes were instrumental in making this great discovery. Was it Douglas or Secker? Or the young writer Parsons, urged on to glorious issues? There is a proverb about new brooms.

"May 25, 1753. In the accounts of household furniture, there appearing sundry articles which are actually worn out, and also an Inkstand in the account of plate which Mr. Wood declares he has never seen since his arrival, as do the linguist and factory brokers who have been thirty years in the factory, it is now agreed that they be wrote off and particular mention be made of the standish in our next advices to the Honourable President and Council."

So the Inkstand was written off in Gombroon, and nobody was hanged. When the waves reached our city there would be some commotion ; but they would soon expend themselves, and find their level on the bastions of Bombay Castle. We have seen that men were not immortal in Gombroon. We now see that they were not infallible. "1752, October 5.—Account salary for one month and six days' salary due to Henry Sewage, Esquire, on his departure, included by mistake in the salary bill dated 31st July last, and now paid back, Rs. 120."

ETCETERA.

The two great bugbears of these times, which have become serious realities in our own, were the Russians and the Afghans—*Offgoons*, a *bizarre* spelling which may please some of the disciples of Sir William Jones or Dr. Hunter. Both the India House and Bombay were extremely anxious to know about the Russians; and the Gombroon factory furnished them with all needful information on the sales of Russian piece-goods and other matters, describing the route taken by the Russian gentlemen with their drabs and broadcloth from Astrakhan to Muscat. I am inclined to think that this is the first notice we have of Russian traders here, an after result due doubtless to the enterprize of Peter the Great. There was an air of great mystery about everything Russian in India, and even the Tapti for a generation later on was considered by intelligent Englishmen to rise in the mountains of Great

Tartary.* Mildew in piece-goods turns up in these old times to vex the souls of the factors, and two other evils of more ancient date affecting the bodies and souls of men, drunkenness and incontinence, which were visited with expulsion *pro tem.* Geologists may be interested to learn that in these parts, and in this age, the sea gained on the land so rapidly as to threaten the English House, and extort a cry to Bombay to sanction means of protection from its invasion. This was the year when the style was changed, and Bombay wrote Gombroon to call the 3rd September the 14th September, and so on afterwards, allowing 11 days to lapse; which was done. The men (*per mensem*) profited by this. Everything for the India House was sent *overland*—that is the word and our age is not the inventor of it—via Bagdad and Aleppo, whence the Consul forwarded the Bombay, Surat, and Gulf letters on to Europe.

We may as well, however, remark that on and after this date down through all the French Re-

* *Nikitin*, the Russian who was in the Bombay Presidency in 1468-74, says:—"And I poor sinner brought a stallion to the land of India. With God's help I reached Jooneere all well, but it cost me a hundred roubles." An amusing and early instance of the horse trade of Arabia with India. If the Russians only read the description which follows, they would surely never think of coming to India. "All are black and wicked, and the women all harlots or witches or thieves and cheats; and they all destroy their masters with poison."

volutionary epoch, this was the orthodox route for quick letters to Europe, *overland*, a great deal more so than the route Waghorn opened up to us through Egypt fifty years ago, and which, it appears, will now hold good to the end of time, unless, indeed, the railway whistle shrieks through the deserted streets of Babylon and Nineveh.* If our memory serves us, there is an allusion in the earliest transactions of the Bombay Chamber of Commerce to an English mail agent being murdered on the Bagdad route. Angria was a name that still sent a tremour through Leadenhall-street; and the factory assure their masters that the great pirate never comes out of his creek or monsoon hiding-place until after September.

Richard Bourchier sits King in Bombay Castle; sometimes styled Governor, and as often President or General.† Two future Governors, Thomas

---

* During the monsoon of 1839 and 1840 letters were forwarded via the Persian Gulf and across the desert to Beyrout, and thence to Europe.

† This was the gentleman with whom Lord Clive had the angry tussle when in Bombay. I can only afford space for the last sentence of a remarkable letter to him which has been preserved. It is dated Bombay, 13th April, 1756:—"Considering the rank I bear of Lieutenant-Colonel in His Majesty's service, of Deputy Governor of St. Davids, of a Member of Committee of this place, I do not think I have been treated by the Honourable Richard Bourchier, Esquire, agreeably to the intention of the Honourable the Court of Directors, who, I flatter myself, will do me justice therein, when they come to hear thereof. I am, with respect, Honourable Sir and Sirs, your most obedient humble servant, ROBERT CLIVE."

Hodges* and William Hornby, sit with him in Council ; and a third, Crommelin, sways the sceptre as Chief at Surat. Brabazon Ellis, the luckiest Englishman of his age in Western India, wields a flowing pen at Bussorah, a man that neither disease nor impecuniosity can touch ; his covenant seems well ordered in all things, and sure ; and Daniel Draper has just finished his career as warehouse keeper at Gombroon. He had not then entered on that ill-starred alliance with Eliza, a lady destined to startle two priests out of their propriety, one famous or infamous in the Church of England, the other famous and infamous in the Catholic Church of France.

THE LORD OF THE HOT COUNTRIES.

We give in a foot-note a specimen letter from this gentleman to an English Captain.† He only owed allegiance to one man.

> " The Bactrian Sophi from the horns
> Of Turkish Crescent leaves all waste behind."

---

* These four men held the Governorship of Bombay 34 years :—Richard Bourchier 1750-1760, Charles Crommelin 1760-67, Thomas Hodges 1767-71, William Hornby 1771-84.

† THE TRANSLATION OF NASSEIR CAUN'S ORDER.
Mahomed Nasseir, slave of God, Prince of Princes, Supreme Lord of the Hot Countries, to whom the Grand Sophi of Persia is alone superiour, sends this his special Order unto the trustworthy English Captain, elected by favour of the Holy Jesus to fill the seat of Christian Dignity at Bunder Abassee.
The Omnipotent Creator of the Universe, who of his great Wisdom has appointed Kings and Rulers to act as his Deputys throughout the world for the support of Justice, and for the

FOUR GRADATIONS OF SERVICE meet the eye in this book. There is the Council at home, the Council at Bombay, the Council at Gombroon, and their subordinate at Bussorah. There is an etiquette in the language they address each other which pleases us to linger over. The India House letters are subscribed "Your loving Friends." Then follow the signatures of twenty individuals—members of the governing body. When Bombay writes Gombroon she follows in the same ancient strain of endearment. A noble house in many ways was this old India House. An inferior may not, however, thus address a superior; so we have in this book every gradation of respect represented from the lowest footstool up to the mighty throne of the Nabobs. "Right Worshipful Sir and Sirs," says Bussorah to Gombroon. "Your

---

universal tranquility of mankind, requires the most unfeigned humility in the reception, and the strictest obedience in the execution of their commands from all subjects and inferiors whatever. Be it therefore known unto you the trustworthy Captain of the English Factory that I, Mahomed Nasseir, slave of God, &c., &c., demand the immediate service of your ship to proceed in company with the Ramawny to the entrance of Shoft river, and in conjunction with her to prevent the King's ship from being delivered into the hands of the Muscat Arabs, which the base Traitor Abdul Shaik has enter'd into an agreement to do, for a valuable consideration in money; and whatever may be requisite to be done in regard to the present business Messey Suttoon, my faithful servant, will advertise you of. Be expeditious and careful in performing that duty which is now incumbent on you, and wait in hourly expectation of my coming.

Seal'd the seal of
NASSEIR CAUN—.

most humble and most obedient servant, B. Ellis."

"To the Honourable Richard Bourchier, Esq., President and Governor in Council in Bombay," writes Gombroon, opening with "Honoured Sir and Sirs;" and in like manner Gombroon heads its London letters "To the Honourable the Court of Directors for affairs of the United Company of Merchants of England trading in the East Indies." Then follows, "May it please your honours;" and concludes with all due respect as becometh, "may it please your honours, your most faithful and most obedient humble servants."*

The Empire of India is complex in its origin; but if it grew out of anything it grew out of a company of merchants.

* The French are great masters of this art:—*Agrees Monsieur l'assurance de ma parfaite consideration avec la quelle j'ai l'honneur d'etre le plus devoue de vos serviteurs.* But there was no greater stickler for the profuse method of concluding a letter than General Wellesley Bahadoor. With a small running hand like a lady's, each line an inch separate, Wellington soon covers a sheet of paper, even the large foolscap of his days. The letter is perhaps one short terse sentence: after which comes the flowing conclusion filling a whole page, "I have the honour to be, Sir, with the greatest respect your most obedient, faithful, and humble servant, Arthur Wellesley." He too addresses "The Honourab e Jonathan Duncan, *Esquire*," a correct designation, we believe, for all Governors and Councillors who are not Honourables in their own right, albeit common use sanctions it not in our day. There is nothing like a letter for bringing a dead man to life again, specially when the talc from the glass sparkles on the name, and has been shaken by the hand of Arthur Wellesley. The particles still glitter on the autograph, though the hand that shook them out has long crumbled into dust.

PEOPLE WERE HERE BEFORE US.

Gombroon was a common place, dull and dreary enough in all conscience; and yet around its shores Nearchus once manœuvred the fleet of Alexander. Hither also (for Ormus is within hail) came in spirit Milton, who has given to it an undying fame, in one line of Paradise Lost, in his description of the devil's throne in Pandemonium, which

"Outshone the wealth of Ormus and of Ind."

There was a Russian proverb, "whatever is produced on earth you find at Ormus."

We would except *Ice*, the mention of which brings us appropriately to William Baffin, who was killed in 1621, at the siege of Kismis, a neighbouring island, and is buried there. His grave is unknown; but his name, in Baffin's Bay, covers several degrees of the Arctic Circle.

THE ENGLISH SIRNAMES OF BOMBAY.

There are historical names which have at intervals occupied the public eye for more than a century, specially in Western India those of

Carnac and Malet.* Such instances are, however, much more numerous in Bengal.

But confining ourselves to the names mentioned in this book, it is strange to observe with what unfailing persistency, and without any genealogical succession that we can see, the same names crop up in our day. Ellis, Graves, Symmons, Wood, Wilson, Hunt, Draper, Sedgwick, Parsons, Percival, Crawley, Sewell, Douglas, Shaw, Forbes, Kerr, stalk across the foot-boards of 1752, and disappear into the darkness. It is no doubt a mere accident; the names are not uncommon, and may continue to repeat themselves in every age of Bombay until

THE END OF THE CHAPTER.

* General Carnac was Clive's second in command at the Battle of Plassey. His tomb in Bombay Cathedral was erected by his nephew, Mr. Rivett, member of Council, and father of the late Sir James Rivett Carnac. The last offshoot from this old genealogical tree was Sir Richard Temple, nephew of the aforesaid Sir James. The Malets have been before the Bombay public for the last hundred years.

HORATIO NELSON:

OR BOMBAY 1775.

CHAPTER IX.

HORATIO NELSON:

OR BOMBAY 1775.

WAS Lord Nelson in Bombay? This question has never been mooted by his biographers, nor by any one else, so far as we know. But everything connected with the early history of a great man is interesting. Our belief has long been that Lord Nelson spent a considerable portion of the time he was in the East Indies in Bombay and neighbouring waters, and that belief is founded on his own words:—"I was placed in the Seahorse, 20 guns, with Captain Farmer, and watched in the foretop, from whence in time I was placed on the quarter deck, having in the time I was in this ship visited *almost every part* of the East Indies, from Bengal to Bussorah."* Nelson was born in 1758, left England in the end of 1773 in the Seahorse for the East Indies, where he remained eighteen months, at the end

* Life of Nelson. From his Lordship's manuscripts; by Clarke and M'Arthur. London. 3 vols.

of which, broken down in health, he was transferred from the Seahorse to the Dolphin, and reached England in 1776. His Indian career is a total blank, and closes like the sea behind his ship. The course of the Seahorse has been hitherto as visionary as the Flying Dutchman, but we are now in a position to establish the fact that the Seahorse arrived in Bushire from Bombay and Muscat on May 12, 1775, that she sailed from Bushire on July 15, reached Muscat on July 31, and arrived in Bombay on August 17, same year. This accounts, at all events, for four months of the Seahorse, during which she was twice in Bombay harbour. There was a reason for her being in Bombay. This was the time we were at war with the Mahrattas, when we took possession of Tanna and Salsette, and Sir Edward Hughes's squadron, to which the Seahorse belonged (this is matter of history), was riding at anchor in Bombay harbour on February 17, 1776, and how long before we know not. We have now before us the journal* of a man who describes the voyage from Bushire to Bombay in the Seahorse, and narrates the incidents of it with graphic power. The journal was

* *Travels in Asia and Africa*; by the late Abraham Parsons, Esq. London: Printed for Longman, 1808.

not published until thirty-three years after it was written—in 1808—three years after the death of Nelson. Had Lord Nelson been alive we are sure that he would have read with much interest the narrative of a voyage when he himself, we believe, was so much prostrated by disease as not to be able to concern himself with anything.

There is no notice, however, of the young midshipman, and we did not expect it. Nelson was then the great unknown, and less likely to be noticed than Scott was at Sir Adam Ferguson's, or Burns when he wandered unknown on the banks of Fail.

Abraham Parsons was a Bristol man, an old skipper, Consul and Factor Marine (whatever that may mean) to the Turkey Company at Scanderoon, the proposed terminus of the Euphrates Railway still *in nubibus*. A shrewd observer, somewhat akin to another captain of a previous generation, who has left us much valuable information on Bombay matters—we mean Alexander Hamilton. One fine morning in 1774 the said Parsons packed up his traps, to wit, twenty camel-loads of merchandise and baggage, not forgetting wine, beer, and rum, and bade adieu to Scanderoon. We do not wonder at it, for it is a beastly place, and has been cursed by all men who have any regard for their healths for well nigh twenty centuries. Like so many a hero in the "Arabian Nights," combining business with pleasure, he set out for Bagdad, and after seeing the City of the Caliphs, found his way to Bushire. Here he found the redoubtable Seahorse. Bear in mind that we have Nelson's own words that he had sailed the Persian Gulf:—

"Bushear, 1775, May 12.—There arrived and anchored in the road his Majesty's ship Seahorse, Captain George Farmer, from Bombay, but last from Muscat, May 24. This day I accompanied Captain George Farmer, by his desire, from the town of Bushear to the road on board the Betty.

"July 15.—At five in the morning, I embarked on board his Majesty's ship the Seahorse. Captain George Farmer, who anchored in the outer road to wait for the (merchant) ships which were to proceed with him to Bombay."

"August 3, 1775.—At Muscat.

"17.—At 2 in the morning we saw the light of Old Woman's Island, near Bombay. At daylight we discovered the town of Bombay; and at 10 in the morning we anchored.

"His Majesty's ship was saluted with the guns from the Castle as usual, which was returned with two guns less than the salute."

We may now draw breath and take a look at the Seahorse as she lies in Bombay harbour. It was on board this ship that Nelson had his first dreams of ambition and glory. We have his own words for it:—"I will be a hero, and, confiding in Providence, will brave every danger." The good angel came to him with this when he was about to throw himself overboard. It was in this ship that a malignant disorder caught hold of him, which Southey, in his Life, tells us baffled all powers of medicine, and he was reduced to a skeleton, having entirely lost for some time the use of his limbs. Parsons here comes to our aid and fills up the spaces between the lines. This voyage of the Seahorse to the Persian Gulf was a most sickly one. Parsons says:—"Fluxes among our crew, combined with excessive heat coming down the Gulph, so debilitated our men, that some days twelve men fell down on the deck through excessive weakness." "Few escaped the disorder, either officer or private man." "The captain and nineteen men out of one hundred and seventy escaped it. Not a man died of those who were attacked."

We do not doubt that this was the sickness Nelson fell a victim to. They were nearly wrecked. "Two lieutenants and the master desired admittance into the cabin, having something of importance to offer to Captain Farmer: they were accordingly admitted, when they explained the necessity of leaving such of the convoy behind as could not keep up with the Seahorse, observing that if the ship could not make any southing, we should fall in with the land to the north of the isle of Diu, where there was no harbour; but, on the contrary, a dangerous shore, and a still more inhospitable set of men, and should they keep on the course which we now held, it would not only endanger the loss of his Majesty's ship, but the lives of every man on board. Captain Farmer thought their reasons so cogent that he followed their advice, and we left those ships that could not keep up with us." Were all officers so faithful and independent in the exercise of the trust committed to them, and all commanders so reasonable and open to conviction as Captain Farmer, we venture to think that there would be fewer wrecks. The Nelson family had some roving connection with Bombay. Lord Nelson's brother had been in the Indian Navy, been murdered, and his murderers were hanged on Gibbet Island in the harbour. Strange to say, that Mackintosh had lived—and a judge—for eight years in Bombay, and never had heard of it—merely heard it from a casual observation which fell from the master of the ship in which he went home. Hangings were few in these days, and we can merely guess that the event *took* place long previously—perhaps thirty years before Mackintosh arrived in the country.

The only other circumstance connecting Nelson with Bombay was his celebrated Battle of the Nile Letter to Governor Duncan of 9th August, 1798. A special officer, Lieutenant Duval, was sent with it, armed with letters to the Consuls and merchants at Alexandretta, Aleppo, Bussorah, &c. Nelson said he would pay the cost of this letter himself if the Government refused to do it. It came in time to save an immense outlay in the war defences of Bombay.

"If my letter is not so correct as might be expected, I trust your excuse when I tell you my brain is so shaken with the wound in my head, that I am sensible I am not always as clear as could be wished. But whilst a ray of reason remains, my heart and hand shall ever be exerted for the benefit of our king and country."

Behold then, reader, if you like, Nelson's first appearance on the Custom's Bunder of Bombay. But in case of misconception, we must ask you to clear away the Refreshment Room, and the bravery and bunting of the Gardens, and the Reclamations, Wellington and otherwise, that have so transmogrified the pristine beauty of this ancient rendezvous. A youth, diminutive in appearance, of 17 years of age, and of a somewhat florid countenance, heightened by the sea-brine, —a midshipman. Negligent in his dress, but as clean as a new gun. Careless of the refined courtesies of polished life, but with an address and conversation of irresistible charm.

His cronie, Tom Troubridge, is with him, and like greyhounds out of the leash they disappear. Bombay was then great in astrologists. One of them had predicted the death of the last Governor Hodges, and it came to pass. But there was no horoscope of this beardless youth, or of a time

> "When Nelson o'er his country's foes
> Like the destroying angel rose."

No cloud yet darkened the manly brow of Troubridge, or presaged his coming woe—the Culloden ashore in the bay of Aboukir, or the Blenheim* engulphed in the Madagascar Seas. Montgomery has written his dirge—

> "On India's long expected strand
> Their sails were never furled;
> Never on known or friendly land
> By storms their keel was hurled;
> Their native soil no more they trod,
> They rest beneath no hallowed sod
> Throughout the living world.
> This sole memorial of their lot
> Remains—They were, and they are not."

Having now, as we think, satisfactorily brought

* Sir Thomas Troubridge sailed from England in 1808. Never heard of.

Nelson to Bombay, our course is plain enough, as the Bombay of 1775 is not difficult to pourtray. We give Parson's account,* and supplement it from some other sources. The town had a population of about 150,000, the walls were complete, William Hornby, Governor; Town House, the old Court House, still standing opposite dock gates; Country House, Parell. James Forbes, the author of the Oriental Memoirs, and grandfather of the celebrated Count Montalembert was here, already Eliza Draper had left, and the ladies abounded in acts of philanthropy and

* The town of Bombay is near a mile in length from Apollo Gate to that of the bazaar, and about a quarter of a mile broad in the broadest part from the Bunda across the Green, to Church Gate, which is nearly in the centre, as you walk round the walls between Apollo and Bazaar Gate. There are likewise two marine gates, with a commodious wharf and cranes built out from each gate, besides a landing-place for passengers only. Between the two marine gates is the Castle, properly called Bombay Castle, a very large and strong fortification which commands the bay; the works round the town are so many, and the bastions so very strong and judiciously situated, and the whole defended with a broad and deep ditch, so as to make a strong fortress, which, while it has a sufficient garrison and provisions, may bid defiance to any force which may be brought against it. Here is a spacious green, capable of containg several regiments exercising at the same time; the streets are well laid out, and the buildings (viz., gentlemen's houses) so numerous and handsome, as to make it an elegant town. The soil is a sand mixed with small gravel, which makes it always so clean, even in the rainy season, that a man may walk all over the town, within half an hour, after a heavy shower, without dirtying his shoes The esplanade is very extensive, and as smooth and even as a bowling green, which makes either walking or riding round the town very pleasant. Near the extreme point of Old Woman's Island next the sea is a very lofty lighthouse, the light of which is so bright and well watched that it may be discerned at five leagues' distance. On this island are two large barracks for the military; sometimes a camp is formed here. It has good grass, not many trees, and a few houses, but neither town nor village. It lies so very open to the sea all round, as to be deemed a very healthy place, whither people after recovering from illness frequently move for a change of air.

benevolence. Several tombstones at Sonapore of this date record the pleasing manners and persons of the deceased. There is no countenance given by Parsons to the *pulla* fish origin of Apollo. It is spelled as we do now-a-days. Bunder becomes *Bunda*, a pronunciation agreeable to all who have been born within reach of the sound of Bow Bells. Nelson, we think, could have had few pleasant reminiscences of Bombay, and would turn his back with indifference on the Colaba Lighthouse, and bid good-bye to a place where the candle of his genius was nearly snuffed out. Had he died here he would have been among the first "inhabitants below" in Sonapore, and his bones would never have been asked for. Nelson and Wellington were two great captains. Bombay could not hold them long. Fired by new ambitions, in other lands, they trod an imperial pathway reserved only for the most illustrious of mankind. And now at the last they sleep side by side under the mighty dome of St. Paul's, and their names live evermore.

NAPOLEON BONAPARTE AT SUEZ, 1798.

CHAPTER X.

NAPOLEON BONAPARTE AT SUEZ, 1798.

"I have Bonaparte's despatches now before me. Bombay, if they can get there, I know is their first object."—Lord Nelson to Governor Duncan of Bombay. Letter dated Mouths of the Nile, 9th August, 1798.

THERE is a marvellous interest in everything connected with Napoleon Bonaparte; and now that his nephew has come and gone like a dream, the interest in no way lessens, but his figure bulks bigger by contrast, for the huge train of events of which he was the creator beggars everything that has come after him. When Louis Napoleon was paving the way for empire he filled the Paris *Théatre Historique* with gorgeous *spectacles,*—Siege of Toulon, Crossing the Alps, Plains of Italy, and the Invasion of Egypt; splendid scenic displays of war horses and fighting men, nowhere more full of startling and brilliant contrasts of East and West than when Italy was left behind for the turbans, scimitars, camels, palms, and pyramids of Egypt.

The invasion of Egypt began by the landing of the expedition, as our readers are aware, in 1798. The date was the 2nd July, and the episode of Napoleon's visit to Suez took place in December of the same year. He spent his Christmas holidays there.

SUEZ.

Now the half-way house between Europe and Asia, is a place of no great antiquity, at least under its present name.* It is here that the traditions of thirty centuries and the wisest expositors of Holy Writ agree in fixing the *locale* of the Exodus and the passage of the Red Sea by the Israelites. Volney in 1790 says:—"The ruinous condition of the houses heightens the melancholy scenery. Nobody remains at Suez

* 1500.

but the Governor, who is a Memlook, and twelve or fourteen persons who form his household."

There are glorious sunrises and sunsets here. Everything is steeped in glowing crimson, and the red light which overspreads the barren hills of Suez has been caught by Herbert in his great fresco in the House of Lords, where Moses is seen descending from Mount Sinai with the Tables of the Law. An English lady once settled here brought out with her a quantity of English earth, of which to make a miniature garden: "a dearer, sweeter spot than all the rest," for the land hereabout seems as if the curse of God lay upon it. It has great associations, but it is a poor consolation to the exile to be told that Suez is mentioned in the Arabian Nights*, that he is living on the sight of Cleopatris, of Arsinoe, or of Kolzium, nay, even that it was here that the angel of the Lord found Hagar by a fountain of water on the way to Shur. Who can bring a clean thing out of an unclean? They say that it is full of vermin. The king of the fleas keeps his court at Tiberias, but he has some most wicked vicegerents at Suez, which seem to combine the poison of Asia with

* Lane's Arabian Nights; Story of Joodar, 1517.

the pungency and active habits of modern Europe. Everybody seems to notice this. Pococke, in his "Description of the East and other Countries," 1737, says, "full of bugs and vermin;" and Sir Charles Napier, reduced to skin and bone in 1851, as we can verify, a "bearded vision," the mere atomy of a man, apparently far beyond the reach of insect attacks, utters these portentous words: "bugs abound." No traveller remains longer than he can help at Suez. An American once went over to the Wells of Moses. He was never seen again,—spirited away by the boatmen or others to the world to come. But this is the Suez of the past.

HIS VISIT AND SCHEMES.

Bonaparte left Cairo on the 24th December with 100 horse and 200 foot, and on the 25th was at Suez. His reasons for visiting Suez we shall see. He was the first man who took the Suez Canal out of the region of myth and dreamland, and gave a practical turn to it by taking with him a body of engineers. They mapped the course of the ancient canal and surveyed the ground deemed practicable for a new one; and when Lepere presented his report Bonaparte uttered these prophetic words:—"*La chose est grande ; ce ne sera pas moi qui maintenant pourra l'accomplir, mais le gouvernement turc trouvera peut-etre un jour sa gloire dans l'execution de ce projet.*" When Bonaparte came to Suez his fortunes were at a low ebb: his army, in a hostile country, was full of murmurs and discontent; and on the 1st August, 1798, the French fleet was destroyed in the battle of the Nile.

It was amid these disasters that in the last days of 1798 Bonaparte came to Suez. One would say that he had other work cut out for him than to drink water from the Wells of Moses, or hold confabulations with the monks of Mount Sinai. It is believed that during these five days that he was in the desert he revolved great schemes. He most probably resolved upon the invasion of Syria which immediately took place, and the invasion of England in 1803 which did not take place. The idea of a canal through the Isthmus had taken possession of him; for he reasoned in this way, that if France were in possession of a ship-canal the power of England in India would be broken. This idea never left him, and he often recurred to it in conversations with Sir Hudson Lowe at Saint Helena. We may well therefore believe that it was on the shores of Suez, with his eye towards the Red Sea, that this man in grey coat, and arms akimbo, with all hope of communicating with France cut off, hemmed in as he was like a wild beast of unconquerable will, meditated and projected great schemes on the fate of India.

He fortified Suez, the Wells of Moses, and Tor; transported gunboats on the backs of camels from Boulak; surveyed each shore of the Gulf of Suez as far as Shadwan*; saw with his falcon eye our troubles, Mysore and Mahratta; saw the unprotected coast of Guzerat, with its rich harvests, food for man and beast; wrote letters to the Shereef of Mecca, the Imaum of Muscat, and Tippoo Sahib of Seringapatam,—mere pasteboard and waste-paper all of them. The sepoys came from Bombay with Baird from the South, and Abercrombie came from the North; and in March, 1801, when the Highlanders, drenched with sea-water, rushed up the sand-hills of Aboukir, they turned the tide of French invasion, or, as Alison hath it, "delivered Egypt from

* Where the P. and O. steamer Carnatic was wrecked abou a dozen years ago.

the Republican yoke and decided in its ultimate consequences the fate of the civilised world."

"Highlanders! Remember Egypt," were Sir John Moore's last words at Corunna. So say we, all of us, highlanders and lowlanders.

CROSSES THE RED SEA.

At 3 a m., 28th December, Bonaparte set out from Suez on his way to the Wells of Moses, "out of respect for Moses." He took 60 foot and as many of the 100 horse as could conveniently accompany him. The cavalcade crossed the Red Sea, at the spot he assigned to the Exodus, and returned to Suez the same night. Being rather late, they made a narrow escape, for they came across the Gulf lower down, where the water was deeper. That there was some confusion, disorder, and shouting in the darkness, and that General Caffarelli's wooden leg insisted on swimming seems undoubted. That there was danger is proved by a native guide lingering behind, doubling the Gulf, and returning by land to Suez next morning. The following despatch is new to us on the *contretemps,* and corroborates the statement that

General Caffarelli became one of the Horse Marines :—

3819, au Général Berthier.
Quartier-général, au Caire, 20 nivose an vii,
9th January, 1799.

Le Citoyen Louis, guide à cheval, est nommé brigadier.
Il lui sera fait présent d'un sabre sur lequel sera ecrit sur un côte. " *Le général Bonaparte au guide à cheval Louis* ;" sur l'autre côté *passage de la mer Rouge.*

BONAPARTE.
Dépôt de la guerre.

Note.—Ce guide avait sauvé le général Caffarelli, dont le cheval, s'était abattu au passage de la mer Rouge.*

We give Kinglake's description from that most delightful of all books of Eastern travel, *Eothen,* 1836 :—

" Napoleon stayed five days at Suez. He made an attempt to follow the supposed footsteps of Moses, by passing the creek at this point ; but it seems, according to the testimony of the people of Suez, that he and his horsemen managed the matter in a way more resembling the failure of the Egyptians than the success of the Israelites. The people at Suez declare that Napoleon parted from his horse, got thoroughly submerged, and was only fished out by the assistance of the people on shore."

There is a charming *naïvete* about this, and it

* Correspondence de Napoleon Ier. Tome Cinquieme. Publiée par ordre de l'Empereur Napoleon III.

contains such a good joke for Englishmen that even Bourrienne's narrative, eye-witness as he was, and the accuracy of a despatch, ought not to be allowed to impair it.

STATE OF FEELING IN BOMBAY.

Geographically, Suez is a great distance from Bombay, politically it is very near, though Arabia lies between, a block so mighty as to cover an area almost as great as that of India itself;* and though there were no telegrams in those days, the sound of these great events soon penetrated to Western India. Early in January, 1800, General Stuart writes a long letter to the Bombay Government on the unprotected state of these coasts and of Surat. Every movement in Egypt was known to us here. Spies, secret agents, renegades (their letters may still be read) made us *au fait*. So when the venue was changed to Syria and the cry in India was "the Persian Gulf," we were prepared. People then did not need Robert Hall's passionate appeal "Recollect for a moment his invasion of Egypt." The fact was patent to us night and day.

* Arabia 1,139,600 square miles, India 1,400,000 square miles.—Keith Johnstone.

The pressing of cotton still went on* and ships were laden for China. But where were the convoys? Scouring the seas in search of that mysterious French fleet which was seen one day at Ceylon, and again at the Isle of France. The mind was on the tenter-hooks, and Sunday gave no rest. When members of Council were at prayers in the Cathedral, they were nudged on the elbow to come *ek dum* to a meeting of Council next door. The editors of the *Courier* and *Gazette*—for both papers then existed—were warned to publish neither arrival nor departure, nor that which was expected. A man was stationed on the mast-head of the Suffolk, at the harbour mouth, on the outlook night and day. There was quite a flutter among the merchants

---

* REPACKING AND SCREWING A BALE OF COTTON Rs. 3-3-36.

Charges for repacking and screwing a bale of cotton in Company's and warehouse-keepers' screws, viz. :—

Hamalage from the present shed to the Marine Bunder or Ramooy Screws	0	0	12
Altering wrapers	0	0	16
Hemp rope	1	2	0
Stretching rope	0	0	8
Twine used in repacking, uncertain but supposing	0	0	12
Screwing bales in the screws	0	0	14
Repacking	1	0	0
Screwing	1	0	0
Twine for sewing the bale when pressed	0	0	12
Weighing at 4 reas per cwt., make per bale	0	0	14
Hamalage from any of the above screws to the bunder-head to be shipped	0	0	40
Shipping off into the boat	0	0	8
Rs.	3	3	36

ROBERT KITSON, Warehouse-Keeper.

Bombay, 10th June, 1800.

when tenders were asked for the Egyptian Expedition. Charles Forbes opens the ball. Then comes Bruce, Fawcett and Co., and Charles Adamson with his big ship. "To all those conversant with shipping it is a point universally known, that small vessels are navigated with much greater expense than large ones." Undeniable. Arthur Wellesley was here, and had he gone in the vessel intended for him, he would never have been heard of. We need not ask whence all this excitement. Napoleon had been at Suez; and the reader of the commonest history-books can see what Bonaparte *did* after this, and he will estimate what his capabilities then were. For who could tell? The world was then in the throes of revolution, and it was an open question whether the vessel of the English State in India might not go down in a sea of anarchy. Nelson, Wellington, and Abercrombie, each in his own sphere, backed by the wisdom of English statesmen and the resources of the English nation, solved for us, under Almighty Providence, the momentous question.

THE SUEZ CANAL.

The two Napoleons, uncle and nephew, I. and III., had much to do with the Suez Canal. We have seen that Bonaparte was the first to put the idea into a tangible shape. Of this the proofs are incontestible, for why did he come to Suez? And Louis Napoleon gave it such material and political assistance as was possible to him. These two men were, in a sense, the Alpha and Omega of the Canal; and had Ferdinand Lesseps erected a monument to either of the Bonapartes as high as the Colossus of Rhodes, he would but have followed the instincts of nature and the dictates of reason, which govern the mass of mankind. But Lesseps is not an ordinary man, and does not work by ordinary methods, or he would have been content with the geographical limits which had been assigned by nature to two seas since the birth of time. He did not make the canal to break the power of England in India or destroy her commerce. Bonaparte to him was merely the shadow of a name, and his nephew a convenient instrument to accomplish his designs. Thus it was when he had brought this great work to a triumphant conclusion, and when any other Frenchman full of Egyptian memories might think of Napoleon, Cæsar, or Alexander "the brave youth of Macedon," he bethought himself of a poor but honest Englishman* who did much in his day to create and further overland traffic, and who spent prodigally his substance, his health, yea, his very life in its accomplishment, "in journeyings often, in perils of waters, in perils of robbers, in hunger, thirst, cold, heat, and nakedness."

But what has all this to do with Bombay? Everything in the world. Bombay has good cause of congratulation in this matter. Waghorn organised, worked, and completed the overland traffic for mails, and we rather think also for passengers, himself, his sole support being the Bombay Steam Committee. This was from 1831 to 1834,—three years on his own hook before the British Government touched it with its little finger. It was then the East India Company, and its Directors, almost to a man, and the Post-office authorities, frowned upon him and his work. But when fortune deserted him, Bombay came to his aid.† The Chamber of Commerce was established in 1838. Chairman—Harry George Gordon. Committee—Peter Ewart, Thomas Lancaster, John Skinner, Thomas Cardwell, G. S. King, and others. Among the first sentences

* Most likely they were acquainted with each other in Egypt.

† Calcutta, Aug. 9, 1836.—"The Overland Mail came in two months from London to Calcutta, the first time such a thing has ever happened."—Hon. Emily Eden's Letters.

of the first report issued by them and it redounds much to their honour—are words of encouragement to Waghorn.* Nor did Bombay rest satisfied until the hour of victory came in 1845, when his messengers ran up the stairs in Leadenhall-street with a letter for the Directors "delivered in thirty days."

Are these things we should willingly let die? If we should, the statue of Waghorn erected and consecrated by the genius of Lesseps stands at Suez to remind us of them, and mute and motionless as it is, seems to beckon the fleets of nations from the Eastern Seas to new enterprise.

"The time shall come when ship-boys e'en shall scorn
To have Alcides fable on their lips;
Seas yet unnamed, with realms unknown adorn
Your charts, and with their fame your pride eclipse.
Then the bold Argo of all future ships
Shall circumnavigate and circle sheer
Whate'er blue Tethys in her girdle clips;
Victorious rival of the sun's career,
And measure e'en of earth the whole stupendous sphere."

THE FORBES LOANS.

The carrying on of war now-a-days seems a

* "Mr. Waghorn has been assured that the members of this Institution, in common with the rest of the mercantile community and the public generally, are fully sensible of the value of his exertions on the particular occasion in question of steam communication in general, which, it is hoped, will be rewarded with the encouragement and support his public-spirited labours so well deserve."—Bombay Chamber of Commerce Transactions 1838-39, page 3.

more complicated and difficult task than in the days of our grandfathers. Everything is now, no doubt, on a larger scale. But we are apt to forget that they had few of the appliances of modern science, and that steam, by land and sea, has reduced the transport of men and material to wonderful simplicity. Any one who saw the water tanks, the compressed hay, and the elephants embarking with the Abyssinian Expedition, will have a faint idea of the difficulties of Sir David Baird's in 1801, in *sailing* ships and without these appliances. The Duke, indeed, while in Western India, was in a perpetual state of unrest, crying out for provisions for his men and forage for his animals. "The troops must have regular supplies of provisions at command, or misfortune or disgrace will be the consequence."* Hence we find that the deaths among the cattle on the march were few and far between. This result requires money; and owing to the terrorism of the Peshwa's agents, money had crept into secret hiding-places, and the shroffs, frightened, and with good grounds, for their very lives, had decamped. We must try to realise a time when the Indian Government had no facility for rais-

* Duke at Ahmednuggar to Jonathan Duncan, 1803, Aug. 13.

ing money by loan, and when she was not strong enough to constitute a public creditor in India, and we will come to the conclusion that the money question was the question of questions. There are no public loans to Government in India before 30th June, 1813.* Twice, in his public despatches to the Governor-General, the Duke calls his attention to the fact that a Bombay merchant had come forward to assist the Government in its hour of need. I will not condescend to go into the question that Sir Charles Forbes knew what he was doing as well as the Duke. The facts remain the same, that the Government wanted money, and Sir Charles gave them it; and everybody is supposed to know what he is doing in businesses of this kind. Did any Native Prince or merchant do, or even offer to do, what Sir Charles did? The amount was not small. At one time there was £500,000 running, equal to a million of our money, lent by Forbes and Bruce, Fawcett and Co.—for they were both interested—and this at a time of scare. It was a kind of advance to Government on their growing crop of cotton from Guzerat, teak from Malabar, sandalwood from Mangalore, at prices

* Notifications relative to the Public Loans of the Government of India republished from the *Government Gazette* 1822 to 1879-1880.

agreed on ; money paid now, and produce taken delivery of afterwards. Interest was to be paid by Government at the rate of ¾ per cent. per month, and 2s. 6d. exchange on such amounts as might be repaid in England,—sicca rupees against 12 months' date bills, we suppose. If they gained anything on these last items, the labourer was worthy of his hire. The loans extended over two or three years. The Forbes loans enabled the war to go on when the war could not go on without them, and supplied those sinews which to the hour and the man were essential to its prosecution. Who knows if Assaye could have been fought without them.

CONCLUSION.

History, as a rule, does not recognise such subjects as we have been discussing, but it is precisely for that very reason that we discourse upon them. The facts are well enough known ; and another reason why we dwell upon them is that we believe they mark distinct eras in the art of government and the progress of civilization in India in which Bombay has borne a most distinguished part. Do the Rupee Loans begin virtually with Forbes, and the Overland Traffic practically with Waghorn ? Both these men died about the same time, the one rich and honoured in England,* the other also in England, poor and in obscurity.† Each in his own sphere contributed something to the building of the commonwealth. But the glory of the one excelleth that of the other. The fame of Forbes is local and temporary; but the name of Waghorn will last to the end of time, or to such a time, if it ever comes, when men will cease to remember the benefactors of their species.

* 1849. † 1850.

THE DUKE OF WELLINGTON
IN BOMBAY.

CHAPTER XI.

THE DUKE OF WELLINGTON IN BOMBAY.

A LOVE-PASSAGE.

"I was feasted out of Bombay, and I was feasted into it."
Duke of Wellington's Despatches.

"I THANK you for the picture, of which, however, I must observe, with my friends here, that the two or three glances which you mention made very little impression on the fair artist, as the picture is as like anybody else, as it is of the person for whom it is intended. I shall write to her, nevertheless, and I propose to tell her that I am glad that those few glances made an impression upon her memory so exceedingly favourable; and I have employed a gentleman here to draw the picture of a damsel in the character of a shepherdess, which I shall also present as the effect of the impression made upon my memory by the fair artist.

"ARTHUR WELLESLEY.

"Seringapatam, 6th Nov., 1801."

This passage is crystallized in one of the Duke's despatches—shall we say like a gem in a lot of rubbish? It is addressed to Jonathan Duncan, Governor of Bombay, and tells the old, old story of romance, love, and flirtation. Poor girl!

When the Duke was a gay young aide-de-camp at the Irish Court he was engaged to Lady Catherine Pakenham. While he was in India she had been attacked by small-pox, and shortly after he left England she wrote to tell him her beauty was gone, and that he was a free man.*

How could a young lady, living in Bombay, be expected to know all this in those days, when betrothals were not proclaimed from the house-tops?

The Duke was thirty-two and an uncommonly handsome man, and we do not need his portrait by Lawrence to tell us this. He is described by Mountstuart Elphinstone, in his Bombay and Poona days, as almost at times boyish in his manners. We need not therefore wonder that a

* But he returned to claim her hand, and her hand was freely given, 10th April, 1806.

Bombay young lady fell in love with the Duke of Wellington. There were dozens more, no doubt.

> " How happy could I be with either
> Were t' other dear charmer away !"

The wonder to us is that the Duke ever got out of the place. Who this lady was we shall never know. Mrs. Hough*, who was with us until the other day, could have told us all about it. There were some good sketchers among the Bombay ladies of this period, and Mrs. Ashburner, the friend of Sir James Mackintosh and Amelia Opie, has left us a beautiful vignette in Basil Hall's travels. But, painter or lover, there is nothing to be ashamed of. It was a pure, a tender, and a lofty passion on her part.

> " As in the bosom of the stream
> The moonbeam dwells at dewy e'en,
> So trembling pure was tender love
> Within the breast o' bonny Jean."

And we may well believe that she never told her love except on this occasion when she confided the great secret to that " Brahmanised Scotsman,"† Jonathan Duncan. His ear was never deaf to the cry of suffering humanity, as we may still see from the bas-reliefs on his tomb in the Bombay

* Mrs. Hough died on 24th June, 1873, aged eighty-eight, and had danced with the Duke in Bombay.
† Mackintosh thus designates him.

Cathedral. "Infanticide abolished in Benares and Kattywar," in capital letters, proclaims him the great law-giver, full of mercy as well as justice. What wonder, then, if he turned away his attention from the contemplation of the sickening land tenures of Salsette to the bright eyes and tenures that bound him to the softer sex? And the Duke—

> "Ave Maria, maiden mild,
> Listen to a maiden's prayer."

The Genius of Flirtation came to his aid in this great extremity.

> "I cannot all day be neglecting Madras,
> Or slighting Bombay, for the sake of a lass."*

Happy thought. "I shall write to her, nevertheless," Reciprocate her affection? No not exactly; pay her back in her own coin; do to her as she hath done to me, send her her own portrait as she hath sent me mine. O, thou Iron Duke!

A glorious picture this! Old bachelor† acting *black-foot*‡ to a distressed damsel, and the hero to be of "a hundred fights" with one more fyghte added to the number.

The Duke indicates that the picture was that of "anybody." There was one distinguishing feature in the Duke's physiognomy that made

* Lord Macaulay. † Ætat 45.
‡ Go-between in match-making.

him differ from most men. I wonder she did not manage to paint his nose. I have half a doubt that the Duke eliminated this portion of his features in his hasty estimate of the portrait, and that at that particular moment the *genius loci*, *à la* Pepper's ghost in the shape of Lady Pakenham, was looking over his right shoulder.

There is a bungalow at Khandalla, erected by Mountstuart Elphinstone (Governor, 1819-27), where he very often resided. It is situated on a knoll overhanging a great precipice, down which a water-fall tumbles 1,200 feet in four successive falls. What if, when the snows of age had descended on the fair shepherdess, at some point near this, she drew from her album the picture which Wellesley had sent her ere his brow had been laurelled by one single victory? You may rest assured that it was brought forth from its hiding-place neither in pain, nor in sorrow, nor in anger, but to a delighted family and friends, herself more delighted than all the rest. And then there was

THE DUKE'S NOSE.

If he never saw his own nose nor the nose in the picture which was gifted to him in 1801, nor any of the hundred duke's noses scattered over the world, it is certain—and who can paint like Nature?—that he saw this one, near Khandalla.

The Duke was very reticent on the subject of the ladies of Bombay or the Deccan. In all the volumes of his Indian despatches, one and only one, comes in for a share of panegyric. Of one he says: "She is very fair and very handsome, and well deserves to be the object of a treaty." He wrote this at Panwell. The lady was a widow, but the treaty alluded to had nothing to do with matrimony. I think it was *tout au contraire* to give the lady a Government pension of Rs. 1,200 per mensem if she did not marry.*

THE DUKE OF WELLINGTON IN BOMBAY AND WESTERN INDIA.

"I am *nimmukwalla,* as we say in the East, that is, I have ate of the King's salt, and therefore I conceive it to be my duty to serve with unhesitating zeal and cheerfulness when or wherever the King or his Government may think proper to employ me."—*Reply of the Duke of Wellington, on a friend remarking to him that he*

---

* The widow of Nana Furnavese.

had been reduced from his high rank to the command of a brigade of infantry.

Hastings.—September, 1805.

THE DUKE IN INDIA.

The Duke of Wellington was about eight years in India (1797 to 1805). He resided in Bombay in March and April, 1801, when he came to hurry off Sir David Baird's expedition to Egypt to meet the Great Napoleon; and again from March to May, 1804, after the battle of Assaye. But from March, 1803, to July, 1804, he was in or about the Bombay Presidency, and his two great victories of Assaye and Argaum* were gained in our neighbourhood†, within 200 miles of Bombay. Bombay may therefore claim to have some part in the military education of this illustrious hero, for Assaye and Argaum are the first in the long roll of his conquests which history records, and it was on the burning plains of the Deccan that Arthur Wellesley first tried his 'prentice hand at the art of war.

THE BOMBAY OF HIS PERIOD

Was not like the Bombay of to-day, except in its topographical surroundings, and even these

* Assaye, 23rd September, 1803. Argaum, 28th November, 1803.

† Your victories have taken place in our neighbourhood.—*Bombay Address*, 1804.

have been modified by land reclamation from the sea. It was "a city fortified," and its walls enclosed a population of about 100,000, with as many outside. The walls were then in as great a state of perfection as they ever had been. For a hundred years men had been stumbling over half-hewn stones and heaps of unslaked lime. There were no houses on Malabar Hill. Our venerable* citizen, Mr. Manockjee Cursetjee, has pointed out to us the site of the house where the Duke resided. The walls of the stable only now remain, and the site is on your right opposite the wood-wharf as you ascend the steep Siri road, now much availed of by foot passengers as a short cut to Malabar Hill and the Ladies' Gymkhana.

There is

A GREAT DEARTH OF MATERIALS

Out of which to frame the story of the Duke in Bombay. The fluctuating nature of the English population here forbids anything like continuous tradition handed down from age to age, as we have in Europe. Moreover, our subject was just then emerging into fame. Somebody

---

* Mr. Manockjee now possesses a gold locket with the Duke's hair in it, and a letter from the present Duke, authenticating the same.

said lately that it was a pity Mrs. Hough burned her diary. Perhaps. There are diaries and diaries. We are certain, however, of this, that it is a real calamity that the diary of Sir James Mackintosh covers none of Wellington's history in Bombay, nor, indeed, in this presidency. Strange to say, the Duke had left a week before he arrived, and was already writing multitudinous despatches under the shadow of that great battlement of trap and laterite which we now call Chowk Point when Mackintosh was sailing over the Fifty Fathom Flat within sight of the promised land of Hindostan. Had it been otherwise we should certainly have had many notes from a profound observer and most accomplished scholar on Arthur Wellesley. All memory of the man has now died out, and we venture to state that there is not a single man alive who recollects the Duke of Wellington in India. Even His Highness Aga Khan Mehilati, the descendant of the Old Man of the Mountain, the hereditary chief and unrevealed Imam of the Ismailis, upon whom sits so lightly the burden of four score monsoons, remembers him not*;—so is it with the Honourable Nusserwanjee Framjee, the Nestor of the Parsees. Ten years ago the case was different, but the "Blind Fury with the

* H. H. Aga Khan died in Bombay on the night of the 12th April 1881.

abhorred shears" has cut the last link. Jadowrow, of Malegaon, came to Sir Bartle Frere in 1867, and pointing to the battlefield of Kirkee, said, "The place is much changed since I was here fifty years ago." He bore arms when the Duke was in Poona, in 1803. There is thus no option to us except to deliver ourselves over to conjecture, or be content with such things as we have, in the shape of the miscellaneous scraps which are furnished to us by the despatches and letters of the Duke of Wellington.

THE DUKE'S TRIUMPHAL ENTRY INTO BOMBAY.

Be it known, then, that the Duke of Wellington, otherwise Major General Wellesley, entered Bombay on the 13th March, 1804. He came fresh from the victories of Assaye and Argaum, and Bombay did him all honour. The route by which he entered the city is still visible to us, and very much the same as it was then, except that a structure here and there

"Battered and decayed
Lets in new light through chinks which Time has made."

It stretched from the Dock-gate opposite the old Court House to the old Secretariat, then known as Government House. The course of the procession was thus the Dock-head to Apollo

Street, which was lined from end to end by all the troops then in the garrison, and packed by a dense mass of human beings, a sea of turbans, with a sprinkling of European and Parsee topis, far as the eye could reach, until it terminated at the Cathedral and Bombay Green. The old Court House had once (1776-84) been the residence of Governor Hornby, and was for its time a palatial-looking building. The porch is a lofty collonade surmounted by a balcony, which afforded a splendid coigne of vantage, as it directly faced the Dock archway, and enabled its occupants to catch, as he emerged, a first glimpse of the illustrious stranger, the hero of Assaye. We need scarcely ask if this verandah, on a day such as this, was chockfull of the youth, beauty, and fair hair of England. So, he looking at them and they at him, the Duke, amid the roar of cannon and the blare of trumpets, made his way to Government House.

Great preparations had been made for his reception, for it had been known for days that he was to arrive from Panwell in the Governor's yacht. The Chamber of Commerce was then inchoate, and the Town Council and Corporation without form and void. Nevertheless a Mr. Henshaw was voted to the chair, and commissioned to present an address signed by 123 non-official Englishmen, we presume. The last tableaux are the Duke, Jonathan Duncan, and Mr. Henshaw, each rising in succession to speak on the great question of the day, all very hot, and though enjoying themselves, glad when the whole business was terminated and gave way to a series of dinners, balls, and theatrical representations. We may here observe that the Duke was a close-shaven man, as were all his contemporaries, Nelson, Lake, Abercrombie, Mackintosh, and Malcolm. The reign of the long-haired savages came in with Sir Charles Napier, "the bearded vision of Sind."

It was a big day—a *burra-deen*. Bombay, with one bound, seemed to burst away from the clouds of misfortune which had enveloped her; and it was no wonder she sought relief, for storm and fire and famine had done their worst, and her cup of misery had been well nigh filled to the brim. Five years had passed—and such five years. The elements of Nature seemed to conspire with the violence of man, and the century had dawned amid gloom and disaster to the settlement. There had been a great storm at the close of the monsoon of 1799, in which H. M. S. Resolution, 1,000 native craft, and 400 lives were lost in the harbour. Then a fire broke out in 1803, which destroyed three-fourths of the Bazaar, Barracks, Custom House, and many public buildings. In 1802-3, the clouds having refused to give their rain, a famine raged* only equalled in intensity by that of 1812; and in 1802 a domestic incident threw the whole colony into mourning, the Persian ambassador having been shot dead by one of our own sepoys in the public streets.†

The period had been thus one of intensest anxiety, fears within and fightings without. Had not Nelson written Governor Duncan that if Napoleon was successful in Egypt, Bombay would come next? As each day dawned the flagstaff on Malabar Point was narrowly watched and the horizon seawards eagerly scanned. It will be remembered that Tanna was then the outpost of British dominion, and the outlook across the creek was black and dismal, and blacker and dismaller on the great plains of the Deccan beyond the Western Ghauts. The farther you went the worse it became. There was a court

---

* Rice was imported into Bombay to the value of 50 lakhs, by which there is no doubt that the lives of 50,000 human beings were saved. —*Mackintosh.*

† They patched up such affairs easily in these days. One lakh in presents, Rs. 50,000 in pensions, and the body sent in a ship of war to Kerbella. It was afterwards remarked in the Shiraz bazaar that we might have ten ambassadors if we paid for them at the same price. —*Malcolm.*

at Poona and a court at Hyderabad. Bajee Rao sits on the verandah of the Somwar Palace and hears with delight the yells of the brother of Holkar as he is being trampled to death by an elephant,* and Holkar's vicegerent, Amrut Rao, by way of reprisal, threatens to give over Poona to plunder and burn it to ashes.

Sydenham, the Resident at the court of the Nizam, considers it as "a sort of experiment to determine with how little morality men can associate together, and seems to think that the most atrocious ruffians from the brothels and massacres of Paris might here be teachers, and even models, of virtue. Holkar had become so besotted a drunkard as almost to have lost his senses; after an excessive dose of cherry-brandy he plucks the turbans from the heads of his chiefs and beats them like the lowest slaves;"† and Scindia was so bad that the Duke of Wellington, on 31st January, 1804, almost driven to desperation by his conduct, wrote Malcolm, then at his camp, "It will not be a bad plan to bribe the prince as well as his ministers."

This represents the rulers of the wide area of

* 1801.

† *Mackintosh.*

Mahratta dominion, but Peshwa, Scindia, Holkar, and Nizam it was all the same. But we must not ignore.

THE CONDITION OF THE PEOPLE.

And our witnesses shall be two men of European reputation who had singular opportunities of extending their observations in the Deccan and Konkan at this period. We premise that their report will not be a one-sided one, neither biassed by senseless prejudice nor overweening indulgence. Neither of them disliked the natives of this country.. When Hormusjee gave a masque ball Mackintosh was among the revellers. When Dady was dying he handed over to Mackintosh the care of his two sons, who afterwards became merchants in Bombay. "I have offered you peace, and you have chosen war," said the great Duke, and the words were uttered by the same man who, on the field of Assaye, sent for a havildar of the 4th Cavalry, who had dashed among the enemy's horse and bore away the standard, and then with a gentle pat on the back said, *Acha, havildar jemadar*. And a jemadar he was made. There was no collusion, as Wellington and Mackintosh never met nor corresponded in India. Indeed, they were political opponents during their lives.

The Duke of Wellington did not disguise from himself or the public the means he had acquired, or the capacity with which he was gifted, for writing on the condition of the people of Western India.

"No man," he says, "has ever had so many opportunities of contemplating the subject in all its parts, and possibly no man has ever adverted to it.

"There is not one of them that can be implicitly trusted.

"Famine rages in the Deccan. Habits of industry are out of the question, and men must plunder for subsistence, be destroyed, or starve; no law, no Civil Government, and no army to keep plunderers in order—and no revenue can be collected; indeed, no inhabitant can or will remain to cultivate, unless he is protected by an armed force stationed in his village.

"Five miles from Poona, a dreary waste overrun by thieves.

"The only system of the Peshwa's Government is that of a robber.

"The Peshwa is callous to everything, but money and revenge."

And on the march to Poona, "except in

one village not a human being was left for a distance of 125 miles from Meritch to Poona."

So much for Wellington: now for Mackintosh. "No police, no administration of justice, except such as the village system of India supplies. It would be difficult to say for what tax is paid, except it be to bribe the sovereign not to murder or rob the inhabitants.

"Carli to Tulligaum. The country is bare and little cultivated, the road is lonely, and the whole district seems unpeopled.

"Jelliall to Bejapore. For fourteen miles the only living creatures that we saw were some pretty paraquets, a partridge, a hare, and a herd of deer. Yet our road was through a country that had been universally cultivated, and within a few miles of what had been once one of the most superb capitals of the East.

"The number of women enslaved and condemned to perpetual imprisonment in such loathsome dungeons, without occupation or amusement, without knowledge or accomplishment, without the possibility of a good quality which could rise so high as to deserve the name of virtue, is, perhaps, the strongest instance of low or depraved tyranny that the world exhibits.

"The insecurity of this country is not occasional or temporary, but its usual and probably perpetual state.

"In the dominions of the Peshwa, Nizam, &c., they in reality exercise no functions of Government except that of collecting the revenue. In every other respect they throw the reins on the horse's neck. In their dominions there is no police, no administration of justice; sovereignty is to them a perfect sinecure."

This is what the people and country had come to. The question now arises, why did we not leave these besotted Governments to work out their own destruction? And this brings us to a second question,

WHY WAS ARTHUR WELLESLEY HERE?

The answer is easy enough to both these questions. The holders of the musnuds of Western India were at this time brewing a sharp poison for us to drink. When the treaty of Bassein, restoring the Peshwa to Poona, in 1802, was signed, Holkar held up his hands and said, "You have taken away my turban." It was to prevent probable combinations among the Mahratta powers, the end of which would have been to have driven the English into the sea. That was the reason why the Duke was here and that Bombay was filled with joy and rejoicing in March, 1804. The answer to the first question is that we did not arrest the decay of these Governments. They literally died from the contempt of the native populations. Conceive any man wishing to get back to such times! The Duke, in February, 1803, was told by the Viceroy that his presence was wanted at Poona. This brings us to

HIS CELEBRATED MARCH TO POONA.*

And the Duke shall be his own historian. "We marched to Poona from Seringapatam, the dis-

---

* We are indebted to an eminent Bombay Civilian for the following, which clears up the topography of the Duke of Wellington's famous march of 60 miles in 32 hours, from Baramati to Poona, on 19th-20th April, 1803. With a force of 10,617 men, of whom 1,709 were cavalry, he left General Stuart's Headquarters at Harihar on 9th March, and crossed the Tumbuddra on 12th March. He reached Mirach on 3rd April, and *appears* to have marched steadily thence towards Poona. Hearing on the 19th that Amrut Rao was still near Poona, and that he was supposed to be about to burn the town, he marched on with his cavalry—412 Europeans and 1,297 natives. The infantry followed, reaching Poona on 22nd. The route was by the "little Bhore Ghaut," a route often mentioned in the annals of 1800 to 1820. The Ghaut is near the eastern end of the chain which runs eastward from Singurh and Boleshwar, and before the construction of the Dewa Bapdeo and Katraj Ghaut was the only practicable road across that range of hills. Though superseded by the Bapdeo and Dewa Ghauts for traffic to Poona by road the Ghaut is still kept up, as it is on the line of communication between the Uroti railway station and Saswad Jejuri and other places on the line of the old Satara road.

tance being nearly six hundred miles, in the worst season of the year, through a country which had been destroyed by Holkar's army, with heavy guns, at the rate, upon an average, of thirteen-and-a-half miles a day; and halting twelve days for orders, we arrived at Poona in two months from the time we marched. On this march we lost no draught cattle. I remained in the neighbourhood of Poona, in a country which deserves the name of a desert, for six weeks, and then marched with the train in the same state. . . It has frequently been necessary for the troops to march for many days together a distance of fifteen to twenty miles daily. The heavy artillery always accompanied them. Upon one occasion I found it necessary to march a detachment sixty miles in thirty hours, and the ordnance and provision carriages, drawn by the Company's bullocks, accompanied them. . . The number of cattle which have died are really not greater than it would have been at the grazing ground." He is now on the march to Ahmednagar, Assaye, and Argaum with the *carte blanche* which was given to him by his brother, the Viceroy, to do, in fact, anything he pleased, either offensive or defensive, the how and when being left entirely to himself. Would any of these victories have been won if the telegraph had then been in operation? We may be certain that more cattle would have died.

DUEL; DISCIPLINE AT NAGAR.

Wellington was glad to take the 78th Regiment of Highlanders with him. Malcolm's feeling was that their Gaelic address would have an excellent effect on the enemy! Our readers will recollect that this was the regiment whose pipers enlivened Poona in 1879, and we may add also the Scots dinner of that year. The following incident occurred before the storm and capture of Ahmednagar on 12th August, 1803. Captain Grant, a young officer of the 78th, gave a party to his friends in camp, and asked Captain Brown's piper to amuse them, so that they might listen to the pibrochs and dance to the reels. Captain Brown was an old man and an Englishman, and it would have been no compliment to have asked him. Nevertheless, his piper having been asked without his knowledge, he took umbrage at this, and at evening parade addressed Grant. Grant replied that he would send for the piper as often as he pleased. "Sir, you are but a boy, and nobody but a boy would tell me so." Then came the *dénouement*. A friend was called in, who recommended a challenge, which was accepted, and in the duel Brown fell dead. General Wellesley turned the friend out of camp, "that such a wretch might not have the opportunity of sharing in the honours of an army which he had thus disgraced." Poor Grant was in a terrible state at the storm, and under arrest as he was, and unarmed, he rushed off the first man at the top of the ladder, from which he fell a corpse.*

NATIVE OPINION OF THE DUKE.

Gockla, a Mahratta residing in camp with a body of horse, wrote thus to his friends :—

"These English are a strange people and their General a wonderful man ; they came here in the morning, looked at the Pettah wall, walked over it, killed all the garrison, and returned to breakfast. What can withstand them ?"

TRAITS.

It would be a great mistake to suppose that the Duke of Wellington in Western India was

---

* Abridged from *Maxwell's Wellington.*

the soldier only, or that he merely changed the soldier's garb for that of the diplomatist to write on mighty themes. We have seen that the condition of the people question was not beneath his notice. He, possibly, was the first man who wrote on the philosophy of an Indian famine; and it would astonish some of our administrators now-a-days to find that their pet schemes and original ideas have been anticipated by him. He contributed something to banking by his celebrated saying that "high interest means bad security." We have no comments of his on foreign exchange, and we suspect that trade in Bombay during these years was so harried that sterling bills were driven out of sight. But no cambist or inland banker in the matter of coins or hoondies could catch him asleep. An unfortunate military man in Poona relegated to conduct the finances received such a castigation that he must have remembered it to the day of his death. "It is useless to write any more on the subject. Should bills be again drawn at Poona, the Government of Bombay will furnish you with an account of the rates of exchange at which they draw their bills and you can regulate your rates accordingly." On the receipt of this the Poona sowcars became *choop* and their countenances fell. He could thus be pleasant and unpleasant; "lofty and sour to those who loved him not, to those that loved him sweet as summer." But not always.

"When in Bombay I had much conversation with mercantile gentlemen there." Yes, he did not think this beneath him; not a ceremonious or "how d'ye do" acquaintance, but redolent, as in Charles Forbes's case, with much talk about money, wine, and horses. He had a great regard for Forbes. The house had been established some twenty years previously. "Forbes," he says, "is a bad judge of horses." But Forbes had money, and this was what the Government at this particular time stood in much need of. The Government had sandalwood in a growing state, trees we mean; in fact, what Charles II. roughly termed "an excrescence of the earth provided by God for the payment of debts," which was evidently the view taken of them by the Government. Forbes could pay the money now—five lakhs, ten lakhs; it was all the same to him—and he did pay it, and cut the wood on the Mangalore coast afterwards. So we find in the last letter which the Duke wrote to Jonathan Duncan, Governor of Bombay, before leaving India, the very words we were prepared to expect: "27th February, 1805. Mr. Forbes's sandal-wood business will be settled to his satisfaction." He had time to note when in Bombay that it excelled all other places in India for making cart-wheels, to which the late Kandahar campaign bore witness. He had time to attend a garden-party at Manockjee Cursetjee's father's house, which you can still see. He had time to groan over his lumbago, and fear that he "would walk like old Pomeroy during the remainder of my life." He went into convulsions over the jokes, written, spoken, or practical, of "mad Malcolm;" and we can solemnly aver that there is a tamarind-tree at the foot of the Seeree road under which he cursed the Bombay Government, for doing which he feared he might be burned in effigy on the Bombay Green. We are bound to believe that he clomb the Siri (ladder) and gave an obolus to the Fakir, *imago mortis*, and was rewarded by a glorious view from Malabar Hill, minus steamers, cotton-mills, and all that sort of thing. Such was Wellington in all his phases. To one he writes, "Give him a hint that I am in the habit of hanging." To another, "I shall send to Mrs. Stevenson in two days some cabbages and celery-plants, and in about a week her rose-trees."

> So various he,
> In all his parts the world's epitome.

HERE ARE TWO NOTABILIA.

"I know but one receipt for good health in this country, and that is to live moderately, to drink little or no wine, to use exercise, to keep the mind employed, and, if possible, to keep in good humour with the world;" and he adds, "the last is the most difficult, for, as you have often observed, there is scarcely a good-tempered man in India."

When the clouds of the monsoon of 1804 were beginning to form he found that 5,000 of the soldiers would be in rags during the monsoon. He solved the difficulty by giving every man his piece of cloth and making each his own tailor.

WAS THE DUKE AT MATHERAN?

We are afraid not; at his "camp at Chowke" he devoured much foolscap and several lengthy despatches of great moment are thus dated.

The question becomes this—whether a man in full power of body and mind, and embued with a strong love of scenery such as Killarney, could have resisted paying it a visit when it was, as it were, at his very elbow. It can be argued on both sides. It was the month of May: that was bad or good; a stiffer pull then than in any other month, but Matheran has then a cooler climate and offers a greater contrast to the heated plains below. One of two things is certain: if he went, he destroyed a pair of Wellington boots; if he remained at Chowke, he had a hot night of it on 18th May. We could forgive his staying away if he had only squelched the maternal progenitor of that scoundrel at the mention of whose name the world still grows pale, and who must have in 1804 been making mud pies somewhere about Chowke.

There was no want of roads. There was "the old Chowke road," up which fifty years afterwards an elephant carried Lord Elphinstone from the Rambagh to the summit, and there was the breakneck ascent at One Tree Hill, where he could have stuck his feet into the notches cut out of the rock (he was not a stout party) and been rewarded by a glorious view from the summit.

He would have seen a plain as big as Esdraelon bounded by the Ghauts, and at his feet the innumerable tents of which his camp consisted, outside one of which were picquetted his two horses, Pat and Diomed* quietly munching their gram. He would have heard the bulbul and the golden oriole, and seen the so-called bird of paradise with its long tail, flitting like a gleam of sunlight from glade to glade. And he would have drunk from those perennial fountains that babble up from the stony valley of the Bund. He would have seen the Dungur wending his way slowly into umbrageous depths to sacrifice a cock at the black stone which he believes came down from heaven.†

> In vain with lavish kindness
> The gifts of God are strewn,
> The heathen in his blindness
> Bows down to wood and stone—

Yesterday, to-day, but not for ever. And if he had remained long enough, he might have bid a final adieu to the lumbago in his back and Dr. Inverarity.

---

* Diomed "kicked" at Assaye, but Malcolm fell in with him afterwards and bought him for the Duke at Rs. 250.

† Dr. Wilson used to remark that there were some grounds for their belief. His opinion was that both this and the Black Stone of Mecca were originally meteoric stones.

THE DUKE OF WELLINGTON'S BOMBAY RESIDENCE.

TO THE EDITOR OF THE "BOMBAY GAZETTE."

Sir,—The writer of a note in your issue of Saturday anent the site of the house in which the illustrious Duke of Wellington resided while in Bombay has awakened in me some dormant memories of by-gone days.

Upwards of six-and-thirty years ago I had the honour of being an occupant of the same house. My landlord was Mr. Cursetjee Manockjee, now long deceased, who was the father of our worthy townsman, Mr. Manekji Kharsedji. (You will please note that, in compliance with the requirements of modern scientific literature, I am compelled to spell the son's name *secundum artem.*)

For the benefit of the curious in such matters and historians in general permit me further to relate that the house, which was called Surrey Cottage, stood at about half-way up the now non-existent eastern brow of Malabar Hill. The excavated *dèbris* of that part of the hill, as many of your readers are aware, was utilized some years ago for the purposes of the Back Bay reclamation. The house comprised a somewhat spacious and lofty hall, with wings and long verandas at the sides and back part. In front there was a porch, to which led two carriage-ways from different directions of the large compound. One of them passed by the still-existing stable near the *siri*. Your correspondent remarks that its walls are standing. He might have added that it has a roof, and that it continues to be used as a stable.

The hall commanded a nice view of Back Bay and a portion of Girgaum, also the Esplanade and the Fort. The Duke, with his eagle eye, must have more than once, I presume, scanned the scene with some interest. Of an evening one of the most striking sights that met the eyes of myself and my friends, as we sat on the landing of the tall flight of stone steps which led up to the hall from the porch, was the long line of lugubrious flaring fires which burned at the Hindu cremation-ground, then not screened, as now, by the high wall on the west, or sea face.

Cholera was frequently rampant in those times. Arthur Crawford (for whom I trust a statue at least is looming in the not distant future) was most probably going to school at that period. A good many years had to elapse before he and his sanitary army invaded the quondam stinking lanes and alleys and bazaars of this city, and cleared away the feculent accumulations of ages, thus removing the fertile sources of manifold dire diseases. By night the fires on the then beach constituted a very correct and significant index of the prevalent mortality, which was in proportion to their number.

Whether the Duke's nocturnal rest was ever disturbed at Surrey Cottage by adventures with reptiles I cannot say, not having heard. It was certainly a *snaky* domicile. On the first night of my occupancy thereof I was rather startled, on entering my bedroom, to find it in possession of two or three young snakes, which were gliding playfully along the sides of the room. They had evidently been enjoying a right of usance for some time previously, and seemed quite unapprehensive of the summary eviction which I had to exercise. The polished chunam floors of the verandas were so cool in warm weather that the neighbouring snakes and serpents (cobras amongst the lot) came and occasionally reposed thereon, as though they feared no disturbance. I remember having been suddenly called up one morning by a friend residing with me to witness the execution of a splendid rock snake, near seven feet in length, which lay extended on the floor of the western veranda, taking a cool snooze. A charge of small shot which my friend discharged at its head from his fowlingpiece consigned it to a permanent slumber.

Mr. Cursetjee Manockjee knew the Duke personally, and had supplied his army with provisions—principally rice, if I am not oblivious of what he told me. He always spoke to me most enthusiastically of the Duke, whom he regarded as a perfect hero. But poor old Cursetjee had his troubles, and they were multitudinous. Out of his transactions with the Indian Government there arose a mighty lawsuit brought by him against the Honourable East India Company. In the midst of his eulogies of the Duke he could not help bitterly reverting to his *case* and his grievances. He had fortified himself with the opinions of great lawyers, one of whom was the eminent advocate Chitty. All of them were in his favour. Equity and right upheld his claims, but alas! he could not succeed against powerful John Company, who, however, offered him a liberal compromise. But Cursetjee had something of the Iron Duke's nature in him. He would not give in, and was game to the last.

Dec. 13. F.

MOUNTSTUART ELPHINSTONE.

CHAPTER XII.

MOUNTSTUART ELPHINSTONE.

SIR EDWARD COLEBROOK has advertised for letters and papers of Mountstuart Elphinstone, to assist him in the preparation of his life, upon which he is engaged, and which, we trust, will soon be given to the public.

In 1861 he presented a memoir to the Asiatic Society in London, and in 1860 Dr. Wilson read a paper on the same subject to the Asiatic Society in Bombay, to both of which we are indebted for most of the information we at present possess of the life and labours of this illustrious man. We may add also Grant Duff's history of the Mahrattas and the masterly minutes which Elphinstone wrote in India, and his paper in 1831 on Indian Policy, which attracted universal attention. Colebrook knew Elphinstone intimately during the last twenty years of his life, and is well fitted for the task; so we have every reason to believe that we will at length obtain a just estimate of the character and career of one whose name is known and revered throughout the whole of Western India.

His will, we understand, debars the publication of his diary, but as Sir John Kaye has already given us a few quotations from it, this prohibition may be ignored. We all know what a zest even the trifles of a day give, for example, to the Bombay lives of Malcolm and Mackintosh. Why do people not burn their diaries, if they object to their publication? This was Mrs. Hough's plan, and she did right.

The great outcry of biographers no-a-days is "no letters." But in his case the letters are voluminous, for Elphinstone was a man who lived before the age of telegrams and penny posts, and kept up the habit of lengthy correspondence to the last days of his life on all sorts of subjects, principally Indian and political, from which we may now fairly claim a full exhibition of the opinions and principles by which he was guided during a long and most eventful period in the history of British India.

ITEMS.

The fourth son of Lord Elphinstone, some time Governor of Edinburgh Castle, Mountstuart

Elphinstone was born in 1779. His cousin tells us he was an idle dog in his youth.

Principally under tutors, some time at the High School of Edinburgh, he sailed for Bengal in 1795. Placed in the diplomatic service under Barry Close at Poona, 1801. With Arthur Wellesley, 1803. Commissioner in Berar, 1804. In 1808-10 he was with the Embassy to Kabul; 1810-17, Resident at Poona; 1817-19 Commissioner; and 1819-27 Governor of Bombay. He spent the rest of his time travelling, but mostly in retirement, in England, and died on the 20th November, 1859.

HIS POPULARITY

Is indicated even in 1881 by Elphinstone College, Elphinstone Schools, Circles, lodges, roads, tanks, and points; a Revenue Commissioner—Robertson—bears his honoured name—a name also given by the historian of the Mahrattas to the son who is among us and is known as Mountstuart Elphinstone Grant Duff.

PORTRAIT.

Mr. Elphinstone was in the forty-first year of his age when in 1820 he became Governor of Bombay, and being a man of temperate and active habits, and fine natural constitution, was in the very prime of manhood, and in the fullest vigour and health. He was close on six feet high, but a slight stoop made him appear somewhat less tall than he was. With this trivial imperfection as an exception, his figure was a noble one; his countenance, as immortalized by the chisel of Chantrey, was in nature's most pleasing mould. It was oval and somewhat thin; the lofty forehead and deep-seated, calm, reflective eye marking the man of talent. His nose was prominent, and slightly aquiline: it was thin, as were the cheeks and lips; his colour inclining to pale; his skin pure and transparent; his hair was light, soft, and silky. His usual expression was that of sweetness, benevolence, placidity, and repose. When excited his whole countenance lighted up with a glow of warmth, his bright eye gleamed out, and his thin lips becoming compressed, showed, though placid, he was far from inanimate—though unusually tranquil, how easily he could be awakened into energy and fire. His hands were soft, white, and beautifully delicate. He was, indeed, the most distinguished and the most popular of the Governors of Bombay, and one of the most able and upright statesmen of modern times. This, we believe, is Dr. Buist's pen-and-ink sketch. It is that of a man of gentle blood, built up by ages of ease and cultivation. This is not the burly form of Malcolm, the farmer's son, nor these the rugged features and gnarled and warped forehead of Colin Campbell.

POLITICAL.

Elphinstone was one of a noble band whom Edinburgh sent forth at the close of the eighteenth century; there was Horner, Murray, Brougham, Jeffrey, Mackintosh, and Elphinstone. These three last were hot republicans in their teens,—a garb soon to be exchanged for more sober livery, the blue and yellow of the *Edinburgh Review*. There seems to have been a doubt in the king's mind, when Mackintosh in 1804, who was then 38, was being sent out as Recorder of Bombay, that the opinions of the author of *Vindiciæ Gallicæ* were too pronounced, but, on being assured on this point, he shrewdly observed: "A man may be allowed to change his opinions; his principles never." Elphinstone, when a boy, sung *Ca Ira* and the *Marseillais*, and his young friends in India on his arrival—by way of burlesque, we suppose—presented him with a tricolor cookade and cap of liberty. "He had no stereotyped prejudices"* but the early views which he imbibed, though experiencing many modifications, never left him, and the Whig peeps out at intervals to the end of his life.

By his accidental meeting with Mackintosh in Bombay in 1811, and afterwards, Elphinstone, though a man of independent thought and action, must have been brought to some extent under the sway of his intellect, which was irresistible and dominated all within its reach. He it was who urged upon him to come before the world and publish his book on Kabul. But under this head, and as illustrative of the strength of Elphinstone's mind or the tenacity of early convictions, it is a curious fact to note that, living in so close proximity with the Duke of Wellington, and sharing with him an entire campaign, at the very outset of his career, and with a mind apparently so flexible, the pupil did not, like Malcolm, fall in with the Conservative views of the great captain. He did not do so, and did not suffer by it. It was George Canning, the author of the *Antijacobin,* who in 1819 recommended him to the post of Bombay Governor, and it was Peel's Government that offered him

* Dr. Wilson.

the Viceroyalty in 1843. And when he became the Nestor of Indian politics, two Governors-General of different shades of politics sought his society before proceeding to their Government, as the greatest authority for the East.

ECCENTRICITIES.

If Elphinstone had lived in the middle ages, he would at one time of his life have been imprisoned like Roger Bacon, or burned for heresy or witchcraft. There was something *eerie* about him—what the world or the *vulgus* of it considers *uncanny*. Once he lived a gloomy and a solitary life. Of women he seldom or never speaks, and neither he nor his nephew Lord Elphinstone, Governor (1853-59), were marrying men*. Wine was poison to him, and he may

* The story goes that Lord Elphinstone's appearance and manners were so prepossessing as to touch the heart—it must surely, if at all, have been the outer cuticle—of the Most Exalted Personage in the realm. In 1839 he was not a stripling but a man of 32. But never mind. The dates harmonise wonderfully. Dates are wonderful things. The great plague in London and the acquisition of Bombay took place the same year. So did the Queen's marriage and Lord Elphinstone's appointment as Governor of Madras, or more correctly 1840 and 1839; and for that matter, tradition informs us that Tenterden Steeple and the Goodwin Sands came into existence the same year. What the year was deponent sayeth not. Moreover, there was a song actually said to have been written by his Lordship deploring his cruel fate. You may still occasionally, when some Afghan business is going on, hear an old colonel on receipt of his marching orders humming a snatch—

"I'll off to the wars again."

The song, it turns out, was not written by Lord Elphinstone at all, but by G. H. Bayley, born 1797, died 1839, the author of be claimed as nearly a total abstainer. He discarded all superfluous articles of dress, and all superfluous articles of food. Instead of a *siesta*, which Mackintosh carried with him to the sofas of England, he merely rested his head on his hands, closed his eyes, and with his elbows on the table, slept the sleep of the just. He gave up the use of beds. It was preposterous in a grown up man in full possession of his faculties, mental and physical, to lay himself down prone in inglorious slumber like the beasts of the stall.* He shook himself out of his chair at the

---

"Would I were a Butterfly" and many other songs. As it belongs to the Elphinstone memorabilia, we give it.

I'll hang my harp on the willow tree,
 I'll off to the wars again;
My peaceful home has no charms for me,
 The battlefield no pain.
The lady I love will soon be a bride,
 With a diadem on her brow:
Oh! why did she flatter my boyish pride,
 She is going to leave me now.
She took me away from my Warlike Lord,
 And gave me a silken suit;
I thought no more of my master's sword
 When I played on my mistress's lute.
She seemed to think me a boy above
 Her pages of low degree:
Oh! had I but loved with a boyish love,
 It would have been better for me.
Then I'll hide in my breast every selfish care,
 I'll flush my pale cheek with wine;
When smiles awake the bridal pair,
 I'll hasten to give them mine;
I'll laugh and sing, though my heart may bleed
 And I'll walk in the festive train,
And if I survive it I'll mount my steed,
 And I'll off to the wars again;
And if I survive it I'll mount my steed,
 And I'll off to the wars again.

* Many years after this he was asked by a friend the reason why. He promptly replied, "Because I was a fool."

unearthly hour of 4 a.m. to read the *Antigone* of Sophocles, when Malcolm, with the "Deil's picture buiks" before him at *Non parell,* was not even wondering whether it was time for his guests to go or stay. Did he, like Plimsol, consider the palanquin, "a glorified coffin?" He delighted to walk on dizzy precipices, with the sound of falling water beneath him, and watch the perturbation of the aides-de-camp in following his example.* He delighted to investigate the manners and customs of the natives, by roaming *incog.* during the night, like the Duke of Sutherland, through the bazaars and fort of Bombay; and once, anxious to experience a new sensation, he was seen on camel-back at midnight, bobbing up and down in the darkness,—an experience which Albert Smith describes "like sitting in an armchair on the top of a hansom cab.

HIS HISTORY OF INDIA

Is his *magnum opus.* While every one admires the zeal which enabled him with much care, research, and accuracy to bring together so great

* There is a tradition at the foot of Torna that a late muscular Governor who ascended it, found himself on the top without any companions. Discretion, however, is sometimes the better part of valour, and his followers need not be ashamed "where braver hearts have failed."

an amount of information in a form so continuous and compact, it is a subject of universal regret that he did not prosecute the history of British India. This book can only be looked upon as an instalment of a great work which his mind foreshadowed, but which failing health, a sense of weariness, or langour, the advice of friends, or the callousness of critics—for though he was indifferent, he was not insensible to human applause—prevented him completing. Or was it the glamour which the appearance of Macaulay's essays on Clive and Hastings (wherein he marshals these heroes on a field of the cloth of gold) threw over all that generation? Whatever the cause, he was bowled away from the subject, and never returned to it again; and the loss is irreparable. For wherein lies the significance of all his labour, if it is not to antedate our times and prepare the reader for the coming day when English rule should put all authority under its feet? What is the history of India to us if it has no connection with Europe? And you may go back, if you like, to the expedition of Alexander the Great. So when we read of Tuglak and Mahmood Begurra, or wade through the annals of Timour or Baber, they seem to us no more than the fights of the kites and the crows, compared with the acts and deeds of the race which rescued India from their oppression.

GOVERNORS OF BOMBAY.

There is not a Governor of Bombay but some evil thing has been said of him. Sir John Child was the brother of him who founded the first private bank in London, that of Child and Co., where Charles II. kept his account, and he was accused of malversation of the Cathedral funds.* Vaux was a traitor. Bartholomew Harris and Thomas Hodges were in league with astrologers.† Of Hornby, whom we have always considered a fine old fellow, we have seen accusations of greed, lust of gain, and that he

---

* Hamilton.

† Ovington and James Forbes.

NOTE ON SIR JOHN CHILD.—He was educated at Rajapor in Rutnageeree, from the age of 10 to 18, with his uncle, Mr. Goodshaw, Chief of that Factory, and being a smart boy, discovered that he carried on private trade with the funds of the Company, and informed upon him! Goodshaw was cashiered, and he at 24 "was laird himself," that is, chief of the said factory. His brother's family in England became not only rich, but allied with noble houses; and it is on record that Josiah Child's widow—he who was chairman of the East India Company, and senior partner of Child and Co.—survived until 1735. This was the *acme* of the Child family, for eleven dukes and duchesses used to ask her blessing, dear old *boodie!* and, it was reckoned, fifty great families would go into mourning for her. Hear that! and this also that no man can tell where Sir John Child's grave is. The *when* he died was 1690, but I have not discovered his place of sepulture in India. Probably it was one of the fine mausolea which were demolished at Mendham's burying-ground near the Cooperage on the eve of the opening of Sonapore in 1760. When Sir John Child died the Cathedral walls were standing fifteen feet high, though *a la bonne heure* he could not go there. The Bombay Cathedral was not for this Child.

was anything but a gentleman.* Jonathan Duncan was a Scotsman. No harder thing could be said of a man in India in the end of the eighteenth century, for a Scotsman was branded, and, like Cain, wandered over the face of the earth. But he was more: a Brahmanised Scotsman, whatever that may mean, and old "havering bodie" who had lost his head.† Even Nepean was a nipcheese and had been a purser in the Navy, and the more credit to him.‡ Malcolm was a fool; but not such a fool. Sir Robert Grant immortalised Love-grove by making the sluices and main drains§ and singing his hymns on the battlements of Poorendhur. Never mind; his hymns will be sung in Anglican cathedral and Methodist meeting-house when you and I are forgotten. Even Gerald Aungier, the first and greatest of our Conscript fathers, the almost impeccable Aungier, is taken to task by the Rev. Mr. Anderson of Colaba as if his religious phraseology savoured of insincerity. O thou Aungier, be not righteous overmuch.||

RELIGIOUS.

Now though Elphinstone was not charged with

* Donald Campbell, 1783.
† Wellington Despatches.
‡ Stocqueler.
§ Oriental Christian Spectator, 1838.
|| Anderson's Western India.

any of these things, he was not allowed to leave Bombay unscathed. And it must be confessed that there was something about his clear, mirror-like mind that attracted the basilisk eye and breath of detraction.

A breath may make it as a breath hath made,

So one fine morning, when his sky seemed perfectly unclouded, a little speck, no bigger than a man's hand, appeared on the horizon, and the words "doubter, sceptic, and unbeliever" were whispered by a field officer—and printed. It so happened that in 1825, shortly before his death, Bishop Heber was guest in Bombay for two months of Mountstuart Elphinstone. He it was who sang—

From many an ancient river,
From many a palmy plain,
They call us to deliver
The land from error's chain.

And this was one of the errors he sought to deliver the land from. He left on record that in all essential points Elphinstone's views were doctrinally correct, and that he had done more for Christianity than any other Governor had ever attempted. It was of little avail where most needed. Thirty-three years after this, when Elphinstone died, an eminent journalist* in London wrote: "His life closed in philosophic beauty and Christian repose." The editor of the journal in which it appeared was taken to task, and the whole question had to be gone into *de novo*. There is an Apostolical succession, and though Bishop Heber was dead, Dr. Wilson was alive; and when in 1860 he appeared before the Asiatic Society in Bombay with a paper on Elphinstone and his services, he took good care to tell his hearers that Elphinstone's respect for religion was exactly as intimated by Bishop Heber, and mentioned by the way that he had been a contributor to the Bible Society, was a friend to the Scottish Mission, and on several occasions had granted plots of land to the Americans. The Doctor adds—"as shown in their annual reports." But why do we speak of such things? Were not the same tactics employed by a coterie in Edinburgh in 1868, in the case of the removal of a renowned principal from Poona, and when the appeal was made to Bombay, wisdom was justified of her children? And did not the same old man whose bones now lie in our Scotch kirkyard again raise his right arm, and by one telegram silence for ever the tongues of the malefactors,

* William Jerdan.

and vindicate the cause of truth and righteousness?

CHARACTER AND ACCOMPLISHMENTS.

If Elphinstone had been a Roman, he would have been the Marcus Aurelius of our school day's something of the soldier, much of the student, and a great deal of the stoic. Did not the Duke of Wellington, after witnessing his bearing at the battle of Assaye, tell him that he had mistaken his profession and ought to have been a soldier? When Bajee Rao from his palace window at Parbutty saw the last of the Mahrattas disappear behind the hills of Gunnesh Khind, he knew whose was the hand that caused their disappearance. No one could guess that under such a mild exterior there was concealed so much firmness and determination. But it was there. When Commissioner at Poona, a conspiracy was detected, consisting of Brahmins and the most desperate of the military class. Elphinstone immediately blew away the ringleaders from the guns. Sir Evan Napean was then Governor of Bombay, and, alarmed at his hardihood, advised him strongly to ask the Governor-General for an Act of Indemnity, which he indignantly rejected. "If I have done wrong I ought to be punished;

if I have done right, I don't want any Acts of Indemnity." He had some terrible nights at Poona—the memory of one still remains. And we have the words of the great Canning that where other master minds failed he foiled the chicanery and machinations of Bajee Rao at every hand.

When he arrived in England, he tells us with characteristic humility that when in conversation with the men of his day he invariably soon found himself out of his depth, and to remedy this he would retire for several months at a time to a roadside inn and pursue his studies with all the ardour and perseverance of a young scholar. Long ere this he was familar with Persian and Hindustani, French and Italian, and with Latin, and when over fifty he perfected himself in Greek.

One fact ought not to be omitted in his Indian days: his devotion to horsemanship and the chase. He had but one pace on horeback, and that was a hand gallop, and, like many other Governors, had a bad fall and broke his collar-bone. He became an active member of the Poona Hunt, and was often seen among a group of eager sportsmen in the grey of the morning after the jackal. But pig was his delight. The wild boar of Scotland had been displayed on the armorial bearings of the Elphinstones ages before the name of India had been heard in the Caledonian forests. So his ancestors having sworn a feud against the gruesome beast, he transferred it from the banks of the Carron to the Mootha Moola, and went at him with a will.

> The bristly boar
> In infant gore
> Wallows beneath the thorny shade.

He had always a native shikaree in his camp, and whenever he brought *kubber* Elphinstone proclaimed a holiday, and it was not his fault if he had not the first spear. A young dragoon—Cooper—was much chagrined that he could not take a spear. Elphinstone mounted him on one of his best horses, which laid the young soldier alongside the hog, and he delivered his spear. "You have won your spurs nobly," said Elphinstone, and made him a present of the horse. And we have seen somewhere that in old age at Hookwood, when his eye was dim and his natural force abated, the presence of a young friend from India would kindle him into animation over some old, old story of "the boar, the boar, the mighty boar." In Bombay we are told that though he was surrounded by young men he never suffered the slightest indecorum, and if any one after dinner indulged in a *double entendre* he would not say anything, but pushing back his chair, broke up the party. He left the bulk of his moderate fortune to his nephew, Lord Elphinstone, who survived him only a few months. They were both buried at Limpsfield in Surrey.

BIOGRAPHICAL.

No man has so peculiarly identified himself, and for so long a time, with the history of Western India. Elphinstone was in Poona in 1801, the year that Bajee Rao put to death Wittojee, the brother of Holkar, by dragging him at the foot of an elephant, and he was in full possession of his faculties when in 1858 he heard from his nephew, Lord Elphinstone, an account of the Indian mutiny. He was present at Bassein in 1802 at the signing of the famous treaty. He went through the whole campaign of 1803 with the Duke: Ahmednugger, Gawilgur, Argaum, and Assaye. He it was in 1808 who first brought to Europe the knowledge of Afghanistan—that country which has twice during the last forty years shrouded so many families in gloom and sorrow. As Commissioner in Poona (1810 to 1817), he foiled the machinations of Bajee Rao, and where Malcolm was hoodwinked, tore away the mask and revealed the enemy of England. He was not terrified by seeing his house, the English Residency, at the Sungum in flames, his library and everything he had except the clothes on his back burned to ashes. He emerged a hero from the glare of the conflagration, and history has blazoned the name of Kirkee on his shield of arms. He settled the Deccan. When he first came to Poona the province was overrun by banditti, and the land around its suburbs could not be let for rent. Look at it now. In 1821 the President was able to write of his Government: "It has repelled predatory invasion, restrained intestine disorder, administered equal and impartial justice, and has almost extirpated every branch of exaction and oppression."* His Government of Bombay (1819 to 1827) was nearly faultless; his efforts for the education of the natives can never be forgotten, for even should the two great structures which bear his name in Bombay crumble to dust by the decay of time or by human or elemental violence, his name will remain as that of a great, a just, and a true Governor, who was content to do the work of a part, when the Government of the whole of India

* Minute on Khandeish.

lay before him, and who with the peerage of England within his reach preferred to live and die an untitled scion of the nobility of Scotland. His statue is placed in St. Paul's, where lie the bones of his great friend and master, the Duke of Wellington.

SIR JOHN MALCOLM.

CHAPTER XIII.

SIR JOHN MALCOLM.

PRELIMINARY.

THE time has now come when the fame of Sir John Malcolm must rest upon books, either books written by himself or the records that remain of his life and doings. There may be still men in Bombay who remember him, and the *sough* of him may still be heard. But tradition is an uncertain monitor, and must soon give up the ghost, leaving us to fall back on the written letter that remaineth. At Mahableshwur, the loved names of Charlotte, Amelia, Kate and Olympia, wife and daughters, have been written by Malcolm on the everlasting hills, and his noble statue still looks down upon us as we enter the portals of the Asiatic Society. But these memorials are local and perishable. Chantrey deals with the outer framework of the man, and a magnificent framework it is, leaving untouched the story of his life. Where Chantrey ends History begins, and the divine chisel shapes the block from Burnfoot into a glorious body, not indeed without spot or wrinkle, but beyond the power of marble to express or delineate.

CALF COUNTRY.

"Noo Jock, my man, be sure whan youre awa, ye kaim yer heid and keip yer face clean. If ye dinna, ye'll jist be sent back agen." Thus moralised his old nurse, while combing his hair for the last time ere he left Burnfoot. He remembered the words didn't he?—aye for many a day retailed at camp fires, from Madras to Ispahan, where "the laugh was ready chorus." There is a world of hard philosophy in the old crone's observations, and it is not for nothing the Scot's "hame coming" is here shorn of its attractions. To George and Margaret Malcolm ten sons and seven daughters were born. The young birds were in fact kicking each other over the nest, and an additional one was given by the old nurse, beyond anything all the schools could hammer into him, to wit, that his days of *neiveing* trouts in the Esk were at an end, and he must now go and do for himself. And she combed his hair to some purpose. It is out of such rough schooling that many Scotch heroes in India have been manufactured. Bear witness Baird, Monro, and last but not least Colin Campbell of Clyde. Gash, douce, prudent woman, may your race be long continued, for God pity the country, when our Indian heroes are in the position of—"Story I have none to tell, sir." Jock was the worst boy in the school, and there never was a row but the teacher observed "Jock's at the bottom of it." Malcolm remembered this, and the story goes that when he published his history of Persia he sent a copy to his old teacher writing on the fly leaf, "Jock's at the bottom of it!" A portrait of Malcolm's mother in the Royal Academy a few years ago attracted much attention, and according to the *Times'* Art Critic she looked in every way a mother of heroes.

THE SOLDIERS' RETURN.

I have seen a story of the return of the two brothers to Burnfoot after they had made a name in the world. It was a fine summer afternoon, and they were posting hard down the rough Langholm road. Suddenly a glimpse reveals to them their old home, with two aged relatives sitting at the hall gate and knitting their stocking in the drowsy sunshine. A river lay between them, and it was a mile to the bridge. Heavily accoutred as they were, they dashed through the stream and were soon hugging their Aunties.

> "Oh gear will buy me rigs and land,
> Oh gear will buy me sheep and kye,
> But the tender heart o leesome love
> The gowd and siller canna buy."

Malcolm "did not wear his heart upon his sleeve for daws to peck at," and did not tell this story to every one, but he had another favourite which will rejoice the heart of the Anglo-Indian and is worthy of Dean Ramsay. A brother officer came back to Edinburgh after twenty years' service in India. His arrival was unexpected, so mounting to the residence of his Aunts, *a flat*, he introduced himself *sans ceremonie*, and found the two at a game of draughts, just as he had left them on his departure, to whom his first greeting was—"What! Have you not finished that game yet?" He was thus a man of infinite humour, and brimful of gaiety and anecdote, his company greatly sought after, and the life and soul of every social gathering. In early life he drank fairly well, but he is no example in this to the present generation, as he was of prodigious size, not corpulent, but capable of stowing away drinks of sorts with impunity. What his favourite drink was in early manhood in Bombay I have no means of knowing. This I can aver, that Cape and Madeira were extensively used, and whisky was unknown. That he was merry, rollicking, even boisterous we gather from Mackintosh, and a "Malcolm row" was not uncommon. This was in Bombay, but even in Paris he himself writes "I was tipsy." This we don't believe, and are rather inclined to think that it is conclusive evidence against the assertion. It is no doubt a case

> "We are no fou, we are no fou,
> But just a drappie in oor ee."

He was "na fou, but just had plenty." However, Malcolm was a man that did not need drink to make him merry. In the tent and field, when floored with fatigue or half-smothered with the *stour* and grime of battle, or amid burning heat, cholera, and other depressing influences, beleaguring Aseerghur, a quiet joke or vigorous sally from him would raise the drooping spirits of his companions in arms, and make them cheerful for the day or night. With Malcolm existence in India was not only endurable but delightful, and men soon began to find this out. The Duke of Wellington averred that there was not a good tempered man in India. It was "the cloimate," no doubt of it, and we presume he excepted himself. So it was thus that among a lot of atrabilious men at Seringapatam he soon discovered that Malcolm could put to flight the demon of dulness. Humanly speaking it is the one thing needful in India to soldier and civilian alike. Even the *medico* and *padre* are not exempt, for they are nothing unless they brighten this world or the next. The jocular may co-exist with the serious, and if Norman Macleod had been a soldier he would have been a Malcolm. Here is an illustration. Henry Martyn, the missionary, came to Bombay in 1811. Though he was vulgarly called "the saint," he was not allowed to pass through the city unnoticed to death and martyrdom. Instead of being relegated to the backslums to munch *chowpatties* in solitude, his conversations with Mackintosh and Elphinstone, such of them as have been preserved, furnish most pregnant material for thought. Malcolm amid all his work had time to write a letter of introduction to Sir Gore Ouseley, our ambassador at the Court of Persia, for him. It says little, but head and heart, Malcolm and Missionary, are equally honoured thereby.*

IN PARIS.

Malcolm went to Paris in 1815 by invitation of the Duke of Wellington. He knew him and did not require the invitation : in fact, Malcolm introduced his friends to the Duke. Emperors were thick as blackberries, and Malcolm was in his glory. He was then 44, so that it was not exactly a case of "Youth in the prow and pleasure at the helm." He had two months of reviews (150,000 men), balls, operas, concerts. *Rouge et Noire* mulcted him eight napoleons at one sitting. Next night he lost nothing. We had thought that *Belvidere* and *Non Parell* had finished his card fancies. But the old Bombay Adam breaks out in Paris.

The Duke. "Ah! Malcolm, delighted to see you," voice and manner, everything the same. He dined about a dozen times with the Duke, and sometimes sat next him talking of "battle, murder, and sudden death." "It was hard pounding on both sides, and we pounded the hardest," said the Duke. He drove with the

* Letter dated February 1811 :—I am satisfied that if you ever see him you will be pleased with him. He will give you grace before and after dinner, and admonish such of your party as take the Lord's name in vain, but his good sense and great learning will delight you, whilst his constant cheerfulness will add to the hilarity of your party."

Duke in his gig. Like the Prince of Wales in Bombay, the Duke was the fastest driver in Paris. No necks were broken. A few Hindustanee words would occasionally creep into the conversation after dinner, and Malcolm would jocularly ask the Duke if he was a *Lootiewalla*, or comparing notes on Talleyrand find a resemblance to some old scoundrel or killedar in Deccany fort which set them alaughing. "Not nearly so clever," said the Duke. At first Malcolm found himself deficient in French, but by the assistance of a master every morning he in ten days, to use his own words, "became quite fluent in French after a bottle and a half of champagne, and was able to recount as many anecdotes as any of them." This was among the French and Continentals. How the Scotch stories fared at his hands in the process of translation we have no means of knowing. We trust that no dark grey man hailing from the north, but hirsute and in Parisian garments, did not, as in Chalmers's case when he had just emerged a full blown member of the Institute of France, and was airing his eloquence fire across the *table d'hôte* "I think, sir, if ye jist speik in braid Scotch, we'll a understan ye a wee better." But joking apart, his powers of application were prodigious. How it came to pass that a Scotch farmer's son in the end of the eighteenth century, who left school at the age of 11, with some eighteen months of academy in London afterwards, should be able to fit himself out in ten days to hold philosophical conversations in French with Humboldt, Volney, Denon, and Silvestre de Sacy, is more than we can comprehend. The secret, perhaps, lies in one sentence in his *Life of Clive*, where he speaks of *that self-education which after all is of all educations the most important*. Sir Walter Scott and Sir James Mackintosh were in Paris at this time : the latter spoke French uncommonly well. We may add that the high living in Paris had its usual effect on Malcolm. He became plethoric and required to be bled

A BIG DAY.

But leaving balls and pleasure houses, let us contemplate Malcolm in a different aspect and with different surroundings, and on a day as the saying is " big with the fate of nations." Malcolm had many red letter days, but this was one that brought out the supreme character of the man, and roused into action its latent wisdom and courage. He always set great store on this day, and the memory of it was sweet to him in after years, for he was brought face to face with a great difficulty with which he had to wrestle without reference to his superiors. That day was the 2nd June, 1818, a natal day for Western India, and on which she may well set up the white stone of her liberties. He was then at a village called Keyree, about thirty miles from Asseergurh. Events had been hurrying on with unexampled rapidity and the Mahratta Empire was in the throes of dissolution. That Empire had been founded by the indomitable pluck of Seevajee, and its limits extended far and wide, so that a successor made the boast that he had watered the horses of the Deccan in the Hooghly. And it was no idle boast. But corruption had long ago settled down upon it. And had one-tenth of the energy of Seevajee been displayed in defending them, the forts of the Deccan would not have fallen before us like the walls of Jericho, and a new chapter* been added to the History of India. Bajee Rao, the last of the Peshwas, for twenty years had been wearying out the lives of our great generals and statesmen by endless intrigue and duplicity. He had wearied Wellington, and he had wearied Elphin-

* Thirty fortresses, each of which, with a Seevajee as a master, would have defied the whole Indian Army, fell unresistingly in a few weeks.—*Lake's Sieges of the Madras Army*, 1825.

stone and Malcolm. He was to weary us no more. A mandate issued from the camp of Malcolm, that he was to resign for himself and his successors for ever all right and title to the government of Poona, in one day leave for "Hindustan," and that if in twenty-four hours he did not present himself in the camp of Malcolm, he and his followers in arms would be put to the edge of the sword.

He came and we all know the rest. It would be no compliment to the understanding of our readers if we set down and leisurely detailed what Bajee Rao's Government was in 1818 and what the state of the country now is in 1881. He who runs may read, and he who sits still may read also, if he is of a doubting mind, in the Rutnageeree section of Mr. Campbell's *Bombay Gazetteer*, a chapter illustrating the infamies of Bajee Rao's rural administration. Suffice it to say that as soon as he left for Benares, Deccan and Konkan breathed freely almost for the first time in their history, and the country set out like a giant in a new race of existence. The land rested from the torments of tyranny and oppression. Life and property became clothed with the habiliments of respect—we mean the respect that a man hath for himself, and that which he oweth to his neighbour, instead of making him a mark for robbery or murder. Henceforward the pathway of Western India was to be no longer through the jungle, on the track of wild beasts and wilder men, but on the broad highway which leads to security and civilisation.

DINNER TO THE ETTRICK SHEPHERD.

In 1832 a dinner was given in Free Masons Hall, and 200 persons were present. Again Malcolm is on the crest of the wave and takes the chair. It was a great night for Scotland. The sons of Burns were there, Lockhart son-in-law of Sir Walter Scott, Galt the novelist, Basil Hall, Lord Mahon, Vice-Chancellor Sir John Stewart, and, a greater than he, Brougham Lord Chancellor of England. Everything passed off magnificently without a hitch. The Shepherd was seen late in the evening in his element ladling out 'whisky toddy to all and sundry from Burn's Punch Bowl lent for the occasion by Mr. Hastie, member for Paisley.

GOVERNOR OF BOMBAY.

In 1828 Sir John Malcolm became Governor of Bombay, and the question arises, why did he accept the office? He was worthy of it, and Bombay was proud to have him. He it was that thought that the Bay of Naples in natural beauty was not so striking as the harbour of Bombay, and that it vied with Corfu and the Albanian hills. But it must be remembered that Malcolm was now 59 years of age. Men have no doubt done wonderful things after 59, witness Napier at Meanee, and Colin Campbell leading the final assault on Lucknow. These sons of Mars were in their element, and Malcolm in Bombay in 1828 we have come to think was a little out of it. "I was a fool for coming to India, and this I have showed every day since I landed." So he did, and we cannot disguise from ourselves that Malcolm had now become a prey to the last infirmity of noble minds, and it is with a feeling of disappointment that we read in his memoirs that he accepted the Bombay post as a stepping stone to the Viceroyalty of India. That event, as we all know, never came. Laudable ambition, praiseworthy endeavour, say some. Perhaps.

There is a tradition that on one of the outlying boulders which jut into Loch Lomond, a Highland Laird, with rod, line, and clip, managed to land in one morning ninety-nine salmon, and that though he fished all day and far into the evening he could not make up the even number.

It is the evening of a long day, and Malcolm still threshes the water after having filled the creel of a giant. So he comes to Bombay—not the old Bombay of Wellington and Mackintosh I ween, but a Bombay full of Judges, writs of *Habeas Corpus*, and worries of all sorts, tear and wear of body and brain, for though both were framed on a gigantic model, the drafts made on them were unusual and incessant, and not to be recouped by any amount of pig-sticking or riding cross country in Kutch and Kattywar. There was no longer the sound of revelry at Parell, but an endlesss decoction of tea and coffee administered six days in the week to a discerning public. For one thing, he had to do with a most disagreeable subject, the reduction of salaries. A man that takes retrenchment in hand has not his sorrows to seek.

"I drink no wine," writes he. Melancholy admission, the days of high jinks are gone, wit banished and mirth nowhere; nothing but an endless caterwauling which followed him to Panwell, up the Ghauts, past Poona, cross the Wye, till the nethermost summit of Mahableshwur was reached, where a statue of retrenchment in the shape of some attenuated official ogled him at the door of his bungalow. How could he drink wine under such circumstances? The wonder is that he survived the ordeal, and we are certainly not surprised to find one fine morning ere his tenure of office is half expired that he chucks up the whole affair. Better for himself that he had never had anything to do with it.

There is an illustration ready at our hand as to how this Bombay Governorship was dealt with by Mountstuart Elphinstone, the immediate predecessor of Malcolm. He at all events did not make this island a stepping stone to Viceregal power.

He was not inferior to Malcolm in intellect, not second to him in administrative ability, and yet he refused twice the Viceroyalty of India. Did he suffer by the refusal? On the contrary, the story adds fresh lustre to his fame and grows brighter by repetition. No feverish ambition or restless anxiety darkened the brow of Elphinstone.

> "Silent he moves, majestically slow,
> Like ebbing Nile or Ganges in his flow."

Greater in this than Malcolm, greatest if you will of all the Bombay Governors, but measured even by a wider scale Elphinstone stands single and alone among the most illustrious Indian statesmen as the one man whom Viceroyalty, the Peerage, and Parliamentary honours solicited in vain. His resolute modesty mocks the courage of wordly ambition, and the feeble health which is said to have dictated it, enabled him by care, contentment, and patience to live to a patriarchal age, for he came to his grave like a shock of corn fully ripe, ere a single ear had been withered by the touch of time or the blighting curse of envy.

REDUCTIO AD ABSURDUM.

This was the era of economy and retrenchment in Bombay, and to everybody connected with Government it must have been a dreadful time, for there was no discharge in that warfare. The measures were necessary, and doubtless Malcolm had his instructions, but I have never heard that he was a man of figures, or had any special aptitude that way. Clearly Malcolm's vocation was to deal with men of increasing not decreasing incomes. It turns his fine spirits into gall. In the clipping process his shears were co-extensive with the Presidency, and he took a hard grip of every man in it, so much so that he actually left Bombay under the idea that he had saved it forty lakhs during his three years' tenure of office. From the resumption of salaries that took place after his departure, we do not doubt that he was merely pumping water out of one part of the ship and that it was coming or would come back somewhere else. There seems to have been too much of the square and rule about this business, as is generally the case of statistical surveys of what the lives and bodies of men can be furnished at the least possible cost. In this roughshod way you can get over a good deal of ground, but the question arises, does it pay in the long run? Had he confined himself to reduction of forces in the field so lately, or in rectifying glaring abuses, the howl of indignation would not have been so marked. But when European officers were asked to give up half their tent allowance, estimate Rs. 70,000, and the three members of the Medical Board each Rs. 9,570, Medical Storekeeper Rs. 6,000, it became beyond a joke. He was a great advocate apparently of the Scot's proverb that "every little maks a mickle," for he actually embodies in the list of items which swell up the amount of forty lakhs, and which was transmitted to the Governor-General, a reduction in the gram rations of the mules in Kutch from 7½ lbs.—their daily allowance—to 5 lbs., Rs. 10,000 saved out of dooly-bearers and camel-drivers, and two peons at Sion causeway, whose united earnings now eliminated effect an increment of Rs. 140 per annum! Some of his reductions were no doubt perfectly proper, *i.e.*, that of Inspector of Deccany Forts, though we can testify that the office is a most laborious one; sending the elephants back to Bengal where they came from; 10 copies subscription, substituted for 20 of the *Bombay Sammachar*.

The Town Hall at this time being nearly finished was a perfect God-send to him. Lath and plaster soon dry in this country, and great was the evacuation of Government servants from their bungalows into those new quarters. All no doubt most wise and proper, but when we read that Grafton and Jervis' survey of the Deccan and the Southern Konkan was discontinued, that the Lunatic Asylum figures for Rs. 600, that by giving up sword exercise and blank cartridge at annual reviews (this statement is supported by the Commander-in-Chief) a saving is effected of Rs. 35,000, and finally that the Government allowance for turf plates to be run by country horses in Guzerat and the Deccan is abolished, "our notions of vice and virtue are shaken to their foundations, and our reliance upon truth and duty at an end for ever." No wonder there was a dinner once a month only at Parell during these very cold seasons, of which could not be said

'Twas merry in the hall
And the beards wag'd all.

for the baked meats not seldom furnished the funeral rites of some unfortunate, and the guests over whose heads the wand of retrenchment had passed no longer saw in the Knight of Burnfoot the joyous reveller of 1804-11, but a gryphon, stern and inexorable, standing with a roll of the names of those whose blood had been shed between his teeth. It would have been well for Malcolm and well for posterity if he had initiated his economical notions somewhat earlier in the day, say at Keyree, when he committed the Government to make Bajee Rao an annual payment of 800,000 Sicca Rupees, which at the then exchange of 2s. 6d. amounted to £100,000 sterling.

VI ET ARMIS.

In addition to these measures which affected so injuriously the condition of man and beast, a strange epidemic seized the Governor and Judges of the Island: whether it was imported from Scotland or indigenous is unknown. It was only skin-deep and cutaneous at first, but broke out into such an astonishing degree of inflammation as to defy the wisest doctors of the State. It killed two Judges in two months—Sir Edward West and Sir Charles Chambers. It closed the doors of the High Court of Bombay for two months. Justice is blind : she then became deaf and dumb, though there never was so much to hear or talk about in Bombay, and it was then the naughty girl threw away her scales. It was all about a little boy at Poona—*Moro Ruganath*. The Judges wanted him in Bombay to try Sir John Malcolm's new road down the Ghauts. The Governor would not have this, and the more the Judges said yes he said no. Let him alone. He was good for Fancy Balls, and that sort of thing. So they set at it hammer and tongs. At first the tourney between the two Scotch Knights—Sir John Malcolm and Sir John Peter Grant—was amusing, but after the words "within these walls we owe no equal and no superior but God and the King" were uttered, the ladies in opposite phalanxes ceased to bow to each other. After this the deluge. It was in vain that Malcolm wandered among the ruins of Bejapore, or fled to Mahableshwur to write letters to Sir Walter Scott. No amount of legendary lore would do away with it. In vain Lord Ellenborough wrote :—" I am sending you a new bishop." A new bishop? The Pope of Rome could not settle it. They only cure was to scatter the byke. So a few months afterwards we find Sir John Malcolm ploughing his way up the Red Sea, in the Hugh Lindsay, that pioneer of steam navigation in these waters, writing enormous despatches to prove that he was right and everybody was wrong. And Sir John Peter Grant, we forget where he went to. It was either Calcutta or Rothiemurchus.

So ends the story of

"The Barrin of oor door, weel !"

PERSON.

Sir John Malcolm when in his prime was the finest looking man in Bombay. He was nearly six feet and a half in height, proportionate and well built, and so muscular as to astonish some of the most powerful carrying natives of Bushire when he took a pipe of wine on his back up the stairs of the Residency. At 60 he was good at the spear, and I observe 32 hogs fell to his party in two days in Guzerat. He had a fine frank open countenance and Shakesperean forehead, and his manner in youth and early manhood was exceedingly genial. His wife also was fine looking. They were indeed a splendid couple. When he took Lady Malcolm to the Langholm district—happening to be in an hostelrie, the landlady, some old acquaintance of the Burnfoot family,—whispered quietly into his ear, "Weel, Sir John, ye've got a top hizzie." But *rus aut urbs* it was all the same. William Jerdan tells us the beauty of Lady Malcolm struck the eye of the beholder in Hyde Park, and inspired some of the sparkling verses of Praed.

CONCLUSION.

Malcolm is now near the end of his journey. He goes home in 1830, writes books, and the Duke tells him that though he were an angel from heaven, nobody will listen to him. And yet another ambition. I will arise and go to my native boroughs, solicit their suffrages and represent them in Parliament. The native boroughs, Dumfries, Annan, and the like, would have none of him, no Conservative, no friend of the Duke of Wellington.

The same event happens every day, the same experience followed by the same result, lessons on the vanity of human wishes written on the sands of time, and of which the lives of great men all remind us.

It is the pace that kills, and it is thus that we see during the last six years of his life, Malcolm rushing to his doom, the unconscious instrument of his own destruction.

He died on the 30th May, 1833, at the age of 64, and on the same day his house of Warfield was completed and ready for occupation.

SIR JAMES MACKINTOSH;

OR BOMBAY 1804 TO 1812.

CHAPTER XIV.

SIR JAMES MACKINTOSH;

OR BOMBAY 1804 TO 1812.

BETWEEN 1804 and 1812 four men appeared in Bombay who ultimately attained the highest object of human ambition in war, in politics, and in literature. There were giants in those days, and we have seen what of Bombay interest centres in one of them, the greatest of them all. Mountstuart Elphinstone was the second. He was twice offered by different administrations the Governor-Generalship of India. John Malcolm, the third, fought his way from the cot of Burnfoot, in Eskdale, to the portals of Parell, and became the life-long friend, the bosom friend of the Duke of Wellington. These were the three mighty men who, by the sword and diplomacy, extended and preserved the boundaries of British dominion; but it was reserved for a fourth to keep alive the flame of liberty within them, and illustrate by his genius the realms which they had either subdued or defended. That man was Sir James Mackintosh. He still appears the most splendid character in the whole range of Bombay history—made to love and to be beloved, with a transparent intellect that shed an electric light on everything it touched, and an imagination that soared far above the common level of mortals. He stands on a pedestal peculiarly his own, and he is more identified with Bombay by a long residence in it. Indeed, so important does this appear to his biographer that he devotes five hundred out of the thousand pages of his life to the Bombay portion of it. He arrived in Bombay in May, 1804, and left it in November, 1812. "The cares and duties of a family oblige me to provide for them in other climates." His mother died in 1779, when he was fourteen years of age. In more senses than one he was a Scottish orphan. When he was Recorder of Bombay he wrote—"In her last letter my mother sent me two Scotch bank-notes, of one pound each, which seemed at that time an inexhaustible fortune."

BOMBAY A DULL PLACE.

"The neighbourhood is beautiful; but what avails all this in a cursed country where you cannot ramble amid these scenes? As for society the back-room of a London book-seller's shop is better. There is a langour and a lethargy in the society here to which I never elsewhere saw any approach. It is all a cheat," he exclaims. "If ever I rise from the dead (he means, no doubt, getting out of the Bombay grave-clothes) I shall be very glad to travel for the sake of seeing clever men and beautiful countries." And again, "Our climate may be endured, but I feel, by its constant and silent operation, existence is rendered less joyous, and even less comfortable. I see around me no extraordinary prevalence of disease, but I see no vigorous, cheerful health." All quite true from his own standpoint, and equally untrue from the standpoint of others, for the Bombay of the period under review, to an ordinary mortal, could not have been a very dull place. There were, no doubt, at that time dull and heavy men in Bombay. We have more than a suspicion that Jonathan Duncan was a dull man. He was the natural leader of society, and his influence must have made itself everywhere apparent. A man cannot live thirty-nine years in India without being somewhat flabby, leaden, or lethargic—*brahmanised,* that is Mackintosh's word in describing Duncan. Hence we fancy that J. D. was as dead as a door nail to the brilliancy of wit or the pathos of sentiment. He was too far gone even for the surgical operation proverbial for Scotsmen, and would sit perfectly helpless amid the subtle flashes of wit that fell flat and pointless on his Forfarshire understanding. Mackintosh may have resented this, found the verandahs of the old Government House in Apollo Street much too narrow for him, took french-leave and sauntered into the Bombay Green to seek for the Southern Cross or soar in regions of transcendental philosophy. And the most likely of all times would be that in which Arthur Wellesley said that Jonathan Duncan had lost his head.

But there was another, and a much more cogent reason, why Mackintosh found Bombay a dull place, and one special to himself and apart altogether from individuals, and having nothing to do with the gloom which we have seen overspread Bombay in 1804. It was two years before Mackintosh cleared his expenses and established himself in Bombay. He was thirty-eight years of age when he arrived, and had already lived one life in London. Not a life in a garret, for though he had made a fruitless start with his Edinr. M. D. at Weymouth to practise as a physician, he soon found his way to London, and made the acquaintance and friendship of some most eminent and gifted men. He had attended the trial of Warren Hastings, had obtained great distinction by the publication of *Vindiciae Gallicae,* had been the guest of Burke the aged at Beaconsfield, and the friend of Charles James Fox, of whom Burke said that he was the most accomplished and brilliant debater that the world ever saw. He had founded in his own house the "King of Clubs," consisting of twenty-five celebrated men. So that coming to Bombay was really like coming to a city of the dead, a copy of the greatest change, as sayeth the preacher, from ceiled roofs to thatched bungalows, from living like gods to dying like men.

He found Jonathan Duncan in place of Henry Brougham, Charles Forbes for Mr. Ricardo, and Dr. Keir, Civil Surgeon, for Hallam the historian. His spirit sank within him, and he uttered those words of despair. In those days steamers were unknown, and it was a very long cry to Loch Awe.* But it is not given to every man to be a Ricardo, and it may have been well

* The English news was often eight months in finding its way to Bombay.

for Mackintosh and well for posterity that eight years of affluent ease and leisure were afforded him to gather up his intellectual wares in the city of Bombay. Besides, dulness is a comparative term, and happiness a measure of the capacity of the individual for enjoying it. "Peebles for pleasure," said an honest Scotsman on his return from that London after which Sir James Mackintosh sighed in the bitterness of his heart; and we daresay that Mr. Henshaw, the voluble mouth-piece of the Wellington entertainments, and of whom history records the *vox et preterea nihil,* was in the seventh heaven of delight, while our modern Prometheus lay chained to the rock of Mazagon, plus mosquitoes and prickly-heat. We cannot, therefore, agree that Bombay was a bad place for Mackintosh. William Erskine came out with him and became his son-in-law, and, if we mistake not, has given to Bombay two generations of Civil Servants. One morning a young man called upon him with a letter of introduction from Robert Hall. He also became his son-in-law, Babylonian Rich, the afterwards Resident at Bagdad.

THE DIARY AND LETTERS OF MACKINTOSH

Let in much light on the Bombay society, 1804 to 1812, and unconsciously on himself. At first we seem to look backwards across the haze of seventy years, and see looming in the distance, at the end of a long avenue, the shadow of a great man under the portals of Parell. But gradually the intervening cross lights disappear, and by the aid ot what he has left us he comes forth from the region of shadow and dubiety, and walks the earth again with a character not dim or tarnished by time, and with an intellect as lofty as ever animated the sons of men.

The feeblest effort of imagination can thus picture Mackintosh as he once lived among us—on the judgment-seat—moving amid his fellow citizens, or in the bosom of his family. His face and form, his daily amusements and avocations are familiar to us. Parell has been given to him as his residence by Jonathan Duncan, who is a bachelor and does not need it. His wife is the first lady in the island, and with five daughters constitutes the household. The dining and billiard-rooms are almost the same now as they were then. The rooms are spacious, and the verandahs long and wide.

HE DID GOOD WORK IN BOMBAY.

His accomplishments were versatile. He wrote observations on the Finances of Salsette for the

Governor, which were gladly availed of by him. At Duncan's request he wrote the funeral sermon on the Viceroy, the Marquis Cornwallis! He wrote to the newspapers. The man who in after years was asked by the noblemen and gentlemen who were then the leaders of the Whig party to write an epitaph for Fox's tomb in Westminster Abbey on hearing of his death did not disdain to send his panegyric to the *Bombay Courier*. He founded, ere he had been many months here, the Bombay Literary Society, which has grown into the Bombay Royal Asiatic Society, and sent out the books which constitute the foundation of the noble library which adorns it. Of that Society he was the first President, Charles Forbes, Treasurer, and William Erskine, Secretary. But above all, and what was not known until after his death, and the value of which increases with the lapse of years, he brought his comprehensive intellect to bear upon those social questions which underlie all Government, and in his delineation of the Deccan in 1805 answers for us, and those who come after us, the question whether our being here in 1881 is a good to the natives of India.

He had the wisdom of the seer and wrote for posterity ;—where there is no vision the people perish. As long, therefore, as the written letter remains, so long will Mackintosh continue to be a most powerful ally of the British Government.*

This will do for

A QUIET DAY AT PARELL.

Our host sends a man to rouse us before daylight. *Sahib, sahib!* Those dreadful words still linger in our ears, uttered by the hamal to the sleeping Christian. O thou merciless heathen! But there is no rest to the wicked. So, quick as thought, we hurry into our clothes, with not a glance to spare for the *silhouette* of Charles James Fox in our dressing-room, rush along the corridors, stumbling over the domestics, who litter the place like the sheeted dead, descend the noble flight of stairs, greet our friend and master in his leather breeches and top-boots, his Scotch terrier Tartar meanwhile giving tongue, mount our Arabs—he on Sir Charles Grey, I on Bobberywallah—and with one long canter are in Mahim woods. The false dawn is past, and already the sun's first rays dart through the trees their silvery sheen.

Here we draw breath. We are told that this

* We have made large drafts on this subject from his writings in previous articles.

noble forest is noted in our oldest maps, and certes it is a goodly sight. Such palms! date, doum, fan, cocoa, betel, and acacia,

> "Bending
> To earth their leaf-crown'd heads,
> Like youthful maids when sleep descending
> Warns them to their downy beds."

Our talk is miscellaneous—Aldourie, Kellachie, and spearing salmon on the Don, with a sprinkling of European politics and Bombay police bills. On and on, until in Salsette a new glory bursts upon us in the *pallas* tree, called the flame of the woods, setting, as it were, with its scarlet flowers, the very forest on fire; and we are told that it gives its name to the battle-field of Plassey. And yet another wonder, the silk-cotton tree, a marvel of floral magnificence, decked in wool and scarlet, like the bride of King Solomon. Neither *gool-mohr* nor *bougainvillæ* adorn the scene.* We return. After a bath we are more buoyant than if we had emerged from a *hummam* in Cairo or Damascus; pass into the verandah, and exchange greetings with a number of young faces, their hair waving in the morning breeze, and

---

* *Ponciana Regia*, a native of Madagascar, introduced into India within the last sixty years.—*Brand's Flora of India*, 1871. Bougainvillæ, so called after a French botanist, and also a comparatively late introduction.

some of whom have never yet set eye on poker and tongs.

The library table groans with new books, a most refreshing sight to a new comer. *Edinburgh Review* in blue-and-yellow livery. Scott's novels and lays, Burns (the Kilmarnock edition), and a curiosity which Elphinstone found at Peshawar, a book printed by Gassendi in Paris, 1646, and presented by him to his pupil Bernier, the great Indian traveller, with Bernier's name written by himself on it.

But hush! Mackintosh reads prayers; he did so on board all the way out, and a *fell** reader he is. Breakfast comes on the scene, which we proceed to demolish. Sir James busy at his kedgeree, two boiled eggs, three cups of tea, and two of coffee. Padre Martyn from Calcutta, vulgarly called "the Saint," has come in, who afterwards died in Tokah, and whose praise is now in all the churches; so we had the novelty of grace before and after meat, all standing. Much discussion on grammar and metaphysics; we read, lounge, write, and loiter away in the beautiful apartments that contain the library. Dine at four. From half-past five to seven walk

* Fell, acute, hot-biting.—*Jamieson*. His voice was nasal.—*Sydney Smith*.

on the terrace and walks of this noble house and garden ; drink tea at seven ; and from half-past seven to ten, bed-time, our host reads to his wife and children aloud in his light vest and white jacket. Addison and Milton are his favourites. But Tasso also and novels, for Scott has just burst upon the scene, and Madame de Stäel comes in by turns. The German governess is gone—married, we suppose—but the girls are not without education, and their father helps them in their study of German, Italian, and French, of the last being such a master that he could correspond with a French statesman, or debate in French in a court of law.

A NOISY DAY AT TARALA.

I happened to be in Bombay in January, 1811. Sir James was then living at Tarala, Mazagon. It was not so ornate a house as Parell, but it was roomy and had a fine view : Parell had none. Lady Mackintosh had gone home. It was the time of the races, and a good deal of fun was going on. The races were then in the morning. We drove to the Grand Stand, Byculla, and there met Lady Ouseley. I remember that Sir James was clothed in white vest, breeches, and a frock-coat of green silk, and Lady Ouseley resplendent in Genoa velvet, with three ostrich-plumes towering overhead and nodding in the breeze. I never saw such roads—they were as finely macadamised as those now in England, and long before the name of that celebrated highwayman was ever heard of.* The Flats were a caution. Rickard's horse won, and he was in ecstacies. Tyler of the Indian Navy pointed out the horses, and knew all about them. The Arab horses, of course, did not run so quick as the English horses at New Market. That evening forty sat down to dinner in the strictest etiquette. Being left out in the cold, I had no lady to take in. I was amused afterwards by a married lady asking me if I had been "ship-wrecked." I had never heard the word before in this sense, and imagined it referred to the voyage out.

I never saw men eat so little. Coming from the land where Lord Braxfield had said that a turkey was an awkward beast to eat—too much for one, and two little for two—I know that my father's retainers near Golspie would have been thankful for, and made short work of, the ghost of the feast, which must have been quite as bulky as when we sat down. Every dish was put on

* Captain Basil Hall.

the table, and the air was heavy and overpowering. I remember that the party was stiff until the champagne passed round. The men drank fairly well: Sir James only cold water. We had been drinking Shiraz, the finest wine of Persia, and Constantia, the finest wine of Africa; but no sooner was it discussed than Malcolm set the table in a roar by his adventures at the Court of Scindia. It was the story which he had told Wellington, and which Wellington sent on to his brother the Viceroy, the Earl of Mornington. During a durbar in the tent of Scindia the rain came down, filling a corner of the flap with half-a-ton of water, and the solemnity of the durbar was suddenly arrested by the falling cataract, "Oh, Jasus!" and a hideous yell from an Irish officer named Pepper, who had been suddenly submerged, at which the grim countenance even of Scindia relaxed. Malcolm was a perfect Jupiter Tonans, six feet and a-half high, and as strong as an ox. Had he not carried for a few feet grain in sacks on his back to the weight of 830 lbs., and a pipe of wine up the stairs of the Residency at Bushire? It was long before the toast of the "outward bound" was given, for the ladies were made much of, and song and sentiment followed each other in quick succession.

"Drink to me only with thine eyes," and a Scotsman out of compliment to the host gave "The Lass of Inverness." We lingered long over the Madeira. Lady Ouseley played beautifully on the piano. A lot went in for billiards. Malcolm, who was an adept at cards, made up several parties.* I happened to join Elphinstone with two lady partners at whist—it was long whist, and a capital game we had. My partner gave me a pinch——of snuff from her box: we were still in the age of "snuffy Charlotte." I never saw a man play a better game than Elphinstone, and so cool, for he was well tried. We had not been long seated before his eye caught the sight of his Secretary, standing like an apparition between the pillars of the verandah. He had just arrived from Poona with bad news, and we knew it, for he had a tell-tale face, and you might have led him with a straw. But Elphinstone never flinched, changed countenance, revoked, nor played a wrong card; and as he claimed the victory—*eight, nine, ten,* he quietly rose, after giving the Secretary a terrible

* Malcolm in his youth was very fond of cards. "I have been in my very early years the victim of such habits, and was only saved by the combined workings of distress from debt, and a strong call from men of whose regard I was proud, and who added to the respect I owed them as superiors all the claims of friendship."—*Kaye's Life of Malcolm.*

quart d'heure. He then saw the ladies into their palanquins, wished them good night, and turning round to the Secretary with a "good evening," heard all he had got to say.* Everybody was in great glee. Mr. ——, glorious, chasing Mrs. —— round the library to obtain a kiss. I looked into the smoking-room, a portion of the dining-room extemporised for this purpose: ten Englishmen squatted on their Persian rugs *à l'Arabe,* and as many hookahs going, with so much gurgle-gurgle and hubble-bubble, as if there had been so many stones in their throats. You could not hear the sound of your own voice, or distinguish one face from another, as the smoke through ten pair of nostrils filled the room to suffocation. The floor was covered with cross-legged men and narghilehs, the twisted coils of which appeared like snakes in many a fold. It was a mercy there were no curtains. I remember nothing afterwards. I had often heard of "a Malcolm row," and a "Bobbery dinner," but I did not see one the whole time I was in Bombay.

CALLS.

I made a number of calls one afternoon with Mackintosh. Nobody then ever dreamed of fore-

* We think the locale of this incident was Poona; but it does not matter much.

noon calls. Some of the bungalows were near Belvedere and Belmont, for example.* The Rickardses were in Belvedere, as the Drapers had been forty years before them, and I heard much of Eliza,† and how she had turned the heads of everybody except James Forbes, who merely viewed the creation of so much beauty and accomplishments as a philosophical study. At Love Grove we met Maria Graham, the author of the charming letters, and she told us the sad story of its name: of the young lover who, in endeavouring to save his sweetheart, shared her grave; both were drowned, and their bodies washed ashore, one at each of the promontories which abut from the Vellard; and how a temple was reared on each for the offerings of the love-sick and the delectation of the fakirs. At Breach Candy Mackintosh pointed out to me the whereabouts of the only battle ever fought by the French and English on the western seas of India,‡ and in which, if I understand the matter rightly, we were "confoundedly licked," said the author of *Vindiciae*

* Belvedere stood on Mazagon until a few months ago.—*Dr. A. Leith's Sanitary Report*, 1864.

† For further information on Eliza see Sterne's Life, Thackeray's Humourists, and Abbe Raynal. She died at Bristol at the age of 33, and is buried in the Cathedral.

‡ The "Apollo" and "Anson" engagement, 1747.

Gallicae, by that gallant nation, though our men fought bravely enough. In this way we pay pleasant visits at the Mount, Randall Lodge, Non Parell (Malcolm's), and Surrey Cottage. The people were so many that I have but a confused recollection of their names: Lushington, Money, Forbes, Abercrombie, Erskine, Warden, and Salt. Old Duncan was so ill that we could not see him; indeed, a few days afterwards Dr. Keir sent us a notice of his death. And short as the distance was between his house and the Cathedral, we all got dreadful headaches at the funeral, by walking in the sun without our hats at four in the afternoon. When I was in Bombay the story of steam navigation in America reached us, and how a passage had been made of one hundred and sixty miles in thirty-two hours from New York to Albany. Mackintosh was in ecstasies. "This," he said, "would ensure a passage from Portsmouth to Bombay in about a hundred days." He exclaimed, "Why were we not born a century later!" Sir James was born in 1765. In 1865 the passage was made in twenty-one days.

On the occasion of the death of Lord Cornwallis Sir James preached by proxy in Bombay Cathedral. He had been asked by the Governor to write the funeral sermon, and he did so, and it was preached by the senior chaplain.* We all went, of course Mackintosh included, and it was most amusing, if such a word can be used in connection with a funeral sermon. The preacher stuttered over some of the finest passages and read others perfunctorily, and with unconcern ; took a pinch of snuff, and sneezed in the middle of the peroration so loud as to shake some monumental medallions on the walls. There was little of death, I assure you, in our heads when we came out, and the laughing was continued at intervals during the following day ; at all events, I can vouch for myself.

ON THE JUDGMENT-SEAT.

Before he delivers his address to the Grand Jury, of which W. T. Money was the foreman, and to give a composed dignity to it, he reads the 1st vol. of Robertson's History of Scotland. The statement seems theatrical, but it is perfectly sincere. At half-past five, it being almost then dark, and within the old Court House, on the afternoon of Monday the 16th of July, 1811, Sir James Mackintosh rises from the judgment-seat.

---

* Printed and published with the Senior Chaplain's name.—*Mackintosh's Life.*

He assumes the black-cap and pronounces sentence of death on James Estelow, an English soldier, for the murder of a mean Hindoo at Goa. From his diary we learn that he never signed a paper with more tranquillity than he did the death-warrant. But he is now pale and emaciated, and his voice falters as he pronounces the words of doom. The circumstances were peculiar. Mackintosh had never done the same before, and will never do it again. In a judicial administration extending over seven years, a population of 200,000 had been governed without a capital punishment, and without increase of crimes. On Saturday morning at five minutes past nine the procession from the gaol to the Esplanade passes his own residence at Tarala, Mazagon. He sees it. Patten, the gaoler, in front in a small carriage. James Estelow follows, dressed in black, handcuffed, and with a rope round his neck, with the hangman in a large car, surrounded by a guard of the sheriff's peons. See in this, O! my Aryan brother, the even-handed justice of the Sirkar; for what does his white face avail him now? The scene closes amid great excitement. Nothing like it since the Malays who murdered Lord Nelson's brother were hanged on Gibbet Island. Fifty thousand natives were on the Esplanade, and most of the European inhabitants were present.

AN UNSPOKEN BOMBAY SERMON.

" I have just glanced over Jeremy Taylor on the beatitudes. The selection is made in the most sublime spirit of virtue. For their transcendent excellence I can find no words to express my admiration and reverence. 'Blessed are the merciful, for they shall obtain mercy.' 'Put on as the elect of God bowels of mercy.' At last the divine speaker rises to the summit of moral sublimity: 'Blessed are they who are persecuted for righteousness' sake.' For a moment, 'O! Teacher Blessed,' I taste the unspeakable delight of feeling myself to be better." This is akin to a meditation of Dr. Chalmers.*

MACKINTOSH AND WILSON.

As we draw this paper to a close we feel the touch of a vanished hand. A name rises that must be still fresh and green in the memory of our readers, the Missionary, Philanthropist, and late Vice-Chancellor of the University of Bombay. Though "their graves are severed far and wide by mountain, stream, and sea," by force of

* Chalmers was the personal friend of both Mackintosh and Wilson.

contrast, by force of comparison, by the like and the unlike, these are Bombay brothers that cannot be divided. Though living at different periods, Mackintosh and Wilson are knit together by a two-fold bond, an intense love of literature and a deep and abiding devotion in the service of the Almighty, not *Abdallah* the slave of God, but the willing and intelligent instruments of his high behests. Caledonia, stern and wild, was the nurse of these gentle and loving natures. No two men in Bombay ever had such troops of friends, the one in his Spartan simplicity on the Cliff, the other at Parell. They had great gifts, but great as they were, greater than the gold and frankincense of India, true wise men of the East, they laid them at the feet of their Master. Memory in the one,* imagination and memory in the other—towers of strength, enabling Wilson to grasp all oriental lore, and Mackintosh to soar in the empyrean of Philosophy and History, without a single compeer in the land of their adoption, and very few in the land that gave them birth. Both mingled freely with the natives, both were most tolerant of other men's opinions, both were brilliant conversationalists,

* We believe that in Dr. Wilson's library there was not a single novel.

and both were easygoing and careless of their own money to a degree. What shall we say more? That they never stooped to anything mean or mercenary, that they never debased their great gifts to the service of sin, that they conquered their position by the hardest industry that ever issued from Highland or Lowland home, that they never bartered away their principles to the powers that be for a piece of bread, and that at last they seemed to reach "that maturity of moral stature in which the conflict between inclination and duty is over, and virtue and self-indulgence are the same." Mackintosh was a great patriot, great on the freedom of the slave and the liberty of man,—on Wallace, on Tell, and Kosciusko; but Wilson's ideal transcends the dreams of philosophy, and argues a virtue beyond that of the purest patriotism. It is not every man who can refuse a comfortable settlement at home when within his reach. It is not every man who would divert away a gift from himself, to even the noblest purposes of the University.* Other men than Warren Hastings have had their Daylesfords. Wilson had none to look forward

* Read the history of the foundation of the Wilson Philological Lecture.

to in this world, except six square feet of earth in the Marine Lines, of which he was at length, full of years and of honours, duly infefted. The valedictory cheer at the Apollo Bunder which awaits the warrior and the statesman had no charm for him, and he did not covet it. It is this that endears Wilson to thousands of his adopted countrymen, and will do so, we venture to say, for generations to come; for to him was reserved this supreme distinction, that he, and he alone of all the conspicuous characters that adorn the history of Western India, Mackintosh included, elected of his own free will, when he was young and vigorous, to live and die in India for the benefit of its people. To this his life was consecrated, and for this he died.

POONA AND THE PESHWAS.

A RETROSPECT.

CHAPTER XV.

POONA AND THE PESHWAS.

A RETROSPECT.

Say not thou : what is the cause that the former days were better than these ? For thou dost not wisely enquire concerning this.—*Ecclesiastes* VII. 10.

When Sir James Mackintosh died those who knew him best and were most capable of judging said that he was the most learned man of his age. During the present century we have had living among us—one great general, one or two celebrated statesmen, and one divine, *ultimus Romanorum*, and many eminent men in almost every department of human labour, but never before or since have we had a man of so much learning, and endowed with such a gift of communicating it to others.

He arrived in Bombay in May, 1804, and resided here seven years.

On several occasions in his correspondence he

calls Bombay "the most obscure corner of India." This surely could not have been the case when we find Lord Nelson* (just five years previously), a few days after the battle of the Nile, and while still suffering from a wound in his head, sitting down to pen to the Governor of Bombay the following lines:—

"I have Buonaparte's despatches now before me. Bombay, if they can get there, I know is their first object, but I trust the Almighty God in Egypt will overthrow these pests of the human race.

"Dated mouths of the Nile, 9th Aug. 1798."

Bombay was then a city of 150,000 inhabitants, and so great a centre of military operations was it that Mackintosh himself mentions the fact that it contained an army of 25,000 men.

Sir James. paid a visit to Poona in 1805. When he arrived at Khandalla he felt, as every man has done, a sense of relief from the unmitigated heat in the plains below. It was the same old road (now remodelled by Malcolm) by which so many European pilgrims have found their way to the Deccan during the last two hundred years. And Berkeley in a range of two hundred miles

* Lord Nelson had a brother in the Indian Navy who was murdered. His murderers were hanged on the Oyster Rock in Bombay harbour.

of the Sahyadree Hills could find no better opening for the railway than through the gorges and rocks of this Bhore Ghaut.

He was now at the watershed. It is recorded that a traveller near the sources of the Amazon ascended a spur of the Andes and descried therefrom the waters of the Pacific.

A similar phenomenon may be witnessed near Lanowlee, where you may see the Bombay group of islands, and the Western Ocean shining like a silver band of light beyond them, while adjacent to you is one of the sources of a great Indian river. This is the Indrayanee which becomes the Bheema, then the Kistna, but call it by what name you please, every drop of surplus rain which falls beyond Lanowlee goes into the Bay of Bengal.

But we proceed to Poona.

Mackintosh was presented to Bajee Rao (the man who died at Bithoor in 1851, the last of the Peshwas), then in the ninth year of his reign, and he afterwards made an extended tour in the Deccan. His journals are exceedingly instructive as to the condition of the Deccan question, and as to the rule of the Peshwas and we would advise any malcontent who is not satisfied with things as they are to ponder well his " firm conviction that the first blessing to be wished to the inhabitants of India was that a civilised conqueror might rescue them from their native oppressors, and that they would find better masters in the worst Europeans than in the best of their own countrymen," and he will discover that his verdict is framed in strict accordance with the facts of history.

For in truth the Peshwas, excepting perhaps Balajee, had never done anything for the advancement of mankind. To have large feet and long arms and not to be able to sign your name were qualities of the first mark among the Peshwas. To see a man dragged to death at the foot of an elephant was their amusement. There is not one book, one piece of architecture that can be called great, or even one notable work of utility, that we can remember except the Kampolee Tank and that was constructed by Nana Furnavese, their Prime Minister. The Katrij aquaduct still conveys some water for six miles to Poona and fills an artificial lake at the base of Parbutty which would do no discredit to a second-rate German watering place.

Bajee Rao planted a million of mango trees. His father, Ruganath Rao, built a lofty tower on Malabar Hill in which he lived in 1776 when

Poona was too hot for him. But it has long since disappeared. The remains of the Palace of Parbutty and the Boodwar are very meagre specimens of architecture; the one was struck by fire from heaven in 1817, the other was lighted up by the torch of an incendiary in 1879. A solitary gateway is all that remains of the Somwar Palace and a few pagodas complete the list. There is an architecture in the Deccan which piled up the battlements of Singhur and Poorundhur. But the men who crowned the scarps of Maharashtra with curtain loophole and embrasure were of a previous generation. Why the Peshwas did nothing in the way of architecture it is difficult to understand except on the supposition that the Mahratta Government was made to be taken and destroyed, for there never was a city more favourably placed than Poona to profit in skill and design in architecture, and none, we venture to say, has done less by its opportunities. Some of those works which have delighted so many generations were staring them in the face right and left. The kings of Bejapoor had left them a dome larger than St. Sophia or the Pantheon and the Sultans of Ahmedabad minarets which surpass those of Cairo in beauty of outline and richness of detail. There was certainly no want of money, and money then had twice the purchasing power it has at present. The sack of Golkonda alone in 1687 netted to Aurungzeb in hard cash 6¾ crores, a sum that would pay the cost of all the buildings, private and public, in the Elphinstone Circle and Esplanade of Bombay, with the fee simple thereof. The question has been asked why Aurungzeb did nothing for Poona. He had come of a family great in architecture. His father had erected in Agra one of the architectural glories of the world, a perfect "dream in stone and lime," and it is the mother of Aurungzeb whose bones are ensepulchred in the Taj Mahal. To whom much is given, of him much shall be required.

He was essentially a man of the Deccan, if anything can make a Deccany man. He was born at Dohud (while his father, Shah Jehan, was Soubadhar of the Deccan) in the Punch Mahals, died at Ahmednugger, and was buried at Rosa, near Dowlatabad, the key of the Deccan, and his sepulchre is with us unto this day. He spent the last twenty years of his life in the Deccan. He had been at, if not in, Poona. He had executed the son of Seevajee within 15 miles of Poona.* His grandson had died in Poona and he had changed the name of it. A wife and a daughter are buried at Bejapoor, and his youngest and favourite son was slain in battle at Hyderabad in the Deccan.

The truth is, he looked upon Poona as the home of that "hell dog Seevajee," "the mountain rat," and his infernal Mawulees who embittered his existence and hastened the downfall of his empire.

To bribe Singhur, to batter Poorundhur, to escalade Torna, to knock down (or attempt it) every Mahratta fort in his way was his meat and drink. He had no time to build. If he erected anything it has fallen to pieces, and Torna and Rajghur are as gaunt and weird as on the day they defied the "Lord of the World." Useless as they are—

> "Time that doth all things else impair,
> Still makes them flourish strong and fair."

Poona is described in these days as "situated on a treeless plain." Not altogether on a treeless plain now, as any one may satisfy himself by ascending the heights of Kirkee or the tower of Guneshkhind. Poona on a treeless plain. So are some of the most renowned cities of the world: Damascus from Lebanon has been com-

* At the junction of the Indrayani with the Bhima. The Indrayanee is the river which the traveller sees from the railway on his left at Kurkalla *en route* to Poona, conspicuous enough during the monsoon.

pared to an emerald. But who cares about Poona, the Neera, the Kistna, the Moota, and the Moola? And yet Abana and Pharpar themselves do not fertilise so much land nor feed so many people.

Men have raved for ages about Damascus, but given a history from the days of Abraham and a few gilded domes and minarets, and Poona from Singhur just after the monsoon, might vie in beauty with Damascus from Mount Lebanon.

And there is no want of roses.

Seventy years ago you might travel a whole day without meeting a man, woman, or child on the high road to Poona. It was the days of "Shamgar." "The high ways were unoccupied and the travellers walked through byeways," and you might go over a thousand miles of country without seeing a detached bungalow or an unwalled village. You can still see marks of this insecurity stamped in uneffaceable lines on the broadlands of the Deccan. Why is the ground better cultivated at a distance from roads? Why are the dwellings of substantial men like the meanest huts on the side you approach them? Simply to evade the Pindaree and the freebooter—the custom having survived long after the object has passed away. Seventy years ago more rent could be obtained for land in the secluded glens of the Neera, than at the gates of Poona, where it was worthless, the executive being insufficient to protect an occupant from plunder and devastation.

Life and property had no security. Seventy years ago there was not a court of judicature nor a judge in the whole Mahratta dominions.*

Education like their alphabet at school was not only written in but built upon sand, and there seemed a curse on their social system from its basement to its topmost story.

"The havildar"—we adopt the Muslim names —" plundered the villager and was himself plundered by the Zemindar,—the Zemindar by the Fouzdar, the Fouzdar by his Nabob or Dewan, and the Dewan by the Peshwa. The mechanic only worked to the measure of his necessities. If he saved money it was taken from him. If he possessed skill he was seized by some men in authority and made to work night and day. When this gradation was interrupted it meant bloodshed."

Seevajee when importuned as to the condition of the common people said with contempt, "give them a *dhotie* it is enough," and the historian of the Mahrattas has left this sentence on the proudest period of their dominion, a "system of

* We do not forget the Punchayets.

plunder and violence had been universal for a period exceeding the life of man."

The age of Seevajee has been glorified by ignorant and designing men, and certain it is that in his time, no man or woman suffered death for religion—that the mosque was inviolate and the Koran respected,—facts which redound to his eternal credit, at a time when toleration was neither practised nor understood in civilised Europe. But on the "condition of the people" question, with which we have now to do, let us, by way of illustration, compare it with the worst period of misgovernment in the history of Scotland. We make bold to say that the Scotch Covenanter of the reign of Charles the Second would have stood aghast at the spectacle, not uncommon in the Deccan, of a man ploughing with a loaded matchlock slung behind his back. And of John Brown of Priesthill, the Ayrshire Carrier—if the Deccan could have produced such a man what would have been the verdict ?

"Died beside his own pack-horse of sheer vexation at the tolls !" Imposts were heaped up until they doubled the original cost of merchandise, and political martyrs fell in numbers, resisting fiscal iniquity and oppression.

There was a proverb in Seevajee's time among his people.

"*Deccan is the bread of military men.*" Exactly so : the bread of Swashbucklers and Budmashes.

It seems as far as we can make out to have been the bread of nobody else.

But it had been nearly the same from untold ages. The earliest European traveller in the Deccan, of whom we have any knowledge 400 years since, and strange to say a Russian, notes " the people are very miserable ; they walk on foot and walk fast." This last is a straw that lets us know how the wind blew over these Deccany plains in the olden times, and nothing has survived the wreck of forts and mud built huts equal to it in importance.

The well disposed were anxious to get to their destination and the intended victim was hurrying from his pursuer. Of some it might be said " their feet are swift to shed blood " and of all " the way of peace have they not known." It was, indeed, a cursed regime, where of the " *all* things " of which Adam Smith says " labour is the first price and original purchase-money," the only *one* thing resultant to rich and poor was a life of extremest misery and oppression.

The system affected alike rich and poor. In 1798 the richest shroffs of Poona were tortured to death, one of the most influential of their number expiring on a heated gun. There are men still living who recollect from 1826 to 1830, so far did its baneful influence extend into the present century. In these years Dhun Raj Seth, Tarachund Setaram, and other shroffs of Bombay, Poona, and Surat had 64 of their money carriers murdered by Thugs and their property carried away. We need not wonder that all confidence between man and man was lost. Mahratta in Mahratta, Mahratta in Englishman, Englishman in Mahratta, it was all the same.

The culminating point was reached in 1804 when the Duke of Wellington penned these memorable words :—

"From the Peshwa down to the lowest cooly in the bazaar in Poona there is not a Mahratta in whom it is possible to rely that he will perform any engagement upon which he enters unless urged to the performance by his fears."

This is all the Peshwas can show after a rule of over one hundred years.

This is the judgment of a great man on the tottering Empire whose Deccany horses had once quenched their thirst in the waters of the Indus and the Hoogly, and whose right to exact tribute had been acknowledged on the banks of the Colcroon.

One word—a praiseworthy word it used to be among the Mahrattas—is stamped on the forehead of every Peshwa, and that word is *deceit*. Their rule began in deceit and ended in deceit. It began with Seevajee's murder of Afzul Khan and ended amid the flames of the British Residency at the Sungum.

It dates from the first day of their existence in 1656 when that Master of Duplicity, Seevajee, decked the brow of the first Mahratta Peshwa with the name, to the last day of their sovereignty in 1817, when from a window in the Palace of Parbutty, Bajee Rao saw the battle of Kirkee with which their dominion passed away.

Their fate was strange. Balajee Bajee Rao died after hearing the fatal message from the field of Paniput in 1761.

"*2 pearls dissolved, 27 gold mohurs lost, copper incalculable.*" Bajee Rao died an exile in our own day. Of his two immediate predecessors one committed suicide by throwing himself from the top of his castle in Poona. The other was murdered, it is said, by Bajee Rao's father Ruganath Rao in the same place.

But we return to Mackintosh.

For a time he lived in Tarala (a Sanscrit compound denoting Palm Green) Mazagon. From this bungalow there is a magnificent view all round—a perfect panorama of Bombay—land and sea, and it is now, we may add, resplendent with the green and gold of the Honourable Byramjee Jeejeebhoy. But from 1804 to 1808 this distinguished man lived at Government House,

Parell, Governor Duncan having given it up to him. It was here he penned his brilliant correspondence with those celebrated men, Dugald Stewart, Francis Horner, Lord Holland, John Allen, Robert Hall, and Flaxman. This was what he modestly, but elegantly expressed as reviving the spirit of ancient Indian commerce by exchanging the drugs of India for the sterling money of Europe. It was to this house he asked the great pulpit orator Robert Hall to share his retirement and come and live with him. In its rooms he read Milton, Addison, and Virgil to his children, and on its verandahs and broad walks night after night, he pondered on philosophy and meditated on his contributions to the history of England.

Doubtless in after years his mind often wandered back to what had once been the centre of his affections and household gods, from the day he wrote his first letter, dated Parell, "in the most obscure corner of India, but *forget me not, forget me not*" to the entry in his journal which records his last dinner party there, when the words "*poor Parell*" were wrung from his lips and the scene closed upon him for ever.

SEEVAJEE'S FORTS.

CHAPTER XVI.

SEEVAJEE'S FORTS.

TORNA.

> **" Her ancient weed was russet gray,**
> **And wrinkled was her brow."**

Torna is about 37 miles from Poona. You can see it from the Library door over-looking the end of Singhur to the right. You can ride and walk to *Pet*, a village at the foot of the hill, in a day, ascend next morning, and do Rajghur, which is three miles from it, on the same day. We did not count on the roughness of the way to it, for when we left our carriage at Gora, two miles from the junction of the Singhur road at Kurukwasla, we purposed doing the rest on a Deccany tattoo, to the foot of the hill. We soon, however, found out that for the greater part of the way our " shanks" was the only possible mode of locomotion. Night found us on the slopes of the Bore Ghaut, the range of wavy hills which the traveller sees from Singhur,

"Ribbed as the shifting sand you see ;"

and below, the valley of Kanind, which divides us from the Torna and the Rajghur range. We had sent on our coolies a day ahead, and missed them among the hills, and had made up our mind to remain where we were until daylight. But our men were capital "night howlers," and shouted continually their long-drawn *Rama Ho Rama-a-a*, a cry so well known in the mountain regions of the Deccan that its echoes and the waving of our lights attracted the attention of some drowsy Dungurs, who eventually came to our relief. Grass-torches were lighted, which were fed continuously, and blazed high a lurid light above our heads, and so we were piloted from ledge to ledge, among boulders and loose stones, the dry bed of a monsoon torrent,—a four mile track, to our destination. I am sure that if Bunyan in his Pilgrim's Progress had "alighted" upon such a place, he would never have seen the New Jerusalem. Visions of General Wade, Burns's "riddlings of Creation," the Auld Wives Lift, Adam's Tomb at Tobermory, with a free coup in the Ninestane Burn came before us. The Duke of Wellington uttered three groans in this Presidency. The first was when he received quinine instead of iron, the second was when he wished to God he had never had anything to do with the Bombay Government, and the third was when he was detained six hours in the dark in this Bore Ghaut (a topographical mistake as will be seen in the paper on Wellington) among cactus bushes, twenty miles from Poona, when he was hurrying on, in his celebrated forced march, to save that city from the fire and sword of Amrut Rao in 1803.

He says, Poona, 20th April 1803, "I made a forced march of above forty miles last night with the cavalry (1,700) and a battalion, and I was detained about six hours in the Bore Ghaut."

Snatching a few hours' repose in a temple of Ramswamy, we were awake at three, and soon on our road. It was a beautiful moonlight morning, and, in a four miles walk up the Kanind Valley, the only sound we heard was the cry of the owl. The drowsy watchers of the green crops —human scarecrows, in their thatched habitations—could not make out our somewhat unearthly visitation.

Looking up in the wan moonlight, the

bastions of Torna were frowning above our heads :—

> "In lonely glens ye like to stray,
> Or where auld ruined castles gray
> Nod to the moon."

This was Burns's "address to the Deil," but for the moment we accept it. At Pet we obtained guides to go up the hill. It took three hours walking, climbing, and scrambling to attain our object. The long flight of almost perpendicular steps for about three hundred feet worn and much displaced; or holes cut in the rock, indurated by use, time, and the elements were at length surmounted, and at 7 o'clock on the morning of New Year's Day, 1880, we were battering at the gates of Torna, *first foot,* at all events, in this region. But the withered hag was as deaf as Ailsa Craig. We may add that, owing to the angle of ascent, the gateway was quite invisible to the eye until we were within a few feet of it, and that in one instance the rock jutted out sheer over our heads.

An event here transpired that we did not anticipate. The door was shut—barred—and there was no reply. We had thus time to sit down with a feeling of relief and "rest and be thankful," and leisurely survey the spot on which we were perched. The folding spiked doors were enclosed by a fine piece of arched masonry, a veritable "strength of stone," or munition of rocks.

It was a curious recess, formed by nature between two scarped rocks. At some geologic period the crest of Torna had been rent asunder, leaving this cleft, "the door of Torna," in the rock. Or had the elements of wind and water been doing their work?

> "Who was it scooped these stony waves,
> Or scalp'd the brow of old Cairngorm,
> And dug these ever-yawning caves?
> 'Twas I, the spirit of the Storm."

We *did* get an entrance eventually, but by what means we are not now going to say. It was neither storm, escalade, nor capitulation. It led, however, to a correspondence between the Punt of Bore and the British Government, but the matter was amicably adjusted. So we made our way to the second gate, which enclosed the *Balla Killa,* or upper fort, where the beleagured could retire in case of need.

Here our shouts were heard and a fine looking youth opened the bars and let us in, and led us to a hut on the summit of the hill. His father, an old man, was at the door, evidently offering up his orisons to the *Tulsi* plant. But when he caught sight of us, he threw down his *kumlee* or blanket, and staggered into his dwelling. It was Elymas the sorcerer, struck with blindness in the cartoon of Raphael. You might have led him with a straw. How two European *budmashas*—one with a fowling-piece—could have reached his door, was more than he could comprehend. By our mild persuasive speech he, however, recovered himself and eventually came out with a dignified salaam ; clothed, and in his right-mind. He was an old man, weather-beaten by innumerable monsoons, but as ruddy as a winter apple. He told us that His Excellency the Governor had been there, and showed us where he had sat. His Highness the Punt of Bore, in whose territories Torna is, had come to the foot of the hill, looked up, shook his head, and departed. We did not see beast or bird, tame or wild (crow or sparrow), except a diminutive cat, licking itself smaller and smaller to inevitable death when the *fauna* and *ferae* of Torna will be utterly extinct. We did not see Seevajee. He had been once here, dug up a marvellous amount of Venetian sequins, gold bars, and sycee silver, and a more unlikely place to find such things we cannot imagine. He took this place when he was a lad of nineteen, and it was well he did so when his bones were supple, and his climbing powers were at the best. Had he waited until his fifty-third year, when he had that bad swelling in the knee-joint which ultimately carried him off at Raighur, he never would have done it. We were two centuries too late to see him, otherwise we might have interviewed him in the language of the Scotch Ballad, with the alteration of two words only—

"As I was walking all alane
Atween a castle and a wa',
O there I met a wee, wee man,
And he was the least I ever saw.
His legs were half an ellwand lang
And thick and thimber was his thie,
Atween his brows there was a span,
And atween his shouthers there was three,
He took up a muckle stane,
And flang't as far as I could see,
Though I had been a giant born
I could na lift it to my knee.
O wee, wee man, ye're wonder strong."

But leaving romance, we must pull a long face as we approach the domain of history.

Torna is a spot of surpassing interest. It was Seevajee's first conquest, the nucleus around which all the others clustered, making it virtually the cradle of that Mahratta empire which shook the throne of the Great Moghul. It has been the scene of many bloody conflicts. On one occasion it was escaladed during the night, and carried sword in hand. This was in 1701. It is specially mentioned that this fort was strengthened and repaired by Seevajee, and we have come to the conclusion that he was not a great builder. The stone and lime in many places are not well put together, which may be very easily accounted for by the troublous times in which he lived. Nehemiah's re-building the walls of Jerusalem, as described by a Scots preacher—"A whinger in the ae hand and a theekíng spurtle in the ither"—is an exact, though coarse, picture of the situation of Seevajee. Torna, therefore, does not rival the great works of his predecessors, for there are piles of mason work in the Deccan which equal in grandeur the hoary ruins of Tantallon or Dunottar. Hence everything is going to ruin, piles of teak heaped together, masses of stones confusedly lying about, half filled tanks, moss grown barracks make up a picture of desolation.

The *Doondzermal*, a long spur fortified in some places, only a few feet wide, like a very long canoe in appearance from the parapet, is very striking, but not the only one of its kind among the Deccan forts. The aneroid barometer shows we are 4,350 ft. above sea level. There is, therefore, a great and glorious panorama around us. If Singhur is the *Lion's Den*, Torna is the *Eagle's Nest*. From our eyrie we may descry St. Mary's Church at Poona, the Bishop's bungalow on Mount Malcolm, and John Sand's bomb-proof *hospice* on the crest of Poorundhur, with the *kala panee* visible at sunset. To one who has never seen them, the Mahableshwur range and the enormous block of Raighur, the scene of Seevajee's coronation and death, are novel and interesting. The natives of this country are our masters in the art of climbing. We envy them their endurance, but still more their machinery of heart and lungs. They do not know what it is to be "out of breath," or "pumped out." As we came to the gate by which we entered a policeman made his appearance. *His* long pull upstairs did not seem to bother him, and he was perfectly unruffled in speech and behaviour, as he politely proffered his services to us. He left the gate ajar, and from the little platform inside where we stood we caught a peep of what was before us. The vignette was very lovely,—the ground floor of the world or a map of Asia Minor, but we begged him to shut out the vision for a minute as we would have enough of it.

Some one has written that "Torna is perfectly safe to those whose nerves are not affected by a precipice above and a gorge below." So with this soothing emollient we proceed. The Bedouins do not use chairs, and we have heard them say that as we are ultimately to go into the earth, we may as well sit on it occasionally—in fact, make use of it, by way of accustoming ourselves to it. Our proclivities being earthwards, we therefore sit down as inert a mass of clay as we can make of ourselves in this sentient breathing universe, and paddle our own canoe down the notched rapids.* There are some very nasty bits, but, as the Governor did not complain, we are not going to do so. The risks are : stumbles, false footings, slips, stepping on loose stones or grass waving above nonentity, lurches outwards, grasping tufts or twigs that come away in the hand, and a tendency in stout parties to roll over and over, of which there could be only one termination. Then there are slopes, slides, devil's elbows, with slanting declinations downwards. All roads lead to Rome, and these are of them *plus* gravitation. So we get up and advise all those who have legs to use them in the laudable

* See some of Whymper's admirable Alpine sketches to illustrate this.

and muscular effort of keeping body and soul together, by planting their feet and hands in such places as art or instinct dictates, and so by grappling rock or bush, and always "making an effort" and avoiding whisky, they will soon find their way to a good breakfast by midday at the foot of Torna. Richard Burton, when in Bombay, suggested the formation of an Alpine Club. There is plenty of scope in the Ghauts and Deccan. We could not advise any promoters of such a scheme for information to a better man than James Burgess, chief of the Archæological Survey. He knows almost every hill for a hundred miles round. He is a better pedestrian than Captain Grose. Besides—

> "He has a fouth o' auld nick nackets ;
> Rusty airn caps and jingling jackets
> Wad haud the Lothians three in tackets
> A towmont gude
> And parritch pats and auld saut backets,
> Before the Flood."

THE FORT OF RAJMACHEE, NEAR KHANDALA.

THE BOMBAY FORTS

Were founded on violence. Many of them were built as fastnesses by the first Arab or Moghul invaders. They were not built like the great structures, for example, on the Esplanade which we have seen rising year after year, and where the workmen received a fair day's wages for a fair day's work. We have no building constructed by forced labour in the Island of Bombay. Our oldest building, the Cathedral, was built by subscription, and the list lies before us, a few jottings from which we give in a foot-note*

* Some of the entries in the list of subscriptions to the new Church show the liberality of the donors, and others are curious as illustrating the manners of the age. The Company's contribution was ten thousand rupees, Governor Boone, who succeeded Mr. Aislabie, gave in various sums Rs. 3,918, and Mr. Cobbe, the clergyman, Rs. 1,427—subscriptions more in proportion to the profits which they made by private transactions than to the limited amount of their salaries. Among other entries are, "a fine upon Bhundarries Rs. 18, and a fine inflicted on Joseph Hornall for a misdemeanour; given by the Governor's order." The average amount of the sacramental collections made every month was about Rs. 29, of those made on Christmas day Rs. 72, on Easter day Rs. 39, and on Whitsunday Rs. 34. "A commutation

This was nearly two centuries ago, and it has been the same ever since. Whether by subscription or the State, the workman has been paid his wages; and as these buildings were not founded on violence, we can aver that their walls have not been stained with blood or crime. Crime is a fearful factor in the tradition and history of old buildings. Witness our own Tower of London, and Holyrood where the blood of Rizzio still cries for vengeance and half-crowns. But in Bombay you cannot point to a single building where a martyr, political or religious, has been immured, or a Hindoo or a Moslem put to death. Now the forts of the Deccan, and we are bold to say the splendours of Bijapur,† owe their existence to forced labour, to the labour exacted *nolens volens* by the Lord Paramount, be he

---

for penance corporal" at Surat was Rs. 150. Cornelius Sodington gives "for my wife when I have her, Rs. 20;" and Mr. Richard Waters Rs. 11, which were allowed him by Mr. Cobbe for performing divine services when the said chaplain was on a visit to Surat. The names on the list of those worthy of remark are Mr. George Bowcher, who gave Rs. 200 in addition to what he had contributed about 30 years before in Sir John Child's days; of Alexander Hamilton, to whom we are so much indebted for our acquaintance with his times, and who gave Rs. 80 for himself and Rs. 50 on account of his ship the Morning Star; and of Cunsha Chungua China men, the one of whom subscribed Rs. 150, the other Rs. 90. The total amount collected was Rs. 43,992 or £5,499 (good remitting exchange in these days). Mr. Boone gave the handsome bell which still tolls its summons to the Christians of the neighbourhood.—*Bombay Quarterly Review, Vol. III.*

† The Ibrahim Roza cost £528,150 sterling, 6,533 workmen were employed; time occupied in construction 36 years 11 months and 11 days.—*From inscription quoted in "Architecture at Bijapur," by Meadows Taylor and James Fergusson*, 1866.

king or killidar. Now-a-days you can either work or stay away. But there were no industries in those olden times which a man could fall back upon from the violence of the oppressor. The people were thirled to their masters, and their "meal and malt" ground out of them until the lust or ambition of their governors was satisfied. If a man in those days were a skilful workman, the fact was soon found out, the wages of mere subsistence were doled out, to him, and his surplus earnings pounced upon by the Ruler. There is not a single fort in the entire Deccan which, if its history is looked into, will not be found to be stained with blood and crime. They were all busy weaving the crimson web of war.

> "See the griesly texture grow,
> 'Tis of human entrails made,
> And the weights that play below
> Each a gasping warrior's head."

There is a tradition that the Fort of Satara was founded on human sacrifice, and the place is shown where a son and daughter of the chief Mahar were built in the wall. This may be true or untrue. But it is within the domain of history that the man from whom the then Peshwa received investiture, Rajah of Satara as he was, and great grandson of Seevajee himself, was kept in a dungeon of it for eleven years and fed on bread and water. It is within the domain of history that the Angrias sewed up members of their family in sacks and threw them down the steep cliffs of Sagurghur, and everybody who has read " Tara " or been at Mahableshwur knows of Purtabghur and the gory head of Afzulkhan. But the list is endless : Asseerghur, Dowlatabad, Raighur, and Singhur, *ad infinitum.*

THE ROAD TO IT.

Rajmachee was once taken and held by Seevajee (1648), after he had seized a great loot from a Government Kaphila near Callian on its way to Bejapoor. This was the first blow he struck at the majesty of Empire ; and when one wanders for days among the ruins, still enormous in magnitude and extent, of the capital, one is confounded with the audacity which prompted a single individual to measure his strength with the resources of such a kingdom as Bejapoor. It was the combat of Achilles with Hector ; and the swift-footed Seevajee in the end gained the day. His dwelling was among the rocks, and his strength the everlasting hills. It was then that the Deccany forts made their great name in history. Called into existence in a semi-barbarous age, when men felt secure only on the tops of the highest mountains, in the hands of the hardy Mawullees of Seevajee, they probed Bejapoor on the one hand, and Delhi on the other, to the quick. Every wild foray seemed to add to their prestige, and when brought to bay, as they were occasionally, the cry was

> "Come one, come all ! This rock shall fly
> From its firm base as soon as I."

At length in the course of time they found themselves masters, and Mahratta Dominion added a new chapter to history. But it was the old story. Conquest precedes luxury, and luxury precedes decline. The Brahmin in Poona was not a whit wiser than the Moslem in Bejapoor. The experience by which he might have profited was a dead letter to him, for that history which teacheth by examples had come and gone ere Poona became the capital of the Mahratta Empire. The Adil Shah dynasty was an old-wives' fable to him, and unwarned by its doom, the Peshwas prosecuted the same career of vice and debauchery without a tittle of its elegance or refinement, for the master-builders of Bejapoor have left behind them miles of majestic memorials which still engage the attention of the connoisseur. The game, however, went on, and we know the termination of these things.

> "The gates of hell are open night and day,
> Smooth the descent and easy is the way."

The traveller who proceeds to Poona by rail, as he nears Kurjut, must have observed a high hill on his left crowned with bastions and encircled with lines of circumvallation. He will see more of it, as he emerges from the tunnel where the great Khandala gorge bursts conspicuously on his view ; and where the carriages seem to creep along the edge of dizzy precipices, this giant again meets the eye of the spectator. It is now observable that there are two hills, and if the day is clear, bastion and curtain are quite visible to the naked eye, on either of them.

This is the Fort of Rajmachee, which, though not much noticed in history, is more familiar to the eye of dwellers in these parts than any other fort in the Bombay Presidency, and will doubtless continue to be so. The scenery here is sometimes one of marvellous beauty, and in the grey dawn of early morn, so familiar to us, presents shifting pictures, as grand and beautiful as Glencoe or Killiecrankie. The best place from which the tourist can attack this fort is Khandala. He can "do" it in one day, but it will be a long day, from dawn to dewy eve. A better way would be to take a *resai* and plaid, and sleep in the open all night, and rise refreshed for the work of inspecting both forts by sunrise. We did it in one day, but it is too much for the ordinary pleasure-seeker to demand of him a start at day-light, a tramp over roughish ground for twelve miles, and then half-an-hour of tough work in which all his sinews will be exercised and put to proof, and then to beat a retreat to Khandala, when he will be fortunate if he is not belated. If it becomes dark or moonlight—for even the moon projects distances to which the eye and foot are unused—the difficulties increase tenfold, and stumbling among rocks and thorny bushes, even under the guidance of experienced coolies, brings out infirmities in body and mind that are quite astonishing. The place is well worth seeing, besides the healthful exercise the trip affords, and the path to it is simply charming. For a part of the way you creep along a monkey path which fringes the plateau which faces you when in the railway train, on the opposite side of the abyss. By-and-bye you skirt the foot of immense walls of rock, those great sheets of trap rising perpendicularly three hundred feet high which constitute the barriers of the Deccan, and its water-shed.

About five miles from Khandala there is a splendid place for a pic-nic, and as tats can do most of this distance, it is all easy work, and to those who enjoy fine scenery and bracing air a morning in December or January in that quarter will not easily be forgotten. There is a considerable amount of cutivated ground at the foot of the cone of Rajmachee which is walled round; the enclosure constituting the *pettah,* or what we should call the grange land of the baron's castle whence the inmates derived their supplies : forage for horses and cattle, food for man, and fuel. The walls, we are told on the best authority, extend 5,258 yards in length, or three miles. They are therefore as extensive as those round the great Fort of Dowlatabad. As we round the base of the block on which the main fort is built, and look up, the view is bizarre and extraordinary, and must have impressed the beholder with much awe and sinking of spirit. The rock here, in colour as black as night, rises sixty feet or more, sheer, when it bellies outward, in an abrupt overhanging corporation, ending two or theee hundred feet from the ground where we stand, on the ramparts which are so built as to meet the edge of the scarp. You cannot tell where the precipice ends and the bastion begins, but one or two loopholes, by all the world like the mouth and eyes of some pictured demon, reveal to us this ancient habitation of Seevajee and the Angria. When you do get into it, there is not much; so Rajmachee,

"Like a tall bully, lifts its head and lies."

But we are not there yet. As we round the cone, the difficulties begin. We know well enough what broken-up staircases are when a hundred feet of them are converted into avalanches of rubbish and loose stones shot down a hill-face at an angle of 35°. You have plenty of that on Raighur and Torna. Here you have the stone stairs kicked about in the wildest confusion, loose and moveable, their interstices a mass of yielding grit. On this blasted peak we found a grass, or straw, or cane in great profusion. What had been forced into maturity by the wild lashing rains of the monsoon now lay in withered swathes, kindly placed for us on those moving masses of whinstone rhomboids resting on a basis of grit, as smooth as the China matting of the Byculla Club. There was no danger to life, but very much to limb; so the instinct of self-preservation induced each man to "gang his own gait," and so not commit murder on the man that was beneath him. Once we got fairly wedged in the hollow of a double wall, for in some places there is a triple belt round the hill, and were advised by a native—there are natives here who, like oysters, stick to the rock—to clamber cat-like along the crumbling parapet. But it was too shifting a material on which to trust our corporations,* so what with hard pulling and tumbling, climbing and scrambling, we at length found ourselves, not, as the reader will have seen, "without impediment," in "the bowels" of Rajmachee. Here are rock-cut cisterns and plenty of the purest water.

THE LOOK-OUT.

We are now 2,730 feet above sea-level (about the height of Matheran), lower fort 2,540. Rajmachee means the Royal terrace. It looks down upon the Konkan. The ancients of this place, in their shirts of mail, could look down

* Danger from Loose Walls.—The ruins of Montpezer, six miles from Bassein. "From the wall of the hermitage Mr. J. Forbes met his death a few years ago. He, it seems, imprudently climbed the wall at a corner with his boots on, where the roots of a pepul-tree served as a ladder. He got safely to the top, and after sitting for a while on the wall admiring the surrounding prospect, in the act of rising, it is supposed, part of the crumbling wall giving way under his feet, he slipped and was precipitated into the court of the temple below, a height of between sixty and seventy feet. He never spoke afterwards, but was carried home to Bombay, senseless, and died the same evening.—*Faupell* in 1838, quoted in *Dr. Da Cunha's* "*Chaul and Bassein*," 1876.

and see all that was going on in the plains below. The Bhore Ghaut was the same then as it is now, not only in physical contour and conformation, but absolutely the only pass through which all the commerce of the Bombay Harbour passed to the Deccan. The railway makes no difference in this respect; commerce is friendly, but war is unfriendly, so sometimes an enemy came, and Rajmachee kept an outlook on him. Kotlighur stood guard below, but Rajmachee was the great bull's-eye lantern held in the face of friend or foe, and flashed upon every man who came from those lower Konkan regions. "Who's there?" was the watchword of Rajmachee. God keep the country, when its vigilance committee is perched up in places like this. We can verify the fact that a great extent of landscape can be seen from Rajmachee. But the following are the places that on a clear day may be easily descried. As for the Duke's Nose, Matheran, Bowmullung, Prubhul, and Kurnala, they are barely worth mentioning,—the mere kernel of a grand panorama. Our guide sung out to us Toong, Tikona, Loghur. But even they are nothing when Beemashunkur is in view; and Hurischandraghur where you may lie on the edge of the precipice, drop a stone, and find it takes eleven seconds to strike the bottom; Nagotna; our old friend of sewing-up-in-sacks notoriety Sagurghur, with the sun setting at Alibagh; and there is Toongar and the Salsette Hills, and across the flat sow-backed Purbhul the harbour, island, and city of Bombay. The upper fort is called Shreevardhan, which means, we understand, "increase of prosperity;" the lower fort, in like manner, Munrunjun, "mind pleasing." The first commands the second, which is as it should be, for without prosperity either of body or soul there can be no permanent pleasure of the mind whatever. We looked round for a seat, but the killidar was dead, and we had no Collector to send us a chair and a table as we had at Raighur last new year.

Laird o'Bucklyvie,
  May the devil rive ye
For biggin sic a toun
  Where there's neither a table
Nor a chair, nor a stule to sit doun.

And with this irreverent snatch we bid good-bye to Rajmachee. This fort was taken by Colonel Prother on the 6th March, 1818.

CONDITION OF THE PEOPLE.

Under this head we will select two dates. The first is the period of the "Noble Queen" Chand Beebee, at the close of the sixteenth century.

Meadows Taylor cannot be accused, with all his gorgeous descriptions of the bravery of those times, of overstating the violence to which life and property were exposed. The neighbourhood is Goolburgah.

"The place had an evil reputation for robbers at all times. There were not only the ordinary cutpurses and pick-pockets, pilchers, and night prowlers of such gatherings, but there were thugs from the neighbouring country of Allund, Gungooty and Kulhavee, as well as those who lived in the city itself, carrying on apparently honest trades and occupations, who marked parties for plunder, joined with them as they departed homewards, and slew them when they had gone a little distance with them. For miles, indeed, in every direction, were the unhallowed graves of hundreds and thousands, perhaps, of those who had been decoyed or destroyed. There were, too, dacoits who attacked the lodgings of pilgrims, or waylaid them on the high roads, and plundered with little regard to consequences. Among the latter were many Jatts and Kaikarees, peaceful-looking people by day, but terrible by night."

Our next author is Grant Duff, the place is Poona, the time is the close of the eighteenth century, and the man described is the Police

Superintendent of that city:—"No instance of greater neglect on the part of an administration, or of more extraordinary criminality in a subordinate officer, is recorded in the annals of any State than in the case of Gassee Ram, Kotwal, or Police Superintendent of the city of Poona. This man, a Brahmin, native of Hindoostan, employed the power with which he was vested in perpetrating the most dreadful murders. People disappeared and no trace of them could be found. Gassee Ram was suspected, but Nana Furnuwees refused to listen to complaints, apparently absurd from their unexampled atrocity. At last, it being suspected that Gassee Ram was starving a respectable Brahmin to death, Manajee Phakray, headed a party of the people, broke open the prison, and rescued the unfortunate Brahmin, which led to the detection of the monster's crimes, and he fell a victim to the vengeance of the exasperated populace, by whom he was stoned to death."

Behold in these extracts from the historian and novelist how people lived for two hundred years under the shadow of the Deccany forts.

STREAMS.

As we neared our home, we crossed a stream with a rocky bed. It is a stream which, after this, leaps from shelf to shelf until it makes that final plunge which we see in all its frothy grandeur during the monsoon from the railway as it thunders down the whinstone precipice at Khandala to the great ravine of the Oolas, where it buries itself, as may be said, in sundry places—

> "Where Deucalion hurled his mother's entrails on
> the desert world."

Where we made the passage all was quiet in the moonlight, with nothing but the sound of rippling water, so delightful to the sun-burnt soul in Hindoostan. The stream was wooded to the water-edge with scrub and brush. A bard in another land has pourtrayed something similar, and, like everything he touched in nature, with a master-hand. Minus the hazel, it will do very well for this :—

> "Whyles owre a linn the burnie plays
> As through the glen it wimpl't,
> Whyles round a rocky scaur it strays,
> Whyles in a weil it dimpl't,
> Whyles glitter'd to the nightly rays
> Wi bickering, dancing dazzle,
> Whyles oookit underneath the braes
> Below the spreading hazel.
> Unseen that night."

The great difference between the Deccan and Konkan streams is in their clearness. Abana and Pharpar are nothing to them. On the road to Beejapur there are no streams so clear, from the Beema itself down to the smallest rivulet. We except those in the Island of Arran, where the streams, rushing down from the granite clefts in Goatfell, become transformed in the plain to apocalyptic visions, clear rivers of the water of life, pure as crystal. This is the great want in our Konkan scenery. Clear sand and water-worn pebbles, in lieu of the leprous margin of the Bassein and Callian creeks, these lovely scenes by moonlight, or the chiaro-scuro of early dawn, would transform them into the beauties of Como or Loch Lomond. The romance is sadly dispelled when one jumps ashore ankle-deep in mud.

THE FORT OF RAIGHUR.

> Adieu thou palace, rarely entered,
> Adieu ye mansions, where I've ventured,
> Adieu ye cursed streets of stairs
> How surely he who mounts them swears.
>
> *Byron's Adieu.*

RAIGHUR HO!

Raighur is a lonely hill. No one cares to go to it, for it is rather out of the way and difficult of access. One English lady has ascended it, and Gell, of pedestrian fame, in his seven-leagued boots. From Bombay the journey is

> Splash, splash, across the sea,
> Tramp, tramp, across the main.

The splashing ends at Nagotna, where we exchange the howling of the bunder-boat men for the tender mercies of the messman. A much-abused man in India is the messman, and yet we could not get on well without him. Let us, therefore, talk of him lovingly as we swoop down upon him at the unearthly hour of 4 a.m. He rises uncomplainingly—it is true with something like a grunt—but I am sure, if I were a messman I should be inclined to say "Get out!" But he is the afflicted man's companion, he strokes him with the hair, and sends him gently away in his tonga at peace with all the world. Forgive him, then, if he sings a shrill requiem to himself on our departure. "A fair wind to him. May he never come back again." The morning is cold. There is much fog as we emerge from this creek town, so the driver blows his horn lustily with a "clear the road" twang, which rouses drowsy men and beasts of burden, for we can hear and partially see them, in the gray daylight, hustling and scuffling out of the way. It was there I saw what would have sent away that great wood engraver, Thomas Bewick, crazy with delight, *a dead horse,* and which, I am not sure, figures in one of his tail pieces. The horse lay with extended legs, thrown out from it, in its last kick, in the attitude in which death had overtaken it, a picture of weary *abandon* and utter *thowlesness,* so difficult for the painter to delineate. There, too, was the dog on its haunches, with closed jaws, *riving* with might and main at the undismembered carcass. Our driver seems up to his work. At all events we have no need to imitate Archbishop Sharpe on Magus Moor and shout to the postilion, "Drive,

drive, drive," for the people are inoffensive, and the temper of Deccany man and beast seem to fit each other to a T, and they go at their work as if they meant it. We bowl along, up hill and down dale, sending stones and dirt spinning right and left, taxing wheels and thews to the utmost, until we feel that we are within an inch of our lives, specially so in those long sweeps, as it were in a chariot of doom, thundering down hill to the foot of a *nullah*, full of boulders and projecting stones, on which we bump, thump, and crash—happily not to our destruction.

VIEW OF NAGOTNA CREEK FROM BOMBAY.

We are now on consecrated ground—consecrated we mean to us by many a bright vision from Malabar and Cumballa Hills, for in the early days of the monsoon we have wonderful prospects from Bombay. It is then that distance lends enchantment to the view. Sometimes the curtain lifts, and the clouds clear away from the island of Caranjah, the high land of Thull, and the broad lagoon which intersects them. There across the harbour lies in all its glory a new heaven and a new earth—a place of broad streams and rivers, fretted with the gold and islands of the blest—a vision to satisfy the weary soul at sunrise, vexed with the miseries of a restless night. One solitary palm tree stands on the extreme verge of the horizon, like a lonely sentinel on the confines of the world beyond. What that world is we now know. No longer mere *glamour* or *chiaroscuro*, blotted out of being by the first rays of the rising sun, but a beautiful country well-cultivated, though prosaic, well-watered and well-wooded, filled with a prosperous people whose *gaums* and farm steadings dot the landscape. Tiffin and a night's lodging at Dasgaum, in travellers' bungalow, whence a short morning's drive alongside the creek takes us to Mhar. The estuary is narrow, but seen in its windings and in the long shadows of early daylight, offers some tempting bits of scenery to the artist, water being always a pleasing and grateful adjunct to Indian scenery. The tuft of bulrush, and heron on one leg was not awanting. Burns in "The wicked town of Ayr" hits off Mhar,

> "Low in a sandy valley spread
> An ancient burgh rears its head.

"When I was at Goa I saw in a principal market place an engine with steppings to go upon, called a *strapado,* which unhinges a man's joints."* Exactly. This is the engine to which you are transferred at Mhar yclept a bullock gharry. The distance to be done is ten miles, and we do it in seven hours, and can assure the reader that had we been the stiffest-necked heretic that ever existed we could not have been more severely punished. It is not only a knock-kneed existence, but the head comes in for a fair share of beetling. You are cuffed on one side, and then, by way of average adjustment, on the other, until you are black and blue, and the only rest you get is when the brutes shamble into some *nullah* full of water and boulders, leaving you like Lord Ullin's daughter in the midst thereof. There is great virtue, however, in an Indian tiffin under a tree. An addition of "a stannin drink like the coo o' Forfar," and a rough walk of two miles take us to Pachad.

PACHAD AND THE STAIRCASE.

At Pachad we spent a very quiet night in the temple of Ramswamy. An owl hooted; and a young jackal threaded its way among the recumbent bodies. There were once 10,000 horsemen stationed here, yet we did not hear the sound of bit or bridle.

---

* Dr. Fryer, 1674.

Pachad is the ancient *peth* of the fort. Somewhat like the grange attached to barons' keep and castle, the *peth* was the depôt of supplies brought in from the surrounding country for the use of the garrison : a strong place to keep watch and ward, and summon all visitors, friendly or otherwise, to parley. The ordeal by touch at Pachad sent a tremor right up to the bastions of Raighur. An early start is the best, so we breast the hill at 3 a.m. This enables us to see the sun rise when we arrive at our destination ; but I am not sure but that all the Deccan hills are best to be done in this way. A lamp to your feet and a light to your path is all you want. The precipices and gulfs profound are better in shadow, otherwise the pedestrian, whose nerves are weak or physical education neglected, may be the subject of groggy and uneasy sensations, so the fine scenery and elixir of the cragsman may become man traps to catch or murder-holes to engulph the unwary. I must say, however, that Raighur is a noble hill, and does not resort to mean shifts. Besides, in the afternoon, the western sun blazes fierce on the exposed pathway all the way up.

When Seevajee built Raighur he counted the cost, and it took him years to accomplish. He ran a stair up the side of Raighur. In the level places it was not wanted, but deflections, up or down, were covered by it as it sidled or zigzaged up the hill. The transverse blocks were laid down or cut out of the living rock, and a through gate cleared away in the rock where needed by gunpowder. The horse, the camel, nay even the elephant, were no strangers to the stair of Raighur. Near the summit, the staircase is nearly perfect, and the topmost tiers as entire as the day they were cut. But time and the elemental strife of two hundred years, to which must be added General Prother's gunpowder in 1818, have done their work upon it.

The monsoon deals death to masoncraft on the hillside, and, like the preacher, writes "Vanity of vanities" on the strongest works of man. Every inch in its downward progress a monsoon torrent increases in strength, volume, and fury, until to-day we see the path of the destroyer marked by avalanches of débris and loose stones, spread out like a fan to the plain below, where all trace of the staircase is lost. Any person in good health may ascend Raighur. There is, of course, a good deal of climbing as well as walking, and breaking of shins in Matheran-cooly-path-work. The foothold of a heavy man sometimes gives way, but a lighter one will scramble up the hill in half the time we have done.

POSITION.

Raighur is not *Rajghur*, which is seen from the door of St. Mary's Church, Poona. They both, however, mean Royal Palace.* Raighur is in lat. 18·12 N., long. 73·38 E. Draw a straight line on the map from Junjeera due east, and it will bisect Raighur twenty miles from the coast. It has been called the Gibraltar of the East,† and of all the hill forts in the Bombay Presidency it is the most interesting. It was built and fortified by Seevajee and became his abode. In other parts he was merely a wayfaring man for the night, but here for sixteen years he gathered around him wives and children, Brahmin statesmen such as they were, gods and their gooroos, goods and chattels, the mighty plunder he levied from cities, kaphilas, and caravels. Whatever wild raids he was engaged in, they all had one natural termination which was when he sat down on this

---

* Torna and Rajghur are in the Punt of Bhore's territory. Raighur is British in the Kolaba Collectorate.

† Not the Gibraltar of Mathew Arnold, in those beautiful lines composed in memory of his brother, who died there on his way from India :—

> The murmur of this midland deep
> Is heard to-night around thy grave,
> There, where Gibraltar's cannon'd steep
> O'er frowns the wave.
>
> April, 9, 1859.

mountain top and counted up his gains; and his endless acquisition of plunder, which was his meat and drink, never knew respite except when its massive gates were closed upon him. If ever he slept soundly, it was in Raighur. Here he was crowned, and through its two-leaved gates, borne upon a litter, came from his bloody raid at Jalna, this restless scion of humanity, for the last time, with his battered body, to lay him down and die. Raighur rises from the Konkan, and not from the Deccan, and in this respect and in height resembles Matheran or Prubhul. Its area is about a mile-and-a-half long by one mile broad, tapering away,—a wedge like Gharbut Point, Matheran. In superficies shape and levels the entire hill resembles an isolated Gharbut, but though there are trees upon it, it has not the dense wood of Matheran.

DESCRIPTIVE.

There are three gates to Raighur. The first is 300 or 400 feet from the summit, flanked by bastions 30 feet high, from which the ramparts diverge on either side. The decay of Mahratta power is written on their fort gates. Raighur stands wide open day and night, you can pick the lock of Torna with a penknife (but don't do it), and a Birmingham padlock marked "patent" dangles idly in the wind on the door posts of Purtabghur. Another gate is passed, and we stumble on the brow of Raighur. Two polygonal towers stand here, vaulted, bomb-proof, and with pointed windows, but without mullions. Architecture, partly Hindoo, partly Muslim. They are two-storied and 30 feet high. Externally much ornamented with projecting masses of masonry standing at right angles from the wall. Pleasure houses or watch towers we know not. On this limited plateau is the largest tank on the hill, and a goodly number of trees, among which some buffaloes are wandering promiscuously.

We now enter the *Balla Killa*. The entrance is by a gateway and staircase, on either side of which rise high walls, well built and in perfect condition, and which may have been covered or arched over. We are now within the inner cincture, where everything was kept that was worth keeping. Kingly crown, holy books, with the gold and women of the sovereign. We will speak of the last first. There are seven *jagheers*; each wife had her own quarter. They are walled enclosures as large as a Scotch kirkyard, and as gloomy with a suggestive precipice beyond. Historically the No. 7

is an error, for Seevajee had only four wives. Some architectural forethought, no doubt, contingent upon his connubial dotage, "We are seven." Then come a congeries of buildings, the walls of which only are now standing, residences of nawabs and gentry of sorts.

ARCHITECTURE.

The buildings (such as they are) are the best of all Seevajee's handiwork, for he was a bad mason. He had too much on hand to busy himself entirely with stones and mortar. When we compare even this, which is Seevajee's best, with Eesaghur and Singhur forts, which were built before he existed, the difference is apparent. As for Torna and Purtabghur, forts constructed by Seevajee, they are slipshod work. The grass grows green or brown between every single stone, while you can barely put a penknife blade between the stones of Eesaghur, where the length of the walls (a thousand yards or more), and the magnitude of the bastions surprise as much even an unpractised eye as do their finish and execution. There is a strong Saracenic element in the earlier fort architecture of the Deccan. Take the Rajghur and Torna arches for example. The gateways remind one of Cairo or

Damascus, and carry us back to those dim and early times when the Arabs first carried their conquests and civilisation into Western India. The Hindoo modified what the Arab began, but the disciple in the Deccan was not worthy of his master.

It may assist us, in filling in the picture, to remember that in Seevajee's time there were 300 stone-houses here, accommodation for a garrison of 2,000 men, offices for the administration and disbursement of his revenue, and for the custody of the archives of the kingdom, a mint which coined not only copper coins but golden pagodas, a bazaar also consisting of a street nearly a mile long, the sides of which you can still see plinth high, and a signboard to describe each quarter, standing at corners like a huge inverted slate, six feet high and two broad. Raighur contains one building which we take to be Seevajee's, and which out-distances in architectural beauty and workmanship anything we have seen in the forts of the Deccan. It is a stone arch which, no doubt, constituted the great gateway or entrance to his palace, court, or durbar, apparently a copy of the one at Beejapoor. Comparing Raighur to Gharbut, the arch would be the hotel, and Seevajee's tomb and temple at Gharbut Point.

It is larger than the arch of Titus at Rome, without posterns, very like it, and is the entrance to a court as big as Solomon's temple.* The arch, of regal magnificence, is seen from afar, and must have been a fine picture when the black eagle of Jooner flapped his mighty wings over Deccan and Konkan plain, which he had learned to strip so bare. It has an inside staircase, a most workman-like structure, almost as perfect as the day it was constructed, save that stalactites, finger length, hang from the roof, showing that two hundred monsoons have forced some moisture into hidden crannies.† We creep up in the dark to have

A VIEW FROM RAIGHUR.

The sun is just rising behind Torna. There is nothing but hills to be seen north, south, east, and west. At our feet is Mhar, where Seevajee spent so many of his youthful days. Here is Singhur, and there Mahableshwur,

* Solomon's Temple, 120 feet long, 35 broad.—*Speaker's Commentary.*

† Until the tape and measuring line of the architect comes to Raighur, we leave on record the foot or "rule o' thumb," measurements :—

Height of arch	60	feet.
Span	8	,,
Sides of arch	12	,, broad.
Length of passage through	24	,,
Length of court	150	,,
Breadth	70	,,

It was an open court, and there was a well in the middle of it, now filled up with stones and rubbish.

and to the south-east the fort of Kangoree, where two Englishmen were imprisoned by the last Peshwa with much cruelty. When we bombarded Wassota (to which they had been removed) sixty years ago, Cornets Hunter and Morrison crept out with grizzly beards and unbleached calico, not much the worse of their durance vile. The best view of Raighur is from a place that not one man in a million will ever go to see—we mean the summit of Torna. It is there that its massive bulk and steep walls of rock heave their everlasting proportions on the eye. As you cross the Nagotna plain, Raighur has little appearance, and the nearer we get to it, the less we see of it, until we arrive at the top, when its external appearance is lost to us. We tried in vain to make it out from the Mahableshwur points, and caught merely a make-believe shadow of it from the *coup d'œil* at Warra* on the Par Ghaut, and from Purtabghur.

Seevajee had a quick ear, and heard further than we can see. One night when he was fast asleep in Raighur he suddenly awoke and said some misfortune had befallen Danda Rajpuree near Junjeera. It was too true. It was the

* Warra.—The travellers' bungalow here is a Gothic building like a Swiss chalêt among the mountains. We can recommend a short sojourn in this delightful spot.

bursting of a powder magazine which he heard, and his fort was taken. Rajpuree was twenty miles off.

WHY SEEVAJEE CHOSE RAIGHUR.

Raighur was neither gifted to him nor heired by him like the *jagheers* of Poona and Soopa, but came to him by right of conquest. The time was probably about 1662 to 1664, when Seevajee looking around him for a nest, and taking the measure of events and his own position among them, his eye was arrested by this great quadrangular block. He was then occupying Rajghur, a strong fort 4,000 feet above sea-level, four miles from Torna, and about thirty-five miles south-west of Poona. Rajghur and Torna are both hills of a breakneck character and well suited for the abode of the youthful chief of a turbulent and unsettled country. But he was now looking for something else. Circumstances were driving him, or he was driving circumstances, to a position, where a broader platform would be necessary upon which to exploit. His success was now in a manner assured. He had many forts; in fact, he left 150 fortified places when he died, and among them were some built before his day and in splendid condition to choose from. But Rairee, as it was then called, offered him such advantages, that though its works, out and in, were perhaps the feeblest of them all, and its area unbuilt upon, he resolved to fortify it, and construct upon it a palace and buildings suitable for his government. His reasons for doing so we will endeavour to present to the reader. At first sight Raighur seems an out-of-the-way place—a lonely hill—but, it must be borne in mind, that Bombay with its population of 60,000 had not then the preponderating weight in the common-wealth it has since obtained. A glance at the map shows that Raighur is nearly equi-distant from Bombay, Poona, and Satara. Moreover, it was only a few miles from Mhar, a shallow seaport, it is true, but a base of operations whence supplies were always available, and in communication with the chain of *droogs* or sea forts which he had established along the coast, and to which, should the worst come to the worst—and this was no doubt among his calculations—he could resort. It must be borne in mind that the empire of India was then ruled from Delhi, and that Aurungzebe in person was hurling masses of men into the Deccan to crush the nascent energies of the Mahrattas, of whom Seevajee was the representative. The first great wave had already broken, and Dowlatabad, Jooner, Chakun, Poona, and Soopa had already fallen a prey to the Moslem. Singhur and Poorundhur might come next (as they did), and the deluge would be upon him. So he stepped back, not reluctantly or cowardly, but as a matter of stratagem. Looking from Raighur to the north-east, in the direction of Poona, the sky line is bounded by a huge breastwork of nature's making, thirty miles away, scarps 4,000 feet above sea-level, crowned by the bastions of Rajghur and Torna; as long as they remained intact he was safe. They were his natural defence, his munition of rocks, between him and the Moghul enemy, and they did remain so during his life, for, so far as we know, they were never surrendered to force or by treaty or stratagem. They were to stand and fall together. Such are some of the political and military reasons which may have induced Seevajee to pitch upon the rock of Rairee. As far as we know it was unstained by human blood. The same could not be said of Singhur, Poorundhur, Loghur and, least of all, of Purtabghur, under whose flagstones lay the gory head of Afzulkhan. Here, at all events, he could stand on his own threshold and worship the *tulsi* plant without being confronted with the evidence of his guilt or the witnesses of his crimes.* Reasons also of a physical and topographical character. Raighur is a great wedge-shaped block, split off from the Western Ghauts, inaccessible on three sides, and wanting only fortifications on the fourth, where a gate flanked by towers and ramparts made it impregnable to his enemies, while it was of easy access to his friends. The avenues leading to it were most difficult of access, and the country round about, being a theatre of mountains, has been described by a contemporary of Seevajee, who travelled over it "as a specimen of hell," which, *à la* Dante or Milton, represents the long and toilsome march of a thirsty traveller among cactus bushes, thorns of sorts, and dry water-courses, until the Moslem saw the precipices beetling above his head, which encircled the home of this troublesome idolator.

> "Black he stood as night
> Fierce as ten furies—terrible as hell."

THE ENGLISH EMBASSY.

During the reign of Charles the Second, when Gerald Aungier was Governor of Bombay, an Embassy was sent to Raighur to assist at the

* All this was changed by Sambhajee, the son and successor of Seevajee. The moment he passed the gate of Raighur, says Grant Duff, he displayed the barbarity of his disposition by putting his step-mother, the wife of Seevajee, to a cruel and lingering death, imprisoning her son and Seevajee's prime minister, confiscating his property, beheading or hurling from the precipices of the rock of Raighur the Mahratta officers who were attached to her cause.

coronation of Seevajee. It consisted of Henry Oxenden and two English factors. Henry Oxenden was of good family; his father was a Knight of England. The tombs of his two brothers, Sir George and Christopher, are still shown at Surat, the former forty feet high. Bombay sent the best man she had, next to the Governor. He had been chief of Carwar, which place had been taken by Seevajee, and presumably knew a good deal of the politics of those countries on the western coast of India. He became Deputy Governor of Bombay in 1676. The baronetcy was created in his person in 1679. He died shortly after. He was about fifty-six years of age when he ascended Raighur. The party went in a *balloon* (not aërial navigation, but) a small sail boat to Chaul, and arrived at Pachad six days after leaving Bombay.

NIL DESPERANDUM.

Throughout the early history of Bombay there is nothing so striking or worthy of admiration as the attitude of conscious strength displayed by the men who upheld the government of the infant colony. One would say that the Great Powers at that time could easily have crushed Bombay, and that they did not do it because they could not do it, in justice to their own selfish interests. At all events Bombay did not blanch or fear either within or without her bastions. The men who constituted the Embassy went on this expedition as on a holiday excursion, or a tour in the districts to collect the cocoanut revenue of Matoonga or Sion. They had heard stories of Seevajee's treachery, cruelty, and lustful ambition—stories too well founded. One of Seevajee's forts he called Singhur, the *lion's den*. It still frowns in lofty grandeur over the valley of the Neera and the Lake of Kurukwasla. But in truth they were all lion's dens, with the footmarks inward. Was not the deed of Afzulkhan still ringing in their ears? So, to many a Bombay household, Seevajee was a Black Douglas, an old Man of the Mountain, or Giant Despair, and the caves of Raighur, the hole in the hill, from the door of which Mercy came trembling away.

And yet not one word betraying doubt, hesitation, or fear exists in their narrative. Gerald Aungier had blotted these words out of the dictionary.

Bombay was not at war with Seevajee. Nevertheless, it redounds greatly to the credit of both parties. Seevajee was not afraid to have the Embassy in his fort, and they were not frightened to go into it and remain there. The Raighur of the seventeenth century was not the Kabul of the nineteenth century.

THE BURST OF THE MONSOON.

Let us try and picture this gray-haired and grizzly Puritan on the heights of Raighur. It need not be a difficult task, for we have only to ask ourselves what are now the precursors of the monsoon on any hill in Western India to know what they were then and there. The atmosphere weighs down everything, man, beast, and bird :—

> " There's not a bird with lonely nest,
> In pathless wood or mountain crest,"

but drops the eye or folds the wing, and the very foliage seems to hang limp and lifeless amid the oppressive and universal stillness. As day succeeds day his troubles accumulate.

I doubt not that Henry Oxenden prayed long and fervently (when the insects would let him), for rain, and for wind too: not " the soughin winnin wind," but " the rantin tearin wind " of the Scotch Minister, one blast to shake his house and the very bed he lay on. For long ere this, you may be sure, had come hunger and thirst for the unattainable, the feverish pulse, throbbing temples and bloodshot eyes, for which there was now little left to look at, but a weird and lurid landscape of sand-devils, chasing each other on the plains below him, or, peradventure, the mirage of his own spectre on the neighbouring hill, to mock or confound him with the delusions of witchcraft.* That he cursed the day he left Bombay Castle or his native Kent is not recorded; but recorded or not, with or without evidence, we take it for granted that Henry Oxenden, in consonance with Saxon human nature in Hindoostan, threw his wasted body on a charpoy, and muttered in accents, not loud but deep:—"It is a weariness of the flesh, when will it be over!" "I have seen your nautches, your prize climbing of precipices, your cock-fighting, kite-flying, hawking, archery, spear and tulwar exercise, performing goats and monkeys, what are they to me? What boots it that Seevajee weighs himself against gold, feeds daily a crowd of hungry Brahmins, or flashes his sword of Bowanee in the morning sun? The Mountain Rat!† His mother dies. Who cares? Or whether he marries a fourth or a fortieth wife? Am I to die and have the earth of Raighur shovelled on me, that the Honourable Company trading in the East

* We ourselves have never seen the spectre of the Brocken in the Deccan, but this display of the mirage is vouched for by Dr. J. Y. Smith in the last edition of his book on Matheran.

† The name which Aurungzebe gave him.

Indies may live, or be spared, merely to exist on goat's flesh* while, for sooth, the fat factors of Bombay fare sumptuously every day on prawn and pomphlet or royster over night on their Bombay Punch !† Give me the hurricane rather than the pestilence, for I would rather see the rack of the monsoon on Raighur than the coronation of ten Seevajees. Woe ! worth the hour ! Woe ! worth the day ! He rises,—gropes his way to the nearest loophole in his dormitory His face is dashed with a whirlwind of dust and leaves swept up the naked surface of the ramparts ; half-blinded he peers into the darkness of the night, when lo ! a flash from heaven pours a blaze of light over half the kingdom of Seevajee, and reveals the blackened sides of Torna, seamed and ribbed with the white

---

* A Muslim butcher at the foot of the hill supplied them with half a goat every day. At the end of weeks he began to be surprised and desirous of seeing the *Bellatiwallahs* who had consumed as much as Seevajee's hordes had done in as many years, so he tottered up the hill to have a look at his customers. He had not seen so many animals slaughtered since he had been at Mecca As for Oxenden and his companion they had nothing else to eat for three mortal months, neither fish, flesh nor fowl, nor good red herring—

Goat young, Goat old,
Goat hot, Goat cold,
Goat lean, Goat tough,
Thank God we've had enough.

† *Punch* and *toddy* are both inventions of Western India.
Punch, five—the five ingredients being lime-juice, rosewater, sugar, arrack, and water.
Tom Coryat, writing in India before 1617, says he is drinking his friend's health in *Tadi*. Scotsmen have taken kindly to the word. The Bombay Presidency has much to answer for, if we are prepared to accept this statement, that it has given birth to the names of the national drink both of England and Scotland.

cataracts of the monsoon. Blessed relief: never-to-be-forgotten vision. Thou turnest my mourning into joy, and my heaviness into laughter.

"Oh when in kindness unto me wilt thou be pleased to come
I with a perfect heart will walk within my house at home."

So with this verse of David's Psalm, done into metre by Francis Rous, we leave him. He will now sleep without rocking.

The day dawns. The thunder has cleared the air. After a wild and tempestuous night of splashing rain, the misty curtain slowly rises from a panorama of endless hills; rift and corrie, peak and precipice, in sharp relief. A glint of sunshine anon flashes into being, here and there a knoll or slope covered by the magic of a night's rain with a mantle of transparent green. Raighur is decked with the same delicate hue, a carpet or rather a gauzy robe, thin as Dacca muslin.

Tanks are filling, frogs croaking, and land crabs scuttling out of their hybernation and myriads of insect life abroad. Wild thyme scents the morning air. The cobra-lily peeps out in the dells, the orchid blossoms apple-like on a leafless trunk, and the wild plantain with its spiked sheath of green and glistering leaves bursts its filaments amid earth and stones, overlapping the sere and rustling fragments of last season's vegetation. Amid these heralds of a new era a Jemadhar announces Seevajee's coronation. But we give the account in the Embassy's own words, capitals and all.

THE CORONATION.

" Accordingly next morning he and his retinue went to Court and found the Rajah seated on a Magnificent Throne, and all his Nobles waiting upon him in Rich Attire; his son Sambhajee Rajah, Peshwa Morah Pundit, and a Brahman of great Eminence, seated on an Ascent under the Throne, the rest, as well Officers of the Army as others, standing with great respect. The English made their Obeisance at a distance, and Narun Sinai held up the Diamond Ring that was to be presented him. He presently took notice of it, and ordered their coming nearer, even to the Foot of the Throne, where being Vested, they were desired to retire, which they did not so soon, but they took notice on each side of the Throne. There being (according to the Moor's manner) on heads of gilded Lances many Emblems of Dominion and Government, as on the Right hand were two great Fish's Heads of Gold, with very large Teeth, on the Left several Horse's Tails, a pair of Gold Scales on a very high Lance's head, equally poised, an Emblem of Justice; and as they returned at the Palace Gate, stood two small Elephants on each side and two fair Horses, with Gold Trappings, Bridles and Rich Furniture, which made them admire how they brought them up the Hill, the Passage being both difficult and hazardous."*

It was the 6th of June 1674. The distance from their house to the palace was about a mile. The equestrian sentry at the gate was doubtless the typical Mahratta horseman in his shirt of mail or case of iron network, his helmet covering the ears and falling on the shoulders. The man who crowned him was Gaga Butt, a Brahmin Shastree from Benares.

Seevajee's titles were *Kshittrya Koolavotumsa, Sree Raja Seeva,* the head ornament of the *Kshittree* race, his Majesty, lord of the Royal umbrella. In other words, as loud as trumpet conch or tomtom could proclaim,—Great is Seevajee, King of the Mahrattas, greater than the gold against which he was weighed or the diamonds that saved his life at Delhi.

Seevajee's standard *Bhugwa-Jhenda* was swallow-tailed and of a deep orange colour, but on a big day like this the *Juree-Putka,* or golden streamer, the national ensign of the Mahrattas,

---

* Dr. Fryer.

no doubt waved from the great arch which still crowns the highest plateau of Raighur.

PORTRAIT.

The man who was the subject of this ovation was forty-seven years of age and of a handsome and intelligent countenance. No portrait of him has come down to us except the one in Orme's History, evidently from an oval on glass by some Delhi painter, and most probably picked up by Orme or his father in their wanderings along the coast of Western India in the early part of the eighteenth century. Their proximity to Seevajee's own time is a partial guarantee of its faithfulness. At all events it is the only portrait that we shall likely ever have. A keen eye, a long aquiline and somewhat drooping nose, a neat trim cut beard and small moustache make up for us a face, stolid, feline, and fair for a Mahratta—somewhat melancholy but a wonderful face, in which knowing even less than we now know, we could descry ability and cunning, and the hardihood and daring of a conspirator against the rights of man—one not easily cowed or alarmed, with a strong faith in himself, and a gift to measure his own capacities, and those of the men who were to be his helpers in his career of aggrandisement. Well worth looking at this man among men ; sash across his breast, himself a Star of India, baleful enough, kingly cowl with its tassel of pearls and feathers. No need of a tiara of the diamonds of Golconda for this man, for his eagle eye (on which all contemporaries are as much agreed as on the eye of Burns) outshines them all, and by the skinny fingers he beckons to the English Embassy, he proclaims himself the undisputed ruler of dusky millions.

HOW THEY SPEND THE TIME.

There was the legitimate Hindoo drama in which Gunputti displayed his histrionic powers, amid battles of the gods, and much sound, fury, and blazing explosions as of a thousand devils. National peculiarities were hit off by the stage player to the life: the Arab mercenary black in the face and bristling with arms ; the Moslem *hajee* with ochry beard redolent of musk and Mecca ; the Portuguese sailor, *gallena del Mare* (hens of the sea) ; the Parsee with hat so big that it toppled over amid roars of laughter ; the Sindi, *abu tassa* or the father of the frying pan ; the hatted man *par excellence,* one of ourselves with veritable swagger, flourishing his cane with much *nonchalance* and calling for drink as if his stomach was an unslaked lime-kiln, and his sun topee dinted and as greasy and ancient as if it had been worn by Tom Coryat, whereat the English laughed much. There were *kuthas*. Seevajee was great at *kuthas*; a mixture of recitation, song and anecdote, with a little acting as byeplay, like Mr. Mathew's or David Kennedy's entertainments of a later date. There was music. Seevajee was passionately fond of it. He was in Delhi about the time that the Emperor denounced music, and may have originated or assisted in the tremendous piece of waggery it called forth.

"Public proclamation was made prohibiting singing and dancing. It is said that one day a crowd of singers and dancers were gathered together with great cries, and having fitted up a bier with a good deal of display, round which were grouped the public wailers, they passed under the Emperor's *haroksha-i-darsan*, or interview window, when he enquired what was intended by the bier and the show. The minstrels said that music was dead, and they were carrying his corpse to the burial.*

Seevajee knew the Ramayana and was perpetually singing snatches of it. It would have been a shame to him if he had not, as Valmiki, the Indian Homer—so says the legend—was born at his very doors. You can see his birth-place

* Kafi Khan.

near Jejooree and the Neera bridge, nestling in the valley beneath, as you look down from the battlements of Poorundhur. The Ramayana contains 20,000 verses. There is no need to translate the whole of it; but the following, done to our hand into English by Dr. Wilson, if ever sung by Seevajee, must have been squeaked out by him in a very low key:—

> "Truth is the foundation of piety,
> In the world the root of religion is truth;
> Truth is the supreme principle in the world;
> Truth is the most excellent of all things;
> Therefore let truth be glorious."

Above all there was the newsman. Henry Oxenden stands convicted of having bribed the press. But, indeed, everybody was bribed, from the sweeper up to the prime minister, nay, even the Maharajah himself. In diamonds and shawls they must have paid the expenses of the Embassy twice over. They were told not to come empty-handed, and paying for early news was surely the most venial of sins, for if you wish news even when the truth is economised you must pay for it. The name of this supple courtier and public intelligencer was *Peta Gi Pundit Vocanovoce. Vak* means word or sentence, sentence-maker; but we must leave this bone for the philologers to pick. The Embassy at once recognised his genius and utility by a bonus, a diamond worth Rs. 125, which meant something more in 1674. News or not news, straw or not straw, he had to furnish his daily tale. That this man was a most adroit liar we have the amplest evidence. He killed Seevajee several times, and the obituary notice was sure to be followed by some instance of daring activity. The dead man generally came to life a hundred miles off. So, when he was waylaying Surat, the sibylline leaves had him in Chaul, or chewing betelnut at Bassein when he was scrambling like a wild cat up the scarps of Hurischundraghur. Five rivers flow from the Mahableshwur range. Four have been identified: this doubtless is the fifth. The infant rills of the press of Western India, garrulous and muddy at the fountain-head, have been clarified and subdued by two centuries of criticism, and now pour their lusty waters, east and west, far as the Bay of Bengal or the Arabian Sea. It is curious to stumble upon

A TRANSACTION IN PIECE-GOODS

on the top of Raighur. It illustrates Seevajee as a man of business when brought face to face with the representatives of the English nation. We had a little bill to settle with him, and had dunned him before without success. The amount was pagodas 10,000, or Rs. 45,000, and it stood at his debit in the Bombay ledger, for damage and loss sustained from his troops by our factories at the sack of Hooblee and Rajapoor. The factors had been taken away also, but we had no claim on account of *them*. Poor bodies ! Now, it may be laid down as a certainty that, if the subject of one nation is dealing with the sovereign of another, the subject will come off second best, and if that sovereign is a Mahratta, so much the worse. Henry Oxenden was a guest, and it was no doubt an inopportune moment to trouble Seevajee in this way on the eve of his coronation and marriage. We have evidence that he chafed over it. You cannot drive a hard bargain with a man when you are his guest. The ambassador doubtless imagined that at such a joyful moment he would concede everything. But in this, good, easy man, he was mistaken; for though Seevajee had a mint of money and an unlimited *abroo*, or credit, there was nothing he disliked more than to part with hard cash. Loot in the shape of piece-goods was different. With these he was well supplied, whether it was *sakluth*, the broadcloth of England, or the painted calicoes of India, destined for the beds and curtains of English matrons : Raighur was full of them.

Now for the facts. The settlement of this claim is a marvel of ingenuity. Seevajee sold the

Englishman piece-goods—the market value at the time being pagodas 15,000—at half price. Noble and generous merchant prince of Raighur!

The goods were deliverable in three years, a long contract, but never mind; time was of little value in the seventeenth century. This would liquidate pagodas 7,500 and leave a balance of 2,500, which His Highness agreed should be wiped out, by absolving us from custom duties on our resuming business at Rajapur until those amounted to the equivalent. Most wise! Most fair! The historian to whom we are indebted for these particulars says:—"It is doubtful whether the English ever received what was settled by the treaty." At all events we hear no more of the treaty of Raighur. It lies on the page of history, a mere expression of amity between Seevajee and the English nation, and of course has no place in Aitchison's "Treaties and Sunnuds of India." A horrible suspicion crosses our mind. It is unworthy of the dignity of history, but we shelter ourselves under the Scots' proverb:—"It needs a lang spune to sup kail with the deil." Did we buy back our own goods?

SEEVAJEE AND THE ENGLISH.

Whatever miseries were inflicted on the natives of Western India, and they were not a few, by Seevajee, the English had no reason to complain. He did not injure them. Not one hair of their head suffered. Even when he was pillaging Surat he exchanged civilities with Bombay. I fancy he knew the power and mettle of the English too well to meddle with them. Every cowrie he took in the sack of their factories at Hooblee and Rajapoor, he repaid in his own way, on the curious principles of Mahratta arithmetic. He agreed to restore them their wrecks cast from time to time on his coasts, an inalienable privilege maintained by native powers from age to age. Native powers ! We asked what we ourselves had not then the ability to grant in our own kingdoms of England, Scotland, or France, the boasted homes of civilisation. He agreed to take our money at the money's worth. After showing poor Mr. Smith in his camp at Surat two or three heads and hands chopped off, he was mercifully restored to his friends, clothed and in his right mind. The two Englishmen taken from Rajapur and confined in a hill fort by him were imprisoned on grounds of accusation, of which there was some reasonable suspicion, and afterwards released on paying a ransom. Some small men, such as his Soubadar at Nagotna, may have bullied a stray English shikaree on the coasts of Caranjah. His entertainment, however, of the Embassy, such as it was for three months on Raighur, proves his respect for the English. That respect may have been heightened, nay even created, by the attitude and magnanimous bearing of his great contemporary, Gerald Aungier. Seevajee may have scowled, fumed and gnashed his teeth. Fryer tells us that he cast daily in our faces, that the very ground we stood on in Bombay had not been obtained by valour but by compact, and that we were fitter to live by merchandise than by arms —carpet soldiers in fact. True, O King, in part! Not by the sword these lands were obtained, but *with* the sword they were defended.*

ITS MEMORIES.

Raighur occupies a large space in the history of Seevajee. Suffice it to say that the wealth of Golconda flowed into it—the plunder of Surat and twenty other cities besides; that he passed out of its gates to Delhi, and through its gates did the fugitive return again. Here on a dark night he despatched across the jungle 1,000 of his Mawulees on their famous raid and capture of Singhur,

"The den is taken but the lion is slain."

Here his heart for once failed him, and he reluct-

* We are sorry to impeach the veracity of Fryer, a most invaluable writer on this period. The judgment of Mackintosh comes up against him. He had gone to Callian to see some grand ruins described by Fryer and did not find them. This is most unlike the meek Mackintosh. "We all agreed that Dr. Fryer whose book induced me to go to Callian ought to have been hanged."—*Mackintosh's Life.*

antly resolved to sign the Treaty of Poorundhur, by which he forfeited twenty forts to the Great Moghul. It was from this place that he set out at the head of his memorable expedition to the Carnatic with 70,000 men, levying *chouth* as far as Madras. Here he heard of his father's death. Here his mother died. Here he was crowned, married, died and burned to ashes with a holocaust of his wives, elephants, and camels. His mausoleum is on yonder knoll, its interior a mass of weeds, trees growing up through the pavement of its *dhurumsalla*; its temple foul and dishonoured, and its god cast down to the ground.*

No man now cares for Seevajee. Over all those wide domains, which once owned him lord and master, acquired by so much blood and treasure, and which he handed down with care to the Rajahs of Kolapoor, the Bhonslas of Satara, and their Peshwas in Poona, not one man now contributes a rupee to keep or repair the tomb of the founder of the Mahratta Empire.†

That palace which resounded with acclamation

* The sacred bull had toppled over and was lying on its back. Something similar elicited a capital *bon mot* from Dr. Wilson—*Sic transit gloria Nundi.*

† The British Government conserves the architectural remains of Tudor and Stewart. Will not the Bombay Government do as much for the tomb, the temple, and the arch of Seevajee? A few crumbs that fall from the archaeological bureau of Western India would suffice to keep in repair memorials of a dashing and most romantic period.

at the installation of Seevajee, king of the Mahrattas, was destined to witness a complete revolution in their affairs. A strange incident is recorded in the annals of their final overthrow. Their dominion had lasted one hundred and forty-four years. It is a long story, but we now approach the end of it. When the clouds began to gather round the last days of the Peshwa, his Ranee was sent to Raighur. It was bombarded by the English and committed to the flames. On the 10th May, 1818, Colonel Prother ascended the hill. Somebody, on looking into the ruins of the palace, observed a native lady crouching amid the embers of the conflagration—the hunted hare of the Poet, or Lucia de Lammermoor of Romance, woe-begone and mocking at fate.

This was the wife of Bajee Rao, the last of the Peshwas, and with her Raighur and the Mahrattas disappear from the page of History. As in the last chapter of Ancient History, graven deep on the coin of Vespasian, it ends with the figure of a woman sitting low in the dust under a palm tree.

BEEJAPOOR.

CHAPTER XVII.

BEEJAPOOR.

"I felt nothing of the usual sentiments inspired by ruins in contemplating those of Beejapoor. We in general on such occasions feel a reverential melancholy, and are lifted above the present time and circumstances. But these sentiments are produced by ruined cities which were the scenes of what is venerable or interesting to us. With these feelings we consider Athens or Rome. But here we see the triumph of force, and the buildings of which we behold the ruins were never the scenes of any other qualities than those of treachery, debauchery, and cruelty, of war without science, or generous humanity without elegance or love."—*Sir James Mackintosh*, 1808.

THESE lines were written seventy-four years ago, and in the main are as true as on the day they were written, and, like everything by Mackintosh, are entitled to the deepest consideration. But they may be applied by the European to every ruined city in Asia, and, we may add, also to a good many in Europe. We cannot absolutely say that war was without science amid such stupendous fortifications as exists in Beejapoor. It seems as good as anything going at the time in this part of the world. Elsewhere he says that war was without heroism* and love without romance, and an answer to this may be found in Meadows Taylor's novels. The truth seems to be that public intelligence has drifted towards the subject of this article during the nineteenth century in a way that Sir James Mackintosh, nor any other man in his day, had little or no conception of. That they had plenty of science in Beejapoor of a particular kind is patent enough from the fact that we are only now beginning to find out how the ancient builders and architects of this city were able to do things that we could not do ourselves. The big dome, we are told, is a wonder of constructive skill ; and the roof in the Roza Mausoleum, hanging as it were in the air, was a mystery which is now only explained by their method of using concrete. These are Fergusson's words, and he says further that nine builders out of ten will tell you that such a flat roof as that in the Ibrahim

* This looks heroic :—A Rajpoot who had made what he thought a prudent retreat from battle, when he sat himself down in his house, was served at his meat by his wife with a brass ladle. On asking for a reason, she replied, "Lest the sight of iron should turn your stomach from your victuals, as it had done from fighting."—*Fryer*.

Roza will not stand. It has stood, however, for a couple of hundred years, and may hold together for as many more. The era in which the work was done requires also to be taken into account, and the place. We must not forget that the glory of Beejapoor had all passed away before a single Englishman had set foot in Bombay, and that Mahmood had placed the gilded crescent on his sepulchre before half the domes now in Europe were thought of. The big gun *Mailik-el-Maidan* surely was a contribution to the science of war. Mons. Meg, at Edinburgh Castle, is nothing to it;* and how it was placed in its present position is a question that no man yet has been able satisfactorily to answer.

MEADOWS TAYLOR.

Had the best of all opportunities for writing on the people and history of the Deccan. He had indomitable perseverance, and he who was once an apprentice in a grocer's shop in Bombay in 1824 is now no mean authority on the history of the Deccan, and his novels are in the hands of all. He admits himself that he owed much in the way of legendary lore to William Palmer. It is

---

* Measurements of big gun—diameter at breech, 4 ft. 10 in.; diameter at muzzle, 5 ft. 2 in.; diameter of bore, 2 ft. 4½ in.; length, 14 ft. 3 in. Cast at Ahmednugger, 1548.

matter of history that William Palmer was allowed to establish a house of business at Hyderabad in the Deccan in 1814, and came down in the Calcutta crash of 1829-32.

Sir John Kaye gives the whole story in his life of Metcalfe, and we gather from his account that the comercial relations of the Nizam with this house were so enormous that at one time the Government of India found it necessary to pay off the liabilities of the firm to the extent of a million sterling, and that bullion was sent to this amount from Calcutta. It did no good to Palmer and Company, but rather precipitated the crisis. Our impression is that the existence of Palmer and Company, with their then relations to the Nizam, was a standing menace to the British Government, and the sooner the firm as then conducted was ended the better.

Meadows Taylor will now tell his own story. "In 1830 Mr. Palmer's house continued to be my chief resort. There was a fascination about him quite irresistable to me, his knowledge was so varied, classical, historical, and political. His father, who had been Secretary to Warren Hastings, had taken part in almost all the eventful scenes of early Anglo-Indian history, and had married, as was very usual then among

English gentlemen, a lady of high rank, one of the Princesses of the Royal House of Delhi, and his fund of knowledge and great store of anecdote made him a delightful and improving companion. On the 25th August, 1832, I was married to Mary Palmer, daughter of William Palmer, Esq., at Secunderabad."

It was in 1839 he became acquainted with Christopher North (Professor Wilson, the editor of *Blackwood's Magazine*), who urged him to write his Indian tales. North was no mean judge, and a life of rambling over every part of the Deccan for thirty years, and his marriage, fitted Meadows Taylor to pourtray every department of Mahratta life, military, social, and domestic, in each of which he now stands unrivalled.

With

THE ACCOMMODATION

provided for us in Beejapoor we had no need to grumble. It was the mosque of the Ibrahim Roza —nothing equal to it, we are told, out of Seville or Cordova. It was a big bed-room, the curtains of which were groined arches. You could not sleep in anything larger except under the canopy of heaven, which may be tried by anyone who likes, with perfect impunity, on the Deccan Hills at this season of the year. Aurungzeb slept here verging on three-score year and ten—a heavy weight of clay! He had just captured the city and wept over it. O! thou old hypocrite and fratricide! He was then worth forty millions a year: Gamelli Careri says eighty millions sterling, but let us take the smaller sum; and that without either license-tax or opium to swell his revenue. I wonder if the people grumbled in those days.

There must have been a soul of goodness about the man, for he it was who invented dak bungalows, and built them from Kabul to Travancore. He also took a *scunner* (Scottice for loathing) at big tombs, very likely at Beejapoor. Avaunt all sycophants and mummers!

> "Go to your sculptured tombs, ye great,
> In a' the tinsel trash o' state!"

Kafi Khan gives us his exact words before his death:—"Carry this creature of the dust quickly to the first burial-place, and consign him to the earth without any useless coffin." So no useless coffin enclosed his breast, for he laid himself down, *aetat* 90, at another Roza, on that steep hill above Kailas and Ellora, in a plot of ground a man might have bought for ten rupees, which you may still see with a tulsi plant and some jessamine covering all that remains of the Lord of the World. He made his tomb, after the injunction of the Prophet, not more than two feet high, and open to the dews of heaven.

No man will disturb him; whereas in Beejapoor rust doth corrupt, and thieves break through and steal.

TOMBS.

What Canopus was to ancient Alexandria that was Toorwah to Beejapoor, a magnificent suburb for garden parties and *fêtes champetres* of sorts. Though there was no afternoon tea in those days, they amused themselves with sherbet and other cooling drinks, among fountains and within the sound of rippling water. Of a truth the dead were well remembered in Toorwah, for here, as in Beejapoor, there seems nothing else than tombs. We wandered a whole morning until the sun was high in the heavens; and there was nothing but tombs. The tall crop of jowaree grew superincumbent on the ruined sites of the palaces of the living, but the mausoleums of the dead seemed to shoot up their bulbous domes everywhere. You walk in all directions, but the beginning and end of all is the inevitable. "O vanity of men whose memorials are as vain as themselves, which in a few short years perish, and that which lasts longest lasts no longer than the world!" Every man seems to have prepared his own sepulchre during his life,—an old custom. "In the garden was a new sepulchre wherein was never man yet laid." Sometimes the work was cut short. There is a great mausoleum, half finished, that was to have surpassed the dome of Mahmood as much as that dome now surpasses all other buildings. But when the first stone was raised, its author and intended occupant, Ibrahim Adil Shah I., was cut off by assassination. The workman threw away his tools, and the cooly his last basketful of earth into the ditch. And now there remains something like the ruins of Melrose Abbey, with this difference, that the rests on which the arch is built, stone and not wood as in our modern times, remain inside the arch. They have never been taken down. The people here seemed, like the demoniacs of the New Testament, to have their dwelling among the tombs. As soon as they arrived at the age of consciousness, they bethought themselves of dying—no, not exactly of dying, but of what design and structure should be the habitation of their carcases. They had no notion, as we have, of the narrow house appointed for all living, for

Mahmood now sleeps in an acreage, over which is suspended a dome as big as that of the Pantheon.

> "Some village Hampden that with dauntless breast
> The little tyrant of his fields withstood"

muttered the words "Six feet will hold him yet." It was an idle imprecation. Six feet! Why, sixty feet was not enough for the Patel or Mamlutdar. If the ghosts of these old Beejapooreans could only now revisit the glimpses of the moon, they would be astounded at the condition of their own sepulchres.

The stronger they were fastened down with stone and clamp the greater object were they of cupidity to those who came after them. Size, strength, durability, and ornamentation, all increased the desire to see what was in them, and so Pagan, Frank, and Tartar, full of the idea of the gold with which the kings and counsellors of the earth buried themselves, have wrenched the granite asunder, hammered to pieces the polished whinstones, and scattered the contents at the grave's mouth. Out of one arched window, tomb of Afzulkhan, if you will within its mullioned frame, stood peering out, and shaking its ears, of all things in the world, a live donkey! A mongoose hastily scuttled down to the vaults of another charnel house on our approach. At the door of a third lay some porcupine quills ; and a fourth, levelled with the earth, bore high, in fruit and foliage, our old friend the custard-apple. Vanity of vanities, sayeth the preacher, all is vanity !

Hence Beejapoor is the biggest ghost of past times in the Deccan. Even during its palmy days, say of Tara or Afzulkhan, the dead were more carefully looked after than the living. Every man had his coffin, so to speak, in his own cupboard, and of course there was a skeleton in every house. The only trade for a century seems to have been building mausoleums, and the only commerce carrying stones to them. You can scarcely move without breaking your shins against a gravestone. The moral of Beejapoor seems to be that men had better look after their own reputation during their lives, and leave nothing to posterity, for posterity has done nothing for them but rifle their tombs and scatter their ashes to the winds of heaven, though they did everything in their power to prevent this consummation.

DOVES

Seem to affect mosques all over the East : witness the mosque of Omar ; and you remember the sacred pigeons of Mecca, which have been noticed by every traveller from Vertomannus to Burton. Burckhardt tells us (1814) that nobody dares to kill them, and that they are called the sacred pigeons of Beitullah, the house of God, and another (1503) that they are believed to be the progeny of the dove that spake in the ear of Mahommed in the likeness of the Holy Ghost. Witness also the two white doves on the body of Hassan at the Mohurrum. Here in Beejapoor, as in Mecca, or for that matter before the Bombay Custom House, a man comes daily with food for the pigeons. I watched these white messengers descending from the sky on Christmas Day, our only visitors—emblems of its peace and purity.

There is no smoke in Beejapoor to soil their wings. See Cromwell's favourite Psalm of David:—

> " Like doves ye shall appear,
> Whose wings with silver and with gold,
> Whose feathers cover'd are."

And the

> " Though ye have lain among the pots "

by way of emphasis.

The sky here is very blue and transparent, and throws the outlines of fretted cornice and graceful minaret in sharply-cut and delicate relief.

The doves alighted with noiseless foot on the great flat pavement that spreads out in one stony sheet between the Mosque and Mausoleum of Ibrahim. As they stood between the living and the dead, on that space where thousands of worshippers had once bent the knee with their faces to the west, invoking the one God and the one Prophet, they seemed to read a lesson of peace and good-will to men.

The voice of war is now hushed over all India. Long may it be so! The doves of the Ibrahim Roza have come here for generations, and will doubtless do so for generations to come. There was one day, however, you may be sure, they did not come. That day was the 15th October, 1686, when Aurungzeb amid the hurly-burly of war stumbled from his scarlet-curtained palanquin, and, drunk with the lust of ambition, piled his bloody garments in the Sanctuary of the Roza.

SHEEP AND DOGS.

Why do black sheep eat more than white ones in India? Because there are more of them. The conundrum is attributed to Archbishop Whately. Very much the case on the way to Beejapoor, where black sheep abound. There are some sheep dogs too. Marvellously like the

Scots colley; and they look quite as astute and sagacious.

> "His breast was white, his touzy back
> Weel clad in coat o' glossy black."

This is his sitting portrait, with his tongue out of his mouth, palpitating, with his eye on, and much exercised about, his flock, more touzy than himself. He slinks away, however, on our approach, with his tail between his legs, and in this fails miserably as the counterpart of Burn's next two lines on the "Twa Dogs:"

> "His gaucie tail, wi upward curl,
> Hung ower his hurdies wi a swirl.

Culture, however, will do much for dogs and men. In the far north a minister was descanting on some dreadful boat accident in India wherein 400 coolies had perished. The word is little known in these regions; and a shepherd's wife in the evening commented with her husband on the dismal tragedy to the dog world, when sheep dogs were five pounds a piece, or when there was no market for them, as "naebody would buy a bad ane, and naebody would sell a gude ane."

Husband loquitur: "Whare would sae mony colleys be ganging tae, dae ye think, Janet?"

Wife's reply: "I ken nae place. Aiblins it was to a Falkirk Tryst"—which, we mention for

57

the benefit of the uninitiated foreign reader, is the greatest sheep fair that is held in Scotland.

FAMINE.

No one, in travelling from Sholapoor to Beejapoor, could believe that this country so lately as three years ago was so mercilessly struck down by famine. You can see nothing of it, everything seemed gay and prosperous. Jowaree and other crops are abundant until within a dozen miles of Beejapoor, when the country partakes of the character of the English downs. Not "all in the downs we lay" of Blackey'd Susan, but good golfing ground, if the likeness to the St. Andrew's Links does not deceive us. Some of the men seemed to want filling up between the ribs sadly, but no doubt this year's crop will supply the deficiency.

We saw one man, but only one, a relic of the famine days, and apparently beyond all remeid a veritable death-and-Doctor Hornbook business :—

> "Its stature seemed lang Scotch ells twa,
> The queerest shape that e'er I saw,
> For feint a wame it had ava ;
> And then its shanks,
> They were as thin, as sharp and sma
> As cheeks o' branks."

THE COUNTRY ABOUT BEEJAPOOR

Far from being a desert, seems capable of extended cultivation, and in its palmy days, with its garden-houses of the nobility, must have been a mass of greenery. The surrounding country, covered with coarse grass, presents a brown and tame appearance; so the city itself must have been seen from afar, a green emerald, like Damascus. There is plenty of water, from wells and otherwise, and in ancient times, like the Damascus of to-day, it ran down the sides of every street, for an aqueduct conveyed water for twenty miles. The Adansonia-trees are African, and of enormous girth; and we allude to them because if they are weighted with a thousand years, they point to remote times, when the Hubshee made his first appearance in the Deccan.* The big dome has been painted white, by whom we know not; but the colour at some distance, and even near at hand, detracts from its bulk, and it is only when the side next the spectator is thrown in shadow that its great size is realised. St. Peter's looks brown from the sea, the tombs of the Kaliphs at Cairo are as grey as the desert, and all other domes, east and west, are either gilded or painted black. Viewed from a distance of twenty miles,

* Goruk Imlee, *Adansonia.* These enormous trees are pointed out, under which the malefactors were beheaded. William Taylor of Patna when here was in search of big trees, and ought to have seen these. They are stumpy, but in girth and consisting of only one trunk must beat anything out of California.

the sense of colour is lost, and it cleaves the horizon without a single object to compete with it, in the view, either natural or artificial, a great hemisphere on the skyline.

GLOBE-TROTTERS.

The first globe-trotter who came to Western India was Tom Coryat. Taylor, the Water-poet, thus eulogises him, and perhaps gives us the germs of the word :

> " Let poets write their best and trotters run,
> They ne'er shall write or run as thou hast done."

The time will arrive when a number of men and women from Europe and America, *blasé* with Greece and the Nile, will come to Beejapoor. The big dome and the Kailas of Ellora will take their places as the two great wonders of Western India. There will be a railway-station there, and the telegraphic wires will bisect the citadel as they do the ruins of Baalbek. We shall no doubt, in due time, hear much that is novel and interesting about Beejapoor. It behoves our Government to see that no so-called improvement mars the antique grandeur and simplicity of these exquisite monuments of antiquity, and that in our zeal for their restoration, we do not accelerate their decay, or the decay of that which is most noble and beautiful (we will not say venerable with Mackintosh's words before us) about them. Time is a ruthless destroyer, but not half so ruthless as that zeal which under the pretence of repair effects only to destroy, and we must beware of this kind of renovation and see that the iconoclasts do not proceed from ourselves.* The greatest living authority on architecture has declared that these buildings are worthy of all the care we can bestow upon their preservation. Our first great duty is therefore to protect them from ourselves, and our second from the hands of our neighbour.

There are pieces of sculpture in the Roza of Ibrahim which we venture to say, as sculptured ornaments throughout the world, are unique, and if destroyed or taken away, to use a mild word, could never be replaced. We mean the stone chains, the links of which, cut out of one block, dangle from the cornice and hang gracefully between each arch. They are thirty or forty feet overhead and far beyond ordinary reach, but they are not beyond the avarice and ingenuity of the

* The last Rajah of Satara, in whose kingdom Beejapoor was, when on a visit amused himself with picking out the gilding, arabesque, and lacquered work with the point of his sword. It is said that the Bombay Government have already spent £80,000 on repairs and preservation, so we cannot be accused of want of interest in Beejapoor.

stone collector, who could soon devise ways and means to attain them. We all know what has been done in this way in Upper Egypt. For preservation, therefore, and in view of an influx of sight-seers, we would recommend the discontinuance of the Roza as a hostelry. The Dome of Mahmood and the Mosque and Mausoleum of Ibrahim Roza, in fact, require each a keeper to watch these buildings, so that travellers may be taken over them, as they are in the Mosque of Omar, or any of the great sight buildings in the world.

The student who may now find his way from Western India to any of the Universities of Europe need not be ashamed of his country. It is a great country, and great in its memorials of ancient times. What India has given to Europe is at present an unknown quantity. In race and language, in physics and metaphysics, in religion—and this is a very unknown quantity, and possibly very small—in commerce and trade, in astronomy and medicine, in the arts and sciences, philosophers continue to investigate and grope their way.

One day it is found that Sanskrit is the basis of all European languages; another that the germs of the feudal system exist in the village community in India; and an American has just made out that India built Palmyra, Tyre, and Alexandria, and that the world is indebted to her for the discovery of America. Columbus was only thinking of India and the way thither when his vessels were driven against the New World. If the student is taunted with the statement that India exported in ancient times only apes and peacocks, he can smite his enemies hip and thigh by telling them that the first iron,* the first silk, and the first cotton came to Europe from India; that it was the frankincense of India that was burned on the altars of Rome, Athens, and Jerusalem; that before Sir Christopher Wren, the architect of St. Paul's, was born, Mahmood had hung in the air a dome, with a larger area than that of the Pantheon at Rome; that when Catholics were being burned at Smithfield and Protestants at Goa, Christians were tolerated at Nuldroog and Raichore, and received firmans

* The supply of iron in India, as early as the fourth and fifth centuries, seems to have been unlimited. In the temples of Orissa iron was used in large masses, as beams or girders in roof work in the thirteenth century, and India well repaid any advantages which she may have derived from the early civilised communities of the West if she were the first to supply them with iron and steel.—*Sir John Hawkshaw's opening address, British Association meeting, Bristol*, 1875. The authenticity of the Book of Ezekiel has never been impeached, and "bright iron and steel" are mentioned by him as items in his great display of ancient oriental commerce.

which still exist from the Sultans of Beejapoor; and that courtesy itself is indigenous to India and sprang unaided by either the chivalry or the Crusades of Europe. Truly, as the poet hath it, the pathway of human progress has been from the East.

> "Westward the course of Empire takes its way:
> The first four acts already past,
> A fifth shall close the drama with the day;
> TIME'S NOBLEST OFFSPRING IS ITS LAST."

THE MARTYRS OF TANNA.

CHAPTER XVIII.

THE MARTYRS OF TANNA.

In or about the year of our Lord 1321 four men suffered death for their religion at Tanna. As the Reformation did not take place for one hundred and twenty years after this, Roman Catholics and Protestants may be supposed to have an equal interest in the event. We are indebted for an account of it to Orderic, a Franciscan friar who arrived in Tanna shortly after. Four minorites, whose names were Thomas of Tolentino, James of Padua, Peter of Siena, and Demetrius, a lay brother, were living in the house of a Nestorian, of which sect there were fifteen families in Tanna. On being brought before the Kazee, and questioned as to their belief, they stated that Christ was the very God, and one of them rashly replied that he believed Mahomet was the son of perdition, and was in hell with his father the devil. The end is easily foreseen. The people shouted out for their death. Tanna is a hot place, and they were first bound and exposed bare-headed (we all know what that means to a monk) in the sun from 9 till 3, the six hottest hours of the day. This had no effect. Then James of Padua was thrown twice into a fire. The result was the same. The ruler of the town then sent them away secretly to a suburb across the arm of the sea. This could not be far from that part where the railway bridge, from Salsette, now joins the mainland. But the Kazee persuaded the Melik or ruler to send men after them to kill them. Thomas, James, and Demetrius were beheaded. Peter, who had not been with the others, was next day tortured and cut asunder. On hearing of this massacre, the Emperor at Delhi, Gheias-ud-din Toghlak, sent for the Melik, and, upbraiding him for daring to inflict death on those whom God had twice preserved, ordered him to be executed.

It is very easy in this age of rosewater to say that they behaved imprudently, and courted martyrdom. The Great Moghul did not think so. The narrative is full of legend and miracle, but the air was dense with these articles of belief, and Thomas of Tolentino, if not a spectator, was certainly alive when the greatest wonder of the age is said to have taken place, to wit, the transmigration of the Holy House of Loretto from the shores of Palestine to very nearly his own door in 1294.

But divested of legend and superstition the facts remain the same. These Italian monks, to whom we owe the first seeds of the gospel in India* were the earliest Christian missionaries from Europe, of which we have any exact record. That the martyrdom took place, we think, there cannot be the shadow of a doubt. Orderic mentions some facts about Tanna, casually, which must have astounded the Europe gentlemen of the fourteenth century. That there were flying foxes—that the rats there were so big that the cats could not kill them,—that ants and other vermin were fed by the charitable, and that there did not appear to be a nail or a piece of iron fastening in their boats. " He that is faithful in that which is least is faithful also in much."

Their bodies were buried at Sopara, about four miles from Bassein, a place identified with the Ophir of Holy Scripture (and famous in 1882

* The vexed question of the Nestorians in India we leave out of sight for the present.

for the unearthing of some fine Buddhist relics) ; but, be that as it may, no gold-dust in the *Aurea Chersonesus*, was so precious to the early Christians. At the distance of 550 years we may well despair of presenting more than the flimsiest sketch of a voyage from Ormus to Tanna. It lasted 28 days—sailing by day and coming to anchor in some creek or harbour for the night. It was their way in those times, and dispensed with observations during the night and gave a clear outlook for reefs and pirates. The custom still lingers in the bandar boat cruise now-a-days. Their longest stretch was from Diu to Damaon across the Gulf of Cambay. At length Danu, Tarapur, Deravi, Versova, and Mahim were passed—giving a wide berth to the fishing stakes. On leaving Versova the tall palmyras on the ridge of Walkeshwur came in view on the verge of the horizon. And so working the "Jehaz" round its columnar cliffs fretted by the everlasting surf they made their way into the greatest harbour of Western India. The buggalow which brought these missionaries from Ormus was driven in by a storm. The places visible to the eye on leaving the open sea we shall endeavour to describe by their old names, as they first heave themselves in sight on the page of history. *Khenry Island,* well wooded; *Walkeshwur* covered with rocks, woods, and long grass amid which were almost smothered the Hindoo sanctuary, and tank of the same name with a temple to the triform god at the very extremity. The *Yoni* or famous stone of Regeneration on the water edge. The two Colabas, mother and daughter, though the sea rushed violently between them, seemed perfectly united, and on *Dewa Dandee,* we will place a beacon light, "impugn it whoso list." Along the ridge of these islands there grew a thin green line of palms. But palms were everywhere from *Cape Bombaim* to the site of the city destined to arise here, covering it, and the ground far beyond it in one continued forest ending in the great woods of *Mahim.* Somewhere hereabouts, we may be sure, appeared (say on the site of the Crawford Market) the proverbial fisherman, and the bittern standing on one leg amid his empire of desolation. There were two islands with strange names, *Deva Devi,* the "isle of the gods," and *Chinal Tikri* (Cross-island), the "hill of the harlots." Between them lay a third—one of the wonders of the world—*Garapooree,* or the "town of excavations," conspicuous by its black colossal elephant and stone horse, and more famous for its caves, so full of idols and of graven images, that it might have been well called by Christian, Jew, or Saracen the " hill of devils."

So sailing on, but now in quieter water, between *Trombay* with its Neat's Tongue and Peer's Tomb on the left, and on the right *Kurnala,* that mighty pillar of basalt which has been for all ages a landmark to the sailor making this port of India, they reach Tanna.

If they entered the harbour from the Arabian Sea on a starry night between April and September, they would see over the high land of Thull, a little above the horizon, the " Southern Cross," the symbol of their faith, and a welcome harbinger to this land of heathendom.

Tanna was visited by Marco Polo about forty years previously. The Tanna of to-day does not seem to be a pleasant place. In the early days of the monsoon when the tide is out and at sun down, with rain falling, the view from the railway bridge is one of the dismallest a man can cast eyes on. Of the young civilian, often sent there on his first outset, we may write—

> "The sun's eye had a sickly glare,
> The earth with age was wan,
> The skeletons of nations were
> Around that lonely man."

We cannot rebuild or repeople in our imagination the Tanna of Marco Polo, but we may be certain of this, however, that though the town was a very different place, the topographical surroundings are still the same, and in this respect Tanna was seen by Marco Polo and these early missionaries very much as we see it to-day. A creek, fringed with cactus and palm, up which twice a day, the tide rushes with remarkable velocity, converting its dry and rocky bed into the dimensions of a navigable river, the creek widening out gradually into an estuary, now the harbour of Bombay, and beyond—the illimitable sea,—for the flapping of the great sails of Cabral and Da Gama's fleets was as yet unheard on the Indian Ocean.

The land side was bounded by a barrier of rugged mountains clothed with teak and iron wood over which could be descried the sharp saw-like edges and peaks of the Chanda and Bhowmalang range and the untrodden solitudes of Matheran.

Not far off was Dewah, a scene that has been taken by many painters and found its way to the Royal Academy. Now-a-days, this scene of surpassing beauty bursts upon the eye of the traveller as he emerges from the first tunnel which pierces the mainland of India, one of the magical reaches of this Indian Bosporus which clasps in its arms the islands of Bombay and Salsette,

> " Whose gleaming with the setting sun
> One burnish'd sheet of living gold,
> And islands that empurpled bright,
> Floated amid the livelier light,
> Crags, mounds, and knolls confusedly hurl'd,
> The fragments of an earlier world."

Of the manner of life of these missionaries we know nothing, but we know a good deal about those among whom they laboured. Velvet weavers, buckram weavers, weavers of *Tanna cloths*, vendors of betelnut, artificers of blackwood, leather manufacturers, noisy horse coupers from Arabia, with wild pirates and lawless fishermen (for in those days there was great shipping at Tanna) a brawling, shouting, seething multitude, every man of them Muslim or idolator. Such was the hostile population amid whose lot was cast the protomartyrs of Christianity in Western India. It is sad to believe that when the Portuguese took Tanna 200 years afterwards there was not a single Christian in it.

NOTE ON THE GOLD OF OPHIR.

But we must now deal with the gold of Ophir which has cropped up in this article. We have a great respect for gold either as ore, bullion, or coin, it does not matter much, and if we can only bring it nearer to Bombay so much the better. We may add that as silver depreciates in value this respect increases all the more, and we will, therefore, endeavour to speak of gold with becoming reverence. Ophir is mentioned in Genesis X, 29, and since that time he has had a troubled existence ; like the dove from Noah's ark finding no rest for the sole of its foot. In our young days Niebuhr placed Ophir in Arabia. It was soon after removed by somebody across the Arabian Sea to Sofala in Africa. After a consumptive existence in Africa, it died out and suddenly under the giant auspices of Max Müller the lusty child reappears on the banks of the Indus at a place called Patalene, and Sir Charles Napier, if we remember rightly, when living in Clifton (Kurrachee) amused himself in the belief that the golden cup of Alexander (Ophir no doubt) lay hidden in the Gedrosian sands thereabouts. This belief again was rudely dispelled by the German critic Lassen who "conclusively demonstrated" that the Ophir of Job and Solomon was in Guzerat. The *réghur*, or black cotton soil of Guzerat, is rather an awkward matrix for gold ; but never mind. It is satisfactory so far, our readers will observe, that Ophir is in the right direction, and coming nearer to us, step by step on the golden ladder. We have mentioned its arrival near Bassein; and the arguments for its localisation here are neither so flimsy nor so unsubstantial as at first sight may be imagined.

Sopara is near Bassein. It is mentioned by Ptolemy and the author of the Periplus. Ophir is spelled in the Septuagint *Sophir*, and Josephus says Ophir is in the *Aurea Chersonesus* which belongs to India. Now, where is there another Chersonesus on this side of India except the Bombay group of islands? From Sopara comes Sophir—*Ophir*. But our readers must make their own deductions. Dr. Wilson used playfully to remark that the Scotch were Scythians and were in India ages ago. Had not the letters *Scyt* been deciphered on the dolmens of Upper India? *Scyt, Scoot Scot.* "So runs the dread anathema." We turn up with fear and trembling Smith's Classical Dictionary, the highest authority we can lay hands on, and under the head *Scythœ* is this sentence which we confess seems to prove the Doctor's theory correct, and is a damning argument against the non-Scythian hypothesis. "The Scythians had no fixed habitations, but roamed over a vast tract of country at their pleasure." This decides the question. Of course, the Scotch are Scythians. Then as to Ophir.

Men like to deal in generalities and will never come to particulars. Arabia, Africa, Sind, Guzerat are fine names, in which it is exceedingly easy for Max Müller and others to place the Land of Ophir, words

> "Full of sound and fury
> Signifying nothing,"

making of it a geographical expression pure and simple. It is a great matter, therefore, to have Ophir, once for all, localised, identified ; moored to one place the latitude and longitude of which can be easily determined. * * * * We had written thus far when an uneasy feeling takes possession of us. After having fixed Ophir on as solid a basis as this terraqueous globe affords, in an evil hour we glanced at the newspapers where some preposterous individual, we had used a stronger word, writes to a Glasgow paper (of all places in the world) that Wynaad is the Land of Ophir.

This is really too much. We cannot afford to have gold passing us in this way. Gold has always been a welcome guest in Bombay. Norman Macleod dubbed us "worshippers of fire and of fine gold." We therefore protest against it. Take our apes and our peacocks, and, even our algum trees, but give us our gold. It is too bad. If this continues, Bassein may become an Irish quaking bog and run away with us. Ophir may drift away from its moorings, and leave us like Pogson at Madras, just in time from our garret window to see it clear our line of vision—a comet of the first magnitude.

We have done all we can to establish Ophir in our neighbourhood. But some men will not believe it. Though we sympathise with their incredulity we say to all such unbelievers what Waller addressed to the Lord Protector of England—

"To dig for wealth, we weary not our limbs,
Gold though the heaviest metal hither swims,
Ours is the harvest which the Indians mow,
We plough the deep and reap what others sow."

THE HON'BLE E. I. COMPANY'S FIRST SHROFF IN GUJARAT.

CHAPTER XIX.

THE HON'BLE E. I. COMPANY'S FIRST SHROFF IN GUJARAT.

TRAWADI SHRI KRISHNA ARJUNJI NATHJI OF SURAT.

TO THE EDITOR OF THE "BOMBAY GAZETTE."

SIR,—I have read with much interest the lively sketch given in your paper of Saturday last (3rd Sept. 1881) regarding Napoleon Bonaparte at Suez in 1798. In the last but one para. of the sketch the writer, while giving an account of the Forbes's loans, challenges inquiry as to whether any native prince or merchant of those days did, or offered to do, what Sir Charles Forbes did. I am not aware of any native prince, of that period, having rendered pecuniary assistance to the Company in the shape of loans; but there is one native banker of the time who was once well-known all over Gujarat and India as the Hon'ble Company's shroff. He financed for the Company on a scale of magnitude which surprised even the Agents of the Company themselves. Unfortunately the monetary transactions of the Company before the 30th June, 1813, when public loans began, find no place in the published records of the period. I do not therefore wonder that, in the absence of such published testimony, it should be supposed that the Company received no loans from native merchants, and that the rupee loans actually began with Sir Charles Forbes. I have, however, seen copies of letters and certificates from the Hon'ble Company's Agents of the time to this well-known banking firm of Surat, which show that long before Sir Charles Forbes's relations with the Company began, the Company supplied its financial needs through the banking house of Trawadi Shri Krishna Arjunji Nathji. The memory of this house as the Company's principal shroffs in those days still lives in Surat and Gujarat. While, therefore, fully sharing in the credit given to the eminent English banker whose name is still a household word in

Bombay, it is fit, I think, that the services of this native firm, rendered as they were at a time when the different European Powers were competing with each other for power and pelf in the East, and which laid the foundation of England's present magnificent Indian Empire, should not be permitted to be altogether consigned to oblivion. The first recorded acknowledgment of the Company's obligations to this native banking house bears, I find, the date of the 23rd November, 1759. It is signed by Mr. John Spencer, Chief of Surat, and four of his Assistants, and runs as follows:—"These are to certify that the house of Trawadi was employed in transacting the money matters at Delhi relative to the procuring for the English a firman for the castle and a sanad for the fleet, in which they acted with great punctuality and fidelity. This writing is therefore given them as testimony of their good behaviour, and to show that the house is deserving of the countenance of the Hon'ble Company in case of any oppression to them." This testimony is confirmed by another from Mr. R. H. Boddam, who writes under date the 4th December, 1783, as below:—"I do hereby declare that since my residence here as Chief of Surat, Trawadi Arjunji

Nathji has always shown great attention and diligence for the interests of the Hon'ble East India Company, and has, by the transactions of his house as shroff, rendered them every assistance and service in his power, which at various times have been very essential." Sir Charles Forbes's transactions with the East India Company were indeed on a very large—I should say, considering the character of the period—stupendous scale, but they did not, it seems to me, begin before the seat of Government was removed from Surat to Bombay, and the trade of India was thrown open to private enterprise. But before and even after Bombay became the seat of Government and private European enterprise found scope to develop itself, the Hon'ble Company had found that its business on its hands had overgrown its legitimate limits ; and what with the advances to native weavers and others on the one hand, and the prosecution of wars with native rulers and European rivals on the other, the demands for monetary assistance pressed too hard upon the Company. And the records of the Company's Office at Surat would appear to bear ample testimony to the fact of Trawadi Arjunji Nathji's rupee loans often proving the turning point in the Company's fortunes, when the prospects of raising money elsewhere seemed quite remote.

Trawadi Shri Krishna Arjunji Nathji was a Nagar Brahman by caste. Originally coming from Benares, his ancestors settled in Surat for purposes of business. In Shri Krishna's time the house was known by the name and style of Trawadi Arjunji Nathji. Before coming into close relations with the Hon'ble Company, the dealings of the house were chiefly with the Arab merchants who arrived in Surat for interchange of goods. The fame of Surat had then extended far and wide. Neibuhr, who visited the city in 1762, describes it "as the storehouse of the most precious productions of Hindustan. Hither is brought from the interior parts of the Empire an immense quantity of goods, which the merchants carry in their ships to the Arabic Gulf, the coast of Malabar, the coast of Coromandel, and even to China. The provinces near the city are full of manufactures of all sorts." Trawadi Arjunji Nathji was about this time reputed to be one of the richest bankers in Gujarat. Much of his wealth was made in course of his dealings with the Arabs. He curtailed these dealings as his relations with the Hon'ble Company became closer and closer. In 1804 the Company was at war with Holkar. Holkar sought the protection of the Chief of Bhurtpore. In the following year war broke out between Bhurtpore and the English. We know the result. The troops under Lord Lake were victorious. But how came the victory to be won? The Company was sorely pinched for money. Jonathan Duncan, in his letters to the Company's Agents at Surat described in pitiful terms the condition of the troops, who were left in arrears, and reduced to misery for want of supplies. Native bankers, seeing the fortunes of the Company trembling in the balance, shrunk back from lending money at a time when it was most needed. Jonathan Duncan, knowing where successfully to apply for loans, wrote to the Chief Agent at Surat to open negotiations with Trawadi Arjunji Nathji. Trawadi consented to make an advance, and a sum of 32 lakhs of rupees was counted out in hard coin. Trawadi's house was situated in Balaji's Chukla in Surat, and the story goes that carts loaded with rupee bags extended in long, continuous rows from Balaji's Chukla to the Nausari

Gate. The joy and thankfulness of the Company on obtaining this loan may be easily conceived. The Government of India were not more surprised by the amount of the loan than by the feelings of fidelity and attachment to their cause which dictated it. Trawadi's services were acknowledged by them with khiluts, medals, and grants, and recorded in handsome terms in minutes for the information of the Company's Directors in England. Trawadi, it is said, was made a member of the Council at Calcutta,—what this means I cannot say,—and officially proclaimed as the Company's Shroff in India.

A little before this the Gaekwar was suffering from pecuniary embarrassments. The pay of his Arab Sebundies had been in arrears for many years. They had sat *dharna*. The Gaekwar himself was deprived of his liberty, and his life was in imminent danger. In these circumstances he applied to the Hon'ble East India Company for help. The Company thought proper to afford him the needed aid, and thereby restore quiet at Baroda. The first step towards this was of course to pay off the Arab Sebundies. How was this to be done? This was the question of questions. The Company had no funds to spare. Jonathan

Duncan earnestly requested Trawadi Arjunji Nathji to advance three lakhs of rupees to the Gaekwar. Trawadi hesitated. At the same time he did not like to displease Jonathan Duncan, who pressed him strongly to make the advance. Trawadi demanded British guarantee to secure repayment of the loan, and on this being accorded the loan was made, and the Gaekwar saved from a very critical and embarrassing position. In recognition of this and other valuable services, the Hon'ble Company procured for Trawadi a hereditary and permanent grant from the Gaekwar, of the village of Shewni, in the pergunna of Timba under the Surat Attavisi Mahals.

On the death of Jonathan Duncan, the Government of India recommended Trawadi Arjunji Nathji to the countenance and favour of the Bombay Government. In a letter dated the 31st July, 1812, the Indian Government pointed out that "although the merit of Arjunji Nathji's fidelity and attachment to the British Government is too well-known to render any letter of recommendation necessary, yet the Governor-General is induced to grant this indulgence as well for the purpose of gratifying his earnest wishes, as in compliance with the custom which has been observed when similar applications have been made on former occasions. In compliance with his solicitations, therefore, I am directed to furnish Arjunji Nathji with this letter to your address, and to desire that you will convey to the Hon'ble the Governor the Right Hon'ble the Governor-General's recommendation of Arjunji Nathji to his countenance and favour."

In 1813 war broke out with Nepal, and Arjunji Nathji supplied funds necessary to prosecute it. What the amount of advances he made to Government was is not stated; but it is a fact that on the successful termination of the war, the Government bestowed upon Trawadi a khilut "for the joy of the capture of Nepal," Mr. Secretary Prendergast recording the following approbation of his services :—"I have no hesitation in saying that the records of the Chief Office bear numerous and very decided testimony of the merit and services of Trawadi, and proofs of his fidelity and attachment to the interests of the Hon'ble Company." In Surat Trawadi built the temple of Shri Balaji, at a cost of three lakhs of rupees, and endowed it with the revenues of the village of Shewni, which had been granted to him in perpetuity by the Gaekwar. Trawadi died in 1822, at the age of 72 years. It is sad to reflect that the descendants of one who was at one time the Rothschild of India are starving at the present day in Surat.—Yours truly,

JEVERILAL U. YAJNIK.

Bombay, Sept. 6, 1881.

JAMES FORBES.

CHAPTER XX.

JAMES FORBES.

In the records of Bombay James Forbes holds a high place. He was an Englishman by birth and breeding, of Scotch descent, and was not related to the Bombay merchants who founded about 1780 the greatest house of its day in India. Sir Charles Forbes, the head of this firm for forty years, was born in 1773. James Forbes was born in 1749, came out to India in 1765 in the Civil Service, returned finally to England in 1784, and died 1st August, 1819. The orthodox pronunciation of this name, we believe, is *Forbés* with an accent on the second syllable. Forbes is pronounced thus by the natives, and so it was by Sir Walter Scott. James Forbes left an only daughter, who married a French Count, and by this marriage came Forbes's grandson, Charles Forbes René Montalambert, the celebrated French statesman, otherwise known as Count

Montalambert, author of the *Monks of the West*, and who died 14th March, 1870.

HIS BOOK

Was first published in four volumes quarto *for the author*, and must have been a most expensive one for him to bring out—quite a *livre de luxe*, we should think—in 1812. We learn, however, that it was very popular. It is observable that he did not publish it until 28 years after he had left Bombay, when he was 62 years of age. So he did not "rush into print," but matured his thoughts, bottling them up like old wine. These *Oriental Memoirs* he dedicated to Sir Charles Warre Malet, whose name is familiar to our readers as Resident in Poona at the Court of the Peshwa during the last decade of the last century. Malet had been the friend of Forbes in his youth, and his companion on several excursions they made together in Western India.*

Forbes and his wife, while travelling on the

* MALET.—Forbes was a great admirer of Malet, and not without reason, as the extracts from Malet's letters and journals which he gives us are conclusive that he was a man of uncommon powers and force of character. Malet married in India Susannah, daughter of James Wales, the artist from Peterhead, who died in Salsette, and is buried, we believe, at Tanna. Their son, Sir Alexander Malet, once well-known in diplomatic circles on the Continent, and an author, still lives, we believe. He married Miss Spalding of the Holm in Galloway, Lord Brougham's step-daughter; and their son, Sir Edward Malet, now Consul-General in Egypt, maintains the hereditary talent of this family, and its connection with the East to the third generation.

Continent during the French war in 1803, were imprisoned at Verdun, but released in 1804. The Royal Society and Sir Joseph Banks interested themselves in his behalf by writing to the National Institute of France. M. Carnot was then President, and Baron Cuvier Secretary, and the grounds of his release were that he was a man of science engaged in the preparation of this great work. From Forbes's own letter we learn that the materials from which he projected its publication consisted of 50 folio volumes comprising 52,000 pages of manuscript letters and drawings by himself and other people. The book is beautifully illustrated with 93 large pictures. The originals of the engravings were drawn by himself, for Forbes was a good sketcher. There are coloured drawings of such specimens of the Bombay animal and vegetable world as were then little known in Europe.

There are three views of Bombay, which are extremely valuable, as they exhibit to us the appearance of the Bombay of his time. One is from the sea, taken in 1773, another from Malabar Hill in 1771, and a third of Bombay Green in 1768. This last is a line engraving by the elder Heath, who was a master in the art. The view is taken from the roof of the Custom House, where Forbes then lived, and the look-out in these days was straight across, without interruption, to the Cathedral and the Old Secretariat in Apollo Street, being then the Government House. The carriage of His Excellency Governor Hodges, drawn by four horses and preceded by a dozen horn-blowers and bandoreen, is a conspicuous object in this picture.

The palanquins are light and airy-looking, being open at the sides, and not the closed coffin-like structures of our day. We observe an Englishman taking his constitutional on the Bombay Green, shaded from the sun by a punkah something after the fashion of the Byculla Club ones, or rather a banner screen perched upon a long pole, which the bearer behind him elevates or depresses as is necessary.

All the houses fronting the sea view are low, for the obvious reason, we suppose, that they would not challenge attack by an enemy in the harbour. Hence the old Court House and Secretariat—and we call them by the names they are known by in 1882—bulk big and stand out conspicuous on the skyline. These buildings, we need not say, are to-day completely obscured from the point of view where the artist has drawn his picture by the numerous buildings which have since cropped up between them and the sea. Bombay Castle from the sea (as becometh in 1773) is one frowning continuous line of bastion and curtain, perforated with loopholes out of which peer the iron arbiters of fate. None of those hideous monstrosities in the shape of barns and cock-lofts have yet dared to show themselves above vault and casemate, and offer a tempting shot to the invader. Why they ever should have done so, we are at a loss to conceive, as there seems plenty of room for them elsewhere. Let us cry—

> "Latium be Latium still! Let Alba reign,
> And Rome's immortal majesty remain!"

One thing, however, has come down to us for which we ought to be thankful. It used to be said that Nature has done much for the Bombay Harbour, and man very little.

Our readers must have often observed a very tall palm-tree in the neighbourhood of the Custom House, towering aloft above all its fellows. A similar tree stands out boldly in Forbes's view of Bombay from the sea. We are told that a palm-tree lives only a hundred years. Be it so; we are willing to believe that this one is an exception to the rule, and, untouched by either cyclone or decay, still vindicates its title as a land mark to those on land or on sea, near at hand or far away. Altogether, this is a spirited picture, the Union Jack where it is to-day, and a pennon streaming gaily in the breeze from a tall flagstaff on the Royal bastion of Bombay.

ARRIVAL IN BOMBAY.

When Forbes came out to Bombay, he had not a single friend in it, nor a letter of introduction. A gentleman who came out with him took him to call at a house, which, from the description of its collonade, flight of stairs, and its overlooking the sea, seems to have been the old Court House in Apollo Street. His host "took him by the hand," and, he tells us, "did not let it go for forty years." He gave him what money he needed, and he says all his success in life was due to this man. Who he was we know not. We know that he became Chairman of the East India Company, bought an estate in Hertfordshire, and lived until he was eighty.

Before young Forbes was introduced to him he had married a widow with two children, none of whom had ever been in England. The boy and girl grew up, and had a most romantic history. Governor Hornby married the young lady, and they had a large family, one of whom possibly signs a lease—Jane Hornby—of the aforesaid building for twenty-one years to the East India Company for a Court House. This was in 1807, and the witnesses are Patrick Hadow and William Crawford.

During Forbes's time there was a great nuisance in Bombay, to wit, divination and astrology. Governor Hodges had petted a Brahmin sorcerer to such an extent that he consulted him about everything. He had prophesied many years before that he would be Governor, but that a black cloud was before him. Hodges took ill, and was recommended to try the hot baths at Desgaum, and had reached Fort Victoria at Bankote. "Freits follow them that fear them," says the Scot's proverb, so necromancy and Hodges travelled in company. According to the Hindu calendar, the 22nd February, 1771, was an unlucky night, so he would not go out that evening and take the air. "This is going to be a critical night for me," said he. Superstition makes short work with sick men; and next morning he was found sitting up in his bed with his finger on his lip—dead. The secret was not on his lips, for everybody knew it. He was brought into Bombay, and buried in that Church which is now our Cathedral. Forbes seems half a believer in the second sight, and recites several cases of events coming to pass that had been all known and talked about years before in Bombay. The Brahmin was thus a power in the State.

William Hornby seems to have had a harder head. Nevertheless, during the thirteen years he was Governor of Bombay, his life must have been rendered somewhat miserable by this pertinacious and unscrupulous Brahmin. Hornby had sent his wife and mother-in-law, the widow aforesaid, home to England; but before going the latter, at all events, had become the victim of the Brahmin's delusions, and it is our opinion that the Brahmin half-killed the daughter and killed the mother outright. The spectacle of the mother walking on the sands of Back Bay, looking out wistfully for the ship which was to bring her son from his education in England, and being reconnoitred by the Brahmin, who told her she would never see him, is as strange as anything that has ever been offered in the history of demonology and witchcraft. Whenever any consolation was offered to these miserable wretches, the only reply was, "Oh, the Brahmin, the Brahmin!"

This is what happens when people barter

away the providence of God for the miserable delusions of witchcraft. The keys of the invisible world are in safe keeping. When any man or woman arrogated to himself or herself the possession of them, the authorities sentenced the man or woman to be publicly whipped at the door of our Cathedral.* This was done, and sometimes with good effect. But it was a very different matter with the victims.

WAYS AND MEANS.

When Forbes arrived in Bombay, his salary was Rs. 30 a month, with house accommodation. For some time he had a hard time of it, occasionally going supperless to bed, and reading Shakespeare by moonlight on the Custom House roof for want of a candle. Duke Humphrey and the Parish Lanthorn were thus often his only companions.

The Civil Servants in these days often com-

---

* WITCHCRAFT IN BOMBAY.—The records of the Court of Judicature show that an ignorant woman, named Bastok, was more than once whipped for what were called "diabolical practices." Like many Europeans of past days in India, this unfortunate creature had imbibed native superstitions, and professed to cure sick persons by the use of charmed rice. Convicted of this offence on the 5th of July, 1724, she was admitted by the Court to have been guilty of witchcraft not from evil intention, but from ignorance. So they enlightened her dark mind in this wise:—The Court orders "that she receive eleven lashes at the church door, and after, she and all persons that are guilty of the like do such penance in the church as is customary."—*Bombay Quarterly Review*, Vol. 2.

plained, but the Company bluntly replied that they might go and get work elsewhere, reminding them that they had some secret advantages. "We wish to God that this were true," say they. The reference here was to the facility of trading. But this facility to nine men out of ten turned out a facility of ruining themselves. Forbes was luckier than most of his contemporaries, for out of the seventeen young Civilians who came out with him, he was the only one who returned to England, the remaining sixteen having gone over to the majority. But even among those who stood the climate, and older men, he was exceptionally fortunate. When Forbes was coming home, he looked in at Goa and found Crommelin there, who had joined the service in 1732. Here he was, at the age of 80, filling the subordinate post of Resident at Goa, though he had been Governor of Bombay twenty years previously. Richard Bourchier, who was Governor when Clive was in Bombay, and gave him a wigging, died pennyless. How Forbes made his money he does not tell us, on the principle, we suppose, of—

> "Aye keep something to yoursel
> Ye dinna tell to ony."

It, however, oozes out. If he had liked he

might have joined one of the Agency Houses, which was perfectly allowable up to 1804, and by which he need not have forfeited a single privilege of the Civil Service. But he did not do so.

He mentions the medium price of cotton when he was at Broach as Rs. 70 to Rs. 80 per candy, equal in these days to £8 to £9, and that it was shipped only to Bengal and China. He adds by the way, "*I had generally large commissions annually to purchase cotton at Baroche for the Bombay merchants.* One of the principal frauds of the cotton dealers was exposing the cotton, spread out, on cowdung floors, to the nightly dews. I often paid an unexpected morning visit to at least a hundred of these small cotton merchants. Like Gideon's fleece spread upon the floor, with an honest dealer the cotton was perfectly dry ; if in the hands of a rogue, you might, like him, wring out a bowl full of water."

Wet or dry, however, Gideon's fleece was a golden fleece ; at all events, the lad who went supperless and candleless to bed was, at the age of 35, master of the situation. What he paid for his passage home he does not tell us ; but in the same ship one gentleman gave 5,000 guineas for the accommodation of himself, wife, and family, and another paid £1,000 for himself and wife.

HIS LIBRARY.

Though he left Bombay at an early age, he never ceased to be a Bombay man. All his feelings, ideas, and interests seem to centre in it. Of Fryer in the seventeenth century he has a profound reverence, which is little to be wondered at, as it is a kind of Bombay Bible, which you shall take up again and again, and always find some new thing. Like Fryer and Dr. Wilson, Forbes was a member of the Royal Society. He had a small library, and delighted much in poetry.

Pope, Goldsmith, Addison, Thomson his favourite bard, Beattie, Akenside, Prior, Mason, and Falconer were all at his fingers' ends, and he quotes largely from them. He found Homer in India, to an extent that would astonish Professor Macmillan. But the book of which he found the most illustrations in India was the Bible, and there is no end to his quotations of manners and customs under this head. Sometimes they are very happy: as, for example, when an English lady was reading of Rebekah carrying her pitcher on her shoulder, a native female observed, " Madame, that lady must have been highcaste."

JAMES FORBES AND THE LADIES OF BOMBAY.

Our author was not insensible to female beauty, or the healthful society of virtuous women; for without being a ladies' man, he was never happier than when he was among a bevy of his countrywomen. In those immortal pictures of his, drawn by his own hand, we can see the types of the Bombay beauties of the time, with hair brushed back from the forehead and towering overhead *à la Pompadour,* reclining here, or seated there, in an Indian wilderness, at a table laden with viands, toast and sentiment going round, say under the shadow of the big banyan-tree on the Nerbudda. We can see him with his sister on the slopes of Malabar Hill, drinking in that view of Bombay and its islands which has delighted so many generations. But, indeed, wherever we espy his coat of cerulean blue we may be sure that a saffron China silk dress or a coal-scuttle bonnet is not far distant. He feelingly bewails the sad havoc which old Sol makes among the roses. "The climate," he says, " is generally unfavourable to the roses of my fair country-women in Iudia, where the blushing flower of love soon decays, and the jonquil subdues the snowy tints of the lily," an allegory, the solution of which we leave to our younger readers.

He speaks of the fair and sprightly nymphs of St. Helena, and the sable beauties of Bankote, with antelope eyes, jetty hair, and garments like the drapery of Grecian statues. Above all, he speaks of Eliza, " a lady with whom I had the pleasure of being acquainted at Bombay, whose refined tastes and elegant accomplishments require no encomium from my pen."

Brave words these from a witness of such a character, though Eliza, at the age of 35, had long since ended her pilgrimage. Probably more sinned against than sinning, this verse may be read by all who cast a stone at her:

> "Herself from morn to eve, from eve to morn,
> Her own abhorrence and as much thy scorn;
> The gracious smile unlimited and free
> Shall fall on her, when Heaven denies it thee." *

There is a tendency now-a-days to magnify the present at the expense of the past:—The

---

* ELIZA'S APPEARANCE AND ACCOMPLISHMENTS.—She had an oval face, and an appearance of artless innocence, a transparent complexion, brilliant eyes, and a melodious voice, with an intelligent countenance and engaging manners. Her conversational and epistolatory powers were considerable. She played the piano and the guitar.—*Bombay Quarterly Review.*

Bombay men of a hundred years ago were very much like ourselves. It is very easy to invest James Forbes with the ridiculous. A long waisted coat, knee-breeches, a queue hanging down at the back of his neck, a three-cornered beaver, and a habit of quoting scripture, and at Stanmore Hill his pet sarus walking behind him like a cassowary. Nevertheless he is

> "An honest man close buttoned to the chin:
> Broad-cloth without and a warm heart within."

We need not be frightened to look into the Bombay of Eliza's period. Here is his account; he is speaking of acts of charity and benevolence. "And here, with all the milder virtues belonging to their sex, my amiable country-women are entitled to their full share of applause. This is no fulsome panegyric; it is a tribute of affection and truth to those worthy characters with whom I so long associated, and will be confirmed by all who have resided in India."

In Sonapore burying-ground and over the dust of several of the fair contemporaries of Eliza are inscribed these unsophisticated words :—

> "From her pleasing person and manners she was much esteemed by all who had the pleasure of her aquaintance"—

Words which we do not deem "tinsel trash,"

but which we are prepared to accept as a last and a just tribute on the part of the survivors to the merits of our country-women in Bombay a hundred years ago.

DIANA AND THE COBRA.

The following is in the best style of our illustrious author. We have heard many people attempt to tell the story, but it is generally bungled :—"Whether our hortensial snakes were evil genii or guardian angels, I shall not determine. Haraby, the head-gardener, considered them as the latter, and paid them religious veneration. On that account I never disturbed them until I had erected a cold bath in an orange and lemon-grove for an English lady, who retired thither at sunrise with her sable nymphs to enjoy one of the greatest luxuries of the torrid zone. This bath, perfectly concealed from view, was more useful than ornamental, and very unlike the lake of Diana or any of the modern hummums in oriental cities. It was, indeed, little more than a humble shed, thatched with the leaves of the palmyra, and though as sacred to chastity as the Speculum Dianæ or the gardens of Susanna, it neither attracted an Acteon, nor an elder of Babylon. It certainly did attract another visitor equally unexpected and disagreeable, for one morning the young lady, in the state of Musidora, was alarmed by a rustling among the palmyra leaves which covered the bath; and looking up beheld one of the garden genii, with brilliant eyes under the expanded hood of a large cobra de capello pushing through the thatch and ready to dart on the fountain. Pure and unadorned as Eve when her reflected beauties first met her eye, the lady and her handmaids made a precipitate retreat through the grove and gained her chamber, heedless of gazers, whether in the form of gardeners, snakes, or monkeys."

THE EXECUTION OF GASSI RAM.

On a former page when speaking of Rajmachee we gave Grant Duff's account of this event, and an intelligent Poona correspondent, in the *Gazette*, added some particulars which have come down by tradition. The account which we give in a foot-note is by Sir Charles Malet, who was resident in Poona at the time—1791. It is more circumstantial than either that of the Historian of the Mahrattas, or the account of the Poona correspondent. It differs from them in several important particulars, but may be regarded, we think, as the more correct version, as Malet was living in Poona at the time, and familiar, no doubt, with all the circumstances of the great tragedy.*

NATURAL HISTORY OF BOMBAY.

"I looked without seeing," said Lord Chesterfield, but the remark could not be applied to

---

* GASSI RAM.—Communicated to me by Sir Charles Malet, as a most extraordinary event which happened during his embassy, at the Mahratta Court, in 1791. On the 29th of August thirty-four men of the caste of Telinga Brahmins having been confined in a chokey or close room by the officers of the cutwal, the head magistrate of police at Poona, twenty-one were taken out dead next morning, and the remaining thirteen were with difficulty restored to life. In the evening the popular clamour became violent against the cutwal, who was a Gour Brahmin, named Gaunseram, a native of Aurungabad, and whose office in a city where the most rigorous police is established, necessarily rendered him an obnoxious character. The Peshwa, improperly yielding to the furious mob, delivered up the cutwal, who was tied backwards on an elephant, and in that manner conveyed to a prison without the town, amidst the scoffs and insults of the populace, while guards were sent to seize his family, dependants, and property. The day following the clamour grew more violent, being encouraged by many persons desirous of mortifying the ruling minister, through the ignominy of his cutwal, his dependant. The unhappy man was tied backwards on a camel, and in that disgraceful manner reconducted into the city amidst the reproaches of the people. Here he was made to alight, and his head having been publicly shaved, he was again placed in the same manner on the camel, and having been carried through the principal streets of Poona, escorted by a strong guard, he was for the last time led to a spot about a mile from the city, and there ordered to dismount. One of his hands was then strongly fastened to the end of a turban between twenty and thirty feet long, and the other end committed to some Hallalcores, the lowest outcastes of the Hindu tribes, who contaminate all other castes by their touch. It was then made known to the Telinga Brahmins that the cutwal was delivered up entirely to their disposal, either as a sacrifice to their vengeance, or an object for their mercy: on which twelve Brahmins of that tribe in the most savage manner immediately attacked the fallen magistrate with large stones. The Hallalcores who held the turban by straitening it kept him at full length running in a circle, pursued by his relentless murderers, who at length by repeated blows on the head and breast brought him to the ground: and then with an eagerness disgraceful to humanity, though merciful to the prostrate object of their cruelty, the Brahminical murderers dispatched him by a succession of large stones thrown violently on his head and breast.

Forbes, for he was a close observer. The earth, the air, and the sea were full of the wonders of the Lord. He dilates on the *fauna* and *feræ* of Bombay with delight, not such small deer as jackals, squirrels, hedgehogs, bandicoots, and musk rats, but he opens with the alligator, fierce as the crocodile of the Nile. There is a sense of disappointment, as in that chapter we have seen somewhere on "Snakes in Iceland," when we read further on, that this brute is seldom seen on the Island. What would he have said had he lived to the day when a tiger was slaughtered in Mahim woods? Malet, who was a great sportsman and writes shikar *con amore*, supplies him with an account of his famous lion hunt in Cambay, and he observes that the ibex or wild goat of India is met with on the Raj Pepli hills.

Flowers are a perfect passion with him, and insects a craze. There are beautifully coloured pictures of the tailor-bird, the bottle-nested sparrow, and the praying mantis. As the legend goes (the scene may have been at Tanna), Xavier, seeing one, requested it to repeat a canticle, which it did! *Mantis religiosa!* The consumption of bullion by whiteants turns out, as we expected, a delusion. The bottom of a treasure-chest was eaten away, the rupees sinking and disappearing in the soft earth by their sheer weight, much to the consternation of the Revenue Collector and Cutcherry Shroff.

Strange to say, neither he nor any other naturalist that we know of notices the golden beetle of Elephanta, sometimes caught as far off as Matheran.

Forbes confounded the Pythagoreans at Baroda, by showing them a drop of water in a microscope, and a view of the animals they swallowed every day of their lives.

In this he anticipated Dr. Wilson's exhibition, fifty years later in Guzerat. The Doctor was more fortunate, as Mr. Forbes's microscope was broken to pieces as being a kind of *Athanasius contra mundum*. Forbes was not a sportsman, though he often went out with parties. He took his book with him, verified the bag, and did not waste gunpowder. He was better employed looking after the commissariat and making the midday meal a success. It was then he would astonish his friends with a young sucking boar roasted in spices and Madeira wine, to whet their appetites and give them a *bonne bouche*, after which his health was, no doubt, drunk all round with all the honours, following which, as in the

Surat week of 1781, the English ladies amused themselves by running races on elephants.

NOTABLE THINGS.

Forbes was attached to the army of Ragobah (Rugonath Row), and if he had written nothing else, his book deserves to be remembered for his account of it: 100,000 men and followers, 200,000 cattle, an immense city or camp moving from place to place and eating up every green thing—all trades and professions in it, from goldsmiths to dancing-girls, realising the fabulous armies of Cambyses, Xerxes, and others.

His time represents the first point of contact of the English with the Mahratta Governments, and the condition of the people is laid bare with an unsparing hand. In these times men concealed wealth as they did murder. Every boy over fourteen was armed, and when you sent for butter and eggs, the peasant brought them with a drawn scimitar.

It had been the aim of the English, when they came to Bombay, to put down cruel and bloody rites, and he tells us with gratification that to his knowledge no woman had burned herself in Bombay for fifty years, "nor do I believe this species of suicide has been allowed since the English possessed it;" and he adds this commentary

—"within six months 150 women, within thirty miles of Calcutta, have sacrificed themselves."

In reference to the suppression of infanticide, "thousands of happy mothers in all succeeding ages, while caressing their infant daughters, will bless the name of Duncan."

He predicts that the introduction of infantry and artillery into the Mahratta armies will be their ruin.

The English in Bombay held slaves, but their lot was very different to their African brethren in the West Indies. Here they were sometimes confidential servants, and their hardest task-masters were the Portuguese. When down the coast he bought for Rs. 20 a boy and a girl as a present for an English lady in Bombay.

Of Forbes it may be said—

"'Twas thine with daring wing and eagle eye to pierce Antiquity's profoundest gloom," so he deals largely in pictorial representations and descriptions of Elephanta, &c. Bombay without Elephanta would be Egypt without the Pyramids.

He lavishes pen and pencil also on the Kanheri Caves, and the less known ones at Mhar resuscitated by Burgess.

At Ahmedabad he is in an ecstasy, and has handed us down the only picture that exists of the Shaking Minarets, more wonderful than the Leaning Towers of Pisa.

Everybody has been at Sarkej, six miles from Ahmedabad, but everybody does not know Sarkej is a facsimile of the great Temple of Mecca.

This, however, can easily be verified by a reference to Carsten Niebuhr's *Arabie*, where there is an engraving of the latter. Some of our musical readers will be able to judge of Forbes's ear for music from the following. As he excepts English melodies, we presume he intends the remark as a compliment to Scotland and the adjacent island.

"Many of the Hindoo melodies possess the plaintive simplicity of the Scotch and Irish; and others, a wild originality pleasing beyond description."

"Early rising, the cold bath, a morning walk, temperate meals, an evening ride, and retiring soon to rest, are the best rules for preserving life in India." So he found them, and lived to the age of seventy.

THE ORIENTAL MEMOIRS.

It is now seventy years since the last sentence of the *Oriental Memoirs* was penned, and the book continues to be prized by all men and women who take an intelligent interest in the history of Bombay. But in truth the reading of it is an oriental reverie, and were it not for its great size it would have more readers. Forbes must have known the difficulty of grappling with a thick quarto in the heat of India. Why did he not then suit the specific gravity of his book to the physical capacity of his probable readers? At the best, man in India is an inert animal, and these big books instead of being a feast of reason and a flow of soul are very much of the latter. Nevertheless he has made these eighteen years, 1766-84, all his own. No man shall usurp dominion over him during this portion of time. Crommelin and Hodges are forgotten, but Forbes is remembered. He was not an old fogy in Bombay, as he left it at the age of 35. His flabby face and double chin may provoke comment; but taking him all in all, we can say to ourselves what Burns said of another—

> "If honest worth to heaven rise
> Ye'll mend, or ye win near him."

THE APOSTLE.

Layman as he was, he holds a place in the history of evangelisation in Western India. Before Chaplain Gray, the friend of Burns and the tutor of his children, died at Bhooj (1830), and half a century before Dr. Wilson landed in India, this veiled prophet, Yacoob Forbes, was scattering the seeds of what Bhau Dajee called the religion of the Prince of Peace and Love, among dusky people under the palm and the banyan-tree. He did not leave his religion at the Cape and find a new one in the wilds of Guzerat. No residence alone for years among people worshipping strange gods cajoled him out of his ancient faith, or made him indifferent to the truths of his holy religion. An admirable man. By no means proud or arrogant, for he who was the friend of Horne Bishop of Norwich and had been the guest at Daylesford of Warren Hastings, did not disdain to receive the consolations of religion at the death-bed of, and from the lips of, a domestic servant, and he was not ashamed to put it in print that he had done so.

He was, he tells us, four years without (and he did not undervalue them) religious services. Religious services! His banyan-tree

> "So like a temple did it seem that there
> A pious heart's first impulse would be prayer;

And of his chamber at Dhuboy might be said—

> "This is the gate of God, by it
> The just shall enter in:
> Thee will I praise, for thou me heard'st,
> And hast my safety been!"

So every new experience and deliverance was

to him an Ebenezer, and he had, like most men in India, some wonderful escapes. He has left us the picture of a cobra, painted by himself. He had, while doing so, been handling it familiarly, believing its fangs had been extracted. Next morning it sprang at the throat of a native woman, and she died in half an hour. When Dhuboy was handed over to the Mahrattas, he left it an hour sooner than he had intended.

His followers on the road coming after him were attacked by a body of 300 Gracias, who demanded the Sahib, killing a cavalry officer and his Parsee butler, and wounding many others. Had he been an hour later he would have been caught in the vortex. So every new abode was to Forbes a Bethel or temple of the living God.

> " Where'er they seek thee, thou art found,
> And every place is hallowed ground."

HIS ATTACHMENT TO BOMBAY.

It is strange how life in India warps itself insensibly round the lives and habits of men. The man who asked after dinner, in Portsmouth, for the road to the Apollo Bunder was drunk. But the Duke of Wellington was perfectly sober to the end of his life, when he preferred the charpoy or camp-bed, with which his early Indian career had made him familiar, to the four-posters or masses of Elizabethan upholstery. And so, in like manner, when all that this world holds was fading away from the eyes of Sir Charles Napier, the hero of Meeanee, the windows of a square apartment in England were opened to the four winds of heaven, so that he might realise the old Indian bungalow. His son-in-law laid the British flag on him; and all was over.

But each in his own way. One man decks his abode at home with the trophies of the Indian chase; another fills his library with the black-wood of Bombay; and a third surrounds his drawing-room with Deccan scenes, or sunny views of Matheran in some grey metropolis of the North. Even a sailor has been known to take home with him an Indian crow. In the wilds of Perthshire there remains the ruins of an Indian bungalow. The mouldering rooms are not now as they stood "near eighty years ago."

The story goes that its owner was much imbued with life in Western India, that nothing would satisfy him but broad verandahs, venetians, and all that sort of thing. We need not tell our readers that in Scotland, in November, the end of these things is death.

The doctor was sent for to the nearest country town, and found our Anglo-Indian after *chota-hazri*, with his teeth chattering, under a mosquito curtain, and the wind off Ben Macdhui howling around his charpoy. The man was saved by the skin of his teeth, but his will was not broken. His friends advised him to leave at once for Occidental India and take his Portuguese boy with him, which he did, to spend the remainder of his days there.

HOME.

Few men who have spent a considerable portion of their life in India leave it without regret of some kind or other. It was so with James Forbes. With him the best view of Bombay was not from the deck of the outgoing ship. A crowd of associations rushed upon him, and he tried to console himself with the fact that the Bombay which he had known in his early days was not the Bombay of 1784. But he was very glad to get home. He ordered supper, but like people, as we have heard, who receive news of a great or sudden acquisition of fortune, he could not eat. Then he went to bed and could not sleep a wink, the greenest land on earth, and its hawthorn hedges, was too much for him. When he left Bombay he took a good slice of it with him, we do not mean in the matter of loaves and fishes, though in this he was well enough. But Stanmore Hill and its surroundings, where he settled down, must have looked for all the world like a bit cut out of Bombay or Guzerat.

The love of Bombay with James Forbes amounted to a ruling passion, and he did all he could to foster it by the writing and publication of these bulky Memoirs. Dhuboy, near Baroda, where he spent so many years, haunted him pleasantly to his dying day ; and no wonder, for it seems a bonnie place, and often in his day dreams, in the glades of merrie England, he would hear the old Indian sounds, the bray of the camel, the Moslem call to prayer from the minaret, or the plaintive refrain of women grinding at the mill, coming as a distant lullaby from the land that was afar off. By night, amid the silence of the Stanmore woods, the nightingale awakened him, but it was only to hear the warblings of the bulbul among the palm groves on Cumballa Hill ; and by day when he was seated in his conservatory in a mimic jungle of babul or camel thorn, the blackbird hopping among his gooseberry bushes, was to him only a *misa*—with yellow legs—and nothing more.

As Livingstone wrote in 1869:

> "I shall look into your faces,
> And listen to what you say,
> And be often very near you
> When you think I'm far away."

So was Forbes at home to the men and things he had left behind him in Western India.

It was in these grounds that he erected an octagon building, which eight groups of sculpture adorned; these he brought from the Gate of Diamonds at Dhuboy. It was situated on the margin of a lake covered profusely with the *nymphea lotus*, to remind him of the tanks of Guzerat. In his conservatory he beheld the tamarind, custardapple, cotton, ginger, turmeric, and coffee-plants. There he gathered ripe guavas from a tree entwined by the crimson ipomea and sacred tulsi. He did not succeed in producing fruit on the mango-tree, though this had been done by the Duke of Northumberland.

Even in that picture which was painted of him at the age of sixty-two and which Mrs. Oliphant tells us still hangs in the library of the Countess Montalambert in France, he is represented sitting under the shade of a banyan-tree, among

Trimurti and his Indian idols, the long hanging tendrils coming down and forming a kind of canopy over his head. India was all to him and he was nothing without India. So when he went home he took his pet sarus with him, as he, no doubt, took his hookah. Orme was his Gibbon, and for him Fryer was Herodotus, the father of Indian history. His two articles of belief were Bombay and the Bible. Out of the one he fashioned a competence for this world, and from the other he obtained an all-sufficiency for the world to come.

"Sought in one book his troubled mind to rest,
And rightly deemed the book of God the best."

SUPPLEMENTARY NOTE.

FORBES'S VIEW FROM MALABAR HILL.

It has been suggested to us, that this view has not been taken from Malabar Hill, properly so called, but from Cumballa Hill at a point near the bungalow occupied by Mr. Perosha M. Mehta, or where the road, as you ascend, turns off at a right angle. A friend has taken the trouble to verify all this, and we accept his interpretation with thanks. He remarks justly, that there is no place on the left of the road as you now ascend Malabar Hill, where a tank could be placed, and that the one in this view is the *Gowalla Tank*, and that the road between it and the spectator is the Cumballa Hill road. The position of the Tower of Silence in the picture corresponds with this point of view. The Malabar Hill road, as a carriage road, was not in existence in 1771, and what we call Cumballa Hill doubtless in these days came under the general name of Malabar Hill. All this may seem a very small matter, but it is not a small matter in the ancient topography of Bombay. The riddle is now solved, for the houses we see in the picture are not on Malabar Hill at all, and where, our readers will understand, there were no bungalows at this early period, but upon the margin of the Gowalla Tank.

"Tankerville," which he mentions, doubtless was one of them.

Another, to which he alludes, the "Retreat," stood upon the Breach Candy sea margin.

We hope that this construction of Forbes's picture will commend itself to all who find pleasure in the contemplation of it. It was done by his own hand, and deserves a little attention.

DR. WILSON.

CHAPTER XXI.

DR. WILSON.

India has not seen an abler or wiser friend and benefactor, or Christianity itself a more loving and judicious representative.—*Dr. Bhau Daji's speech in Town Hall,* 1869.

SEVEN years have passed away since the death of Dr. Wilson. That space has been crowded with stirring events, but they have not dimmed his memory. He now stands far away from us, like a lonely hill. The light is clearer on it after sunset, and its boundaries well defined. We can see that the shadows are softened, the inequalities smoothed down, and the mists having cleared away, the bulk, proportion, and contour lie before us. We cannot know him better or love him better, but we may correct our views or sober our judgment, and so command a better observation than when he was alive; for distance not only lends enchantment to the view, but sometimes contributes accuracy to the vision.

This intervening space has added nothing to his story; for not one item cropped up after Dr. Wilson's death that we did not know during his life. Had it been otherwise, the vultures of Biography would soon have been down upon him, and had he illused his wife or denied the faith, we would soon have heard of it.

But he was too transparent for this sort of thing; his character was like his own bungalow, *char durwaza cola,* open to the four winds of heaven. We may also look forward and form a kind of judgment how Time, that great arbiter, is likely to deal with him, and whether the reputation he earned during his life is going to be confirmed by posterity, or fade away like so many indistinct Indian reputations. We hear of jubilee missionary meetings at which his name is not mentioned, we see in the libraries dust lying thick on his book upon Caste, while his *magnum opus,* "The Lands of the Bible," has long ago been superseded by "Palestine Exploration."

But with Galileo we cry, *Il muove!*—still it moves. Labour so continuous and unflagging, and prosecuted with faculties unimpaired, from the day he read his first thesis to that in which his sun set

> " Not, as in northern lands, obscurely bright,
> But one unclouded blaze of living light,"

makes us believe that as he left his mark on the age in which he lived, so his works will follow him to future generations. There is one guarantee that Dr. Wilson's name will not readily perish. It is enshrined in the hearts of the people. Specially is it a heritage of the sons and daughters of our schools and colleges, who will not willingly let it die. It rests, therefore, on a sure foundation ; for he gave himself and all that he had to ameliorate the condition of the men and women of India. And in this respect he was unlike any one of the conspicuous men who have added to the renown of our Bombay commonwealth ; for the greatest of them all were birds of passage, here to-day, there to-morrow.

John Wilson was a monument of Scotch education. That system owes its origin to John Knox in the sixteenth century. It still exists in the School Board, modified to meet the wants of the age ; but there is nothing special about it to any age or country, for you may assert, without fear of contradiction, that it is the duty of the State to place education within the reach of all. He was gifted by nature with uncommon powers of memory, indeed it was averred by some that this was his strong forte, and that herein lay all the difference between him and other men, at all events a *sine qua non* for the linguist. But he had also uncommon powers of observation and apprehension. "I looked, but did not see," was not his motto; rather, like White of Selborne, the smallest fact did not escape his observation. To this was added intense powers of application, for he often sat up whole nights, until the spear-like shafts of the Eastern sun smote him at dawn of day. He took twice the work out of the twenty-four hours that did most men, and he soon out-distanced all competitors. And so he toiled on until on the long hill up to Mahableshwur which seems to have no ending, he met the presage that his work was done. It was in vain that Sir Bartle Frere came to him and asked him to accept from the Prince of Wales his deepest sympathy and regard.

He only uttered, "Vain is the help of man." Dean Swift says of somebody, "He had been a screen between me and death." That screen was now to be taken away.

His sermons by most men were considered

prolix; the heat and languour of the Indian climate make people intolerant of what would be not merely endurable, but delectable, in a northern latitude; but we can vouch from our own experience that his most public utterances—for example, his lectures on the Eastern Churches in the Music Hall of Edinburgh in 1844, his addresses as Moderator of the Free Church in 1870, and his prelections as Vice-Chancellor of the Bombay University, were spoken to attentive and crowded audiences, and that there was no weariness of the flesh while he poured forth in all their exuberance the richest stores of Eastern learning. His prayers were models of devotional propriety, couched in language full of Hebrew diction worthy of Carstairs and the days of old, a phraseology which now seems antique in these times of fervid Evangelicalism; and though he scorned the theology of Blair and Robertson, he had caught something of their stateliness, for he had sat at the feet of the men who were their friends or pupils. One of his professors had been tutor to a Scots nobleman, as he was wont to relate, and in his travels found himself at Lausanne. When there he called on Gibbon, and in conversation imprudently deplored the infidelity of the modern historians—which was, no doubt, true enough; but time and place for everything. Gibbon coloured, walked to his book-case, and throwing a volume on the table exclaimed, "Do you call that the work of an infidel?" It was Robertson's History of America.

It would be a lamentable exhibition of the little we had profited by the friendship with which Dr. Wilson honoured us, if we attempted any analysis, far less an estimate, of his scholarship and labours in the wide field of Oriental research. A jury empanelled from the most eminent Orientalists in Europe would alone suffice for the task. But we may be permitted to say, while skimming thus on the surface, that the gifts of one were the inheritance of many, and that he scattered broadcast on the earth, among his fellow-men of every race, the seeds which God and his own right arm had placed in his disposal. It was well known to Dr. Wilson's friends that shortly before his death he had expressed a desire to live. It was decreed otherwise, and he was quite resigned. But in truth there was much in his position to make life attractive to him. His books, his coins, his troops of friends, his correspondence, the view he had from his house, and, above all, the holy work in which he was engaged, with the many schemes incidental to it, left no idle moments.

Bombay was his home, and it is a mistake to imagine with the men of Edinburgh that Dr. Wilson was making a great sacrifice when he came out for the last time. The bitterness of expatriation, if he ever felt it, was all past when he first laid down his life and work for India; and he came out to end his days where he had spent the most of his life in congenial work. It is true he had his trials, but he bore them with fortitude and equanimity. His righteous soul must have been vexed from day to day by protégés who not only fell short of what he expected, but disappointed and absolutely cheated him, and converted his philanthropy in many instances into a barren conquest. The number of subjects unworthy of his charity and righteous designs was known only to himself, for no murmur escaped his lips. Sometimes, also, his motives were misinterpreted and his acts misunderstood, but he outlived them all. It was not without reason that his hand shook in his later years as if with incipient paralysis, for he passed through some fiery trials.

Two of his first wife's sisters were accidentally drowned, a third was buried at sea. His wife also died—a few years only in India,—his memoir of whom was a great favourite of the ladies of a past generation. And now came his crowning act of self-denial, when he gave up his State emoluments and withdrew from the Church of Scotland, casting himself on the bounty of the Scotch people. The deed of demission of the Free Church rang throughout Europe, forty years ago, but the sacrifice was greater, at all events the courage which dictated the sacrifice was greater, when men who were placed as Dr. Wilson was placed among races of alien religions threw away their means of subsistence. It might be supposed that having forfeited State support, he would forfeit the friendship of the Governors of India. But he did not do so, for Governor after Governor and Viceroy after Viceroy paid him court, and he was seen at midnight in the autumn of 1857 walking unprotected through streets suspected of hatching rebellion, when all men were quaking, except perhaps Lord Elphinstone, Forjet, and himself, in the blank amazement of a great fear. And thus it was when any treasonable document required to be deciphered, when a new heir was wanted to the *gaddee* in Baroda or an Abyssinian expedition projected, Dr. Wilson was called in by Government, for even Sir Robert Napier found something to interest him about Magdala ere he dreamed that this "awful mouthful of a word," as he expressed it in after years would become the badge of his distinguished name. We cannot suppose that any man in our generation will take up the position of Dr. Wilson. It was unique in its duration, and unique in this—that he had piled up a great heap of multifarious knowledge on Western India subjects such as probably few men will ever do again. This knowledge he did not keep for himself, but scattered wherever and whenever opportunity offered; and his intellectual capital was in ready money. To every question of "Do you know?" he had but one answer, "Yes." And forth came the gushing well-spring to refresh the thirsty soul. That the man who on three several occasions, delivering his blows one after the other in quick succession, brought down his sledge-hammer on Hinduism, Mahommedanism, and Zoroastrianism should have made friends among and been courted by the leading representatives of them all, is the most brilliant spectacle that has ever been offered to the world of the missionary in heathen lands. And it is a lesson that need never grow old, for grace, human and divine, is always worth the possessing; and he was endowed with both to a very large extent.

To many people who did not know him, or knew him but little, Dr. Wilson appeared a bundle of contradictions. To one he was garrulous, to another taciturn, to another he talked of big friends and acquaintances. He was a minister of religion, and yet he refused to be called "the Reverend." He was a voluntary in practice, but in theory for a Church established by law. He liked a good "hard psalm," but he was very fond of Sir Robert Grant's hymns, which all Bombay men are glad to see have found a place in Palmer's Book of Praise. He managed to pull well with his own denomination, though, perhaps, an exception may be found to this, as also with other denominations of Christians; and it is sometimes more difficult to do this than to take common ground of action in philanthropic schemes with the disciples of the old creeds of India. He asked the Bishop of Bombay to join the Bible Society, which the Bishop declined to do. But he wrote him on his death-bed a letter which leaves nothing to be desired, and still sheds its fragrance over the grave of this good man as he sleeps under the shadow of the great Rock of Weem. As a student he had seen Sir

Walter Scott walking, or rather limping, on the streets of Edinburgh, yet he cared nothing for the Waverley Novels.

Of course, everybody knew that he abjured instrumental music in church, and thought a sermon ought to be at least half an hour in length. But it is not so well known, and will surprise many to learn, that Dr. Wilson was a man of humour. He had not the *bonhomie* of Norman Macleod nor the incisive wit and satirical jest of Archdeacon Jeffreys, who was a kind of Bombay Sydney Smith, though he delighted to relate the latter's brusque reply to the lady who asked if there was any choice of climate in this Presidency. "Yes," said he, "you may be stewed in Bombay, or grilled in the Deccan." There's a stane in my fit, my lord"* tickled, we had almost said put many a

---

THERE'S A STANE IN MY FIT, MY LORD.

* Jemmy, a half-witted body, had long harboured a dislike to the steward on the property, which he paid off in the following manner :—Lord Lauderdale and Sir Anthony used to take him out shooting; and one day Lord Maitland (he was then) on having to cross the Leader said, "Now, Jemmy, you will carry me through the water"—which Jemmy duly did. Bowmaker, Lord Lauderdale's steward, who was shooting with them, said, "Now, Jemmy, you must carry *me* over." "Vera weel," said Jemmy. He took the steward on his back, and when he had carried him half way across the river he dropped him quietly into the water.—DEAN RAMSAY.

The other story was that Jemmy, with his lordship on his back, halted in the middle of the stream and pulling up his leg, "There's a stane," &c. His lordship offered him a six-pence if Jemmy would land him on the opposite bank. "Na," said Jemmy, "the factor has given me a half-crown to let ye doon in the water."

mess in a roar twenty years before the first edition of Dean Ramsay saw the light, and as it hails from Lauder, is, no doubt, the Doctor's own story. But as he got older he became more chary of his best, and even his old friend, Colonel Day, could not extort from him more than one *recherché* tit-bit of Robin Gray, Malcolm's *protégé*, and whilom Police Magistrate of Bombay. He sometimes tickled his audience in the Town Hall with a touch of sly humour, as, for instance, speaking in succession to Mr. (now Sir William) Wedderburn, he alluded to his grandfather's career in Guzerat, and said he had a most exact knowledge of the science of finance and figures, men of this kind being a great desideratum just at present. It so happened the news had just arrived of some arithmetical miscalculation in Budget or other returns not uncommon in Calcutta, adding, as it were, the "year of our Lord" to the pounds column*; and the remark was received with great laughter.

John Smith, of Smith, Fleming and Co., accompanied him in 1843 throughout his long

---

YEAR OF OUR LORD IN THE POUNDS COLUMN.

* A successful merchant in the north having at the end of the year entrusted his assistant to balance his books, was so overjoyed at the result when announced to him, that he summoned his friends and neighbours and held a gaudeamus in celebration thereof. Next morning he discovered that his profits had been swelled out by an error of £1860." My certe, &c. &c.

wanderings in the Sinai Peninsula and Syria, but one of his fastest friends, and one for whom he also entertained the greatest respect, was David M'Culloch. He was a man for whom John Connon had an unbounded admiration, and Sir Erskine Perry, addressing a jury, uttered this eulogium from the judgment seat, "We all know and respect David M'Culloch." David was the scion of a small, but ancient, estate which had been held in Galloway by the M'Cullochs of Ardwell for generations. Indeed, we believe that for a very short time before his death he was actually "laird" himself, though he never entered upon possession. He died in 1858, and was buried in the Scotch burying-ground, where his tomb may be seen to this day. He was very charitable; among other benefactions he gave Rs. 30,000 to the building fund of the Free Church, and being a bachelor and a man of means, had much money to dispose of in this way, and the will to do it.

Our readers will recollect a scene in the closing days of the poet Burns, and which is given by most of his biographers. The poet was then in low water in Dumfries, say in 1792, when M'Culloch, of Ardwell, who knew him well, recognised him sauntering on the shady side of

Queensberry-square, and rallied him to go and join the general throng on the other side of the street, who were then discussing a county ball to be given that evening in Dumfries. The poet repeated the verse of a ballad, a melancholy refrain, indicating that his dancing days were over. This friend of Burns was the father of David M'Culloch. David, in Bombay, lived what seems a gloomy and solitary life. He kept geese and canary birds, and was careless about his dress, and to his other eccentricities added the harmless one of taking one long walk in the year. The place was Tanna and back, and the day he chose for this was New Year's Day, the coolest time of our Bombay season.

It was on one of these excursions that Dr. and Mrs. Wilson met David in Tanna, and while there accompanied them to a silk manufactory, for which, in mediæval times, Tanna was so famous. While there Mrs. Wilson gently reminded Mr. M'Culloch, on looking over the silks, that he might profit by his opportunity and invest in a silk dress, which he could present to the lady highest in his estimation. David yielded—consented also to give up the latter half of his walk, and to accompany them in their carriage to Bombay. They saw nothing of David for several weeks, but one evening on coming in from their drive they observed a bulky parcel on the lobby table. It was addressed "To Mrs. Wilson, with D. M'Culloch's best compliments."

On another occasion the Doctor met David coming through the Bombay Green, carrying with him a small spade and a dead canary bird in a paper bag. In answer to the Doctor's inquiry as to where he was going, he told him he was going to dig a grave and bury his pet bird. Dr. Wilson must have smiled an incredulous smile, as David quickly added, "May be that wee bird will be the first to welcome me into Paradise." Dr. Wilson was early enough in India to know Gray, a missionary of the Church of England, buried at Bhooj, and we think he was content to finish that translation of the new Testament into Mahratta which Gray begun. Gray was no mean poet, for he is commemorated by Hogg in the "Queen's Wake."

He had been the friend of Burns and the tutor of his children, and his letters furnish the most valuable account we possess of Burns' family life while he dwelt in the three-storeyed house in Bank-street, Dumfries. By the time Wilson knew him Gray had worn away the vain asperities of youth, and Wilson has placed on record that he was not only a man of talent, but a good man. This is one link that connects Burns with India, but there are others which we may state without travelling much from our subject. The first statue, perhaps, that was ever erected of Burns is in the National Gallery of Edinburgh, and bears on its pedestal that the movement which ended in its erection was initiated by a group of Bombay merchants. A grandchild of the poet Burns lies buried at Kaladgi, and the wife of one of the poet's sons at Jhansi, facts recorded on the Burns' Mausoleum in Dumfries. It would be vain to cite any man in Western India so accomplished all round as Dr. Wilson. Other men may be found more skilled in special branches of knowledge, but none of such universal attainments. Men were attracted to him like steel filings to a magnet; but whatever the motive that brought them to his presence, each went his way, warmed and filled with the bread that does not perish in the using. He had no favourite race, and he rose to the height of his great vocation when he asserted that as regards aptitude of receiving information there was no difference between the Hindoo, the Parsee, and the Moslem; that all were the same in this respect, Aryan and non-Aryan, Jew and Greek, bond or free. Though he was among the first to cast in his lot with the Free Church, he considered it no part of his duty to anathematise the State Churches of Great Britain, and though he was not called upon to enter the vexed sea of politics, the British name and authority in India had no more ardent, enlightened, or judicious supporter than Dr. Wilson.

When Lord Mayo laid the foundation-stone of the University, the Governor of the day, Sir Seymour Fitzgerald, uttered these words: "There is a name on that stone, that of John Wilson. That name will endure long after all memory of my transitory dominion has passed away"—words which reflect as much honour on the speaker as they do upon the subject of his eulogium. We have spoken of his versatility. To one friend he would discourse on the Arsacidae, and show him on the Parthian coin the effigy of the man who defeated Crassus; to another he would talk of the botany of Arabia, and assert that it had made little or no progress since Forskal's time; to a third, the leading physician of the day, who in describing the ailment of a common friend had hazarded the remark that he could proceed no further without using technical language, "You need not fear," said the white Brahmin.

"I spent two years at the medical classes." A snake would be killed; the name and qualities were soon forthcoming; and this would give occasion for him to dilate on the wonderful concentric rings in the skeleton, to be produced by boiling it down (destroy the chatty afterwards). And he added, "Some of the aborigines would consider this a *bonne bouche*."

Or David Livingstone would drop in. "Were I ten years younger I would go with you to Africa and see the Fountains of the Sun." And he would have done it, for he was a great and an unwearying pedestrian,

> "From Ahmed's Moslem fanes and regal bowers,
> To towns far distant on Konkan shores."

But he had drunk of another fountain. The day he received a letter from him by the hands of Stanley was a memorable one. Five years had passed away. And it was a picture to see the old man reading over the faded manuscript, written on thick foolscap with a reed, in which he denounced some of the Nassick boys as committing every crime under heaven. "Remember me to dear Mrs. Wilson," he faltered out, the tears dropping from his eyes. Mrs. Wilson had been dead for years.

It has been said that Dr. Wilson had no imagination. The first Mrs. Wilson had. She was a woman whose nerves were finely strung, and sometimes burst into song, and her gifted son, Andrew Wilson, inherited all her genius in this respect. He it was who ten years ago wrote the "Songs after Sunset":

> "Again the scene shifts. Ten years hence I see
> A city grand and pleasant to the eye,
> Bombay, as it will doubtless one day be
> Freed from caste prejudice and rivalry;
> Broad roads to view, and noble buildings fair,
> Green shaded walks beneath umbrageous trees,
> With fountains playing 'neath the sunny blue,
> Tempered and softened by a cool sea-breeze."

Dr. Wilson lived more than forty years in India. "Can a European live as long here as at home?" "Yes," he would reply, and after a pause: "I would advise him to go out of Bombay two months every year." And so he generally contrived to do, and in early life hardened his frame by pedestrian excursions and seasons of innocent relaxation. He was always a welcome guest, and he never could have obtained the reputation he had in Bombay, even, with all his gifts, unless he had had a most winning and gracious presence. He had wonderful tact in adapting himself to the age, sex, or position of a chance companion. It was all the same, Viceroy or the last arrival beginning a Governmental or mercantile career.

Though imbued as few other men have been with the dignity and responsibility of his office, he was able to extract such materials as lightened for himself and others the burden and heat of the day, and cheered them on in the journey of life. He served God with his mirth as much as some men do by their sadness. It was averred that his auditors required to be good listeners or they felt a sense of weariness, but that was their affair, and possibly due to the lateness of the hour, or the heat of the climate, neither of which tended much to allay the vigour of his spirits. There is a tradition founded on fact that Lord Magdalla actually fell asleep all unobserved by his guest who sat beside him, and to the great amusement of the party, who were much profited and instructed by the largeness of the discourse. He lived in Spartan simplicity, never drove in anything but a one-horse shigram, and a bottle of cold tea was his meridian. Not that he abjured drink; when he returned from the ovation given to him in the Town Hall by the Governor and his fellow-citizens, he drank of the wine that maketh glad the heart of man, and rose like a giant refreshed. Not without a touch of gay humour was Sir Seymour Fitzgerald's remark, looking at the figure of Wilson, whose coat had been exquisitely cut in bas relief on the silver salver presented to him. "Tell him," said he, "with my compliments, that Terry has made the best coat I ever saw him wear." That message, we need scarcely add, was not delivered.

He was very proud of his membership of the Royal Society. Consciously or unconsciously he wrote for posterity, and, like Mackintosh and Mountstuart Elphinstone, from habits of deep thought and close observation, and making it his study to note dates and references with accuracy, his works will ever reward the student of India's religions and history.

His memory remained intact. A day or two before he died a friend repeated the line—

> They also serve who stand and wait;

and added, "Cowper?" "Milton—on his blindness," was the quick reply. And he could be solemn enough on occasion. One racked by pain and fever, and half demented, told him that for three days and nights he had been so bad that he could neither read his Bible nor say his prayers. "HE knows that," pointing with his finger to the sky.

It must be remembered that, his attainments and the rewards which accompanied them, however lofty in themselves and worthy of human ambition, did not bring Dr. Wilson to India. They were means to an end. That end was the salvation of India, a word much abused in recent times. It was no word with a vague meaning to Dr. Wilson. The salvation of India meant to him security of life and property to the natives thereof in this world, and the hope of an immortality in the next. What had Dr. Wilson to do with life and property in India? some may say. We reply that the effort of his life was to complete the work commenced and carried on by Duncan and Walker for the abolition of infanticide. Had that nothing to do with the preservation of life? And everything he wrote was in the interest of good government, which, if it means anything at all, means protection, to life and property.

What he began, he strove to complete, for he could not rest contented until the coin was deciphered, the flower classified, or the word harked back to its parent root. But some things he finished, and some things he could not finish; and as the end drew near he bewailed that his performances had borne such a feeble proportion to the magnitude of his conceptions. Had John Wilson lived a hundred years it would have been all the same. There would still be absurdities in men and things to demolish, something to add to his book on Caste, or some new conquest to effect in the wide field he had mapped out for himself. He would still be getting himself stung by bees in the Konkan, or poring over the rocks of Girnar, or dipping into Joseph's well for another lost Bible, or holding confabulations over the mysteries of religion with a new generation of Jejeebhoys or Sassoons, or interrogating another Rabbi Duncan at Pesth, until Duncan was forced to exclaim with Bathsheba that half even of the wisdom of this modern Solomon had not been told him.

But not until the rocks of Petra and Asoka had yielded up to him their last lithographic secret, not until John Knox's great ideal was realised in India, not until the gospel had been preached to every creature, would he have seen of the travail of his soul and been satisfied. For him there was always something to do or suffer, or something to complete, even on that day when he bid adieu for the last time to that fair scene from the Cliff, over which the eye of the missionary and philanthropist had so often wandered, those boundless fields consecrated to him for evermore.

BOMBAY DIRECTORY—1792.

CHAPTER XXII.

BOMBAY DIRECTORY—1792.

THE HONORABLE MAYOR'S COURT.

The Worshipful P. C. Bruce, Esq., Mayor.

ALDERMEN.

Alex. Adamson, Esq., Senior Alderman.

Robert Kitson, Esq.
John Forbes, Esq.
James Tate, Esq.
James Tod, Esq.
John De Panthieu, Esq.
George Stevenson, Esq.
Charles Elphinstone, Esq.

George Simson, *Sheriff*.
Philip Samuel Maisler, *Registrar*.
Augustus William Handley, *Examiner*.
Henry Fawcett, *Accountant General*.

ATTORNIES.

Henry Forrester Constable.
William Paddock.
William White.
Bryt. Brooksbank.
James Anderson.
Phinehas Hall.
Stephen Cassan.
Edward Popham.
William Ashburner.

THE HONORABLE COURT OF APPEALS.

Major General Robert Abercomby.

George Dick, Esq.
Daniel Crokatt, Esq.
William Lewis, Esq.
John Morris, Registrar.

INSURANCE SOCIETY.

Mr. Forbes.
,, Bruce.
,, Ashburner.
,, Henshaw.
,, Rivett.
,, A damson.
,, Constable.
,, Tate.
,, Nesbitt.
,, De Souza.
,, L. B. De Souza.
,, Simson.
,, Fawcett.
,, Stevens.

Mr. Hadow.
,, D. Scott.
,, J. Ferguson.
,, Sir F. Gordon, Bart.
,, H. Trail.
,, T. Graham.
,, J. Griffith.
,, J. Ried.
,, Dady Nasservanjee.
,, S. C. Senoy.
,, N. Goolabdass.
,, N. Manockjee.
,, P. Bomanjee.
,, F. Nanabhoy.

LIST OF MERCHANTS.

EUROPEAN.

Adamson (Alexander).
Bruce, Fawcett and Co.
Forbes and Co.
Harding (Joseph).
Rivett and Wilkinson.
Souza, Mignel de Leuis.
Tate (James).
Taylor and Agnew.

NATIVE.

Gantoo Caste.

Manordass Rupjee.
Vituldass Keussowram.
Sunkersett Baboolsett.
Pandooset Sewajeesett.
Bhimjeh Ramsett, *Tobacco Farmer.*
Lallbhoy Goverdhondass Minter.
Sewker Sinoy, *Goa Agent.*
Lalla Jairam.
Hurjevan Sirput.
Narondass Nowrotumdass.
Moorlither Sumboo.
Jugjeevun Anoopdass.
Nawrotumdass Motichund.
Moorlither Pursotum.

SHROFFS.

Munordass Duarcadass.
Gopaldass Manordass.

Bengal Shroffs.

Javerchund Atmaram.
Vizbhucan Tapidass.
Pittamber Chutoobhuz.
Balmucan Nursindass.
Goverdhon Jugjivandass.
Ramdass Bhugwandass Narondass.
Hemraze Goccull.
Davaldas Pittamber.
Luckmichund Nanabhoy.
Galla Jewa Moody.
Wirziall Bhugtey.

Natoo Sumboo, *Broker.*

PERSIC CASTE.

Dady Nasservanjee.
Hirjee Jeevanjee.
Nasservanjee Manockjee.
Pallanjee Bomanjee.
Sorabjee Muncherjee.
Framjee Nanabhoy.
Dorabjee Furdoonjee.
Byramjee Motabhoy.
Burjorjee Dorabjee.

CHINA AGENTS.

Rustomjee Dadabhoy
Eduljee Bomanjee.

MUSSULMAN.

Mahomed Soffee.
Bhorjee Curimjee.
Gassamjee Mottabhoy.
Mullickjee Cassimjee.

ARMENIAN.

Aniet Sarkize.
Calslan Satour.
Panwass Seemon.
Sahak Moorad.
Pogus Satour.
Simon Markhar.
Jacob Pedross.

By the courtesy of the Hon. Sorabjee Shapoorjee Bengallee we are enabled to present our readers with all that is contained in the Bombay Directory of 1792.

The two leaves in this squat volume compared with the Bombay Directory of to-day bring forcibly to view the small beginnings of our almost imperial city. It is a lesson in the history of great cities, and like the London Directory of 1792 is a very miniature booklet compared with its Brodignagian successor of 1882. Here, then, is a list of our prominent citizens, European and Native, ninety years ago. The European firms are eight in number. Alexander Adamson, a name long prominent in Bombay, figures as "the good Samaritan" in one of Malcolm's Persian sketches, and his signature is familiar to us in letters about ships and shipping in Wellington's time. He joined the East India Company in 1782, as a Civil Servant, and is now what is termed a "Junior merchant." He is styled "Transfer Master and Assistant to the Treasurers." Bruce, Fawcett and Co. are represented in 1882 by Messrs. Remington and Co., established after 1805. This firm consisted in 1792 of two Civil Servants; Patrick Crawfurd Bruce, Land Paymaster. He is the Worshipful P. C. Bruce, Esquire, Mayor, and is a "senior merchant." Henry Fawcett is the Accountant General, and is "a junior merchant."

We are particular in defining the position of these gentlemen, so that we may give illustrations of the fact which we pointed out lately, that prior to 1804, Civil Servants were allowed to become partners in commercial firms or Agency Houses, without forfeiting any of the privileges belonging to the service of the East India Company.

Of James Tate, Dr. Hové writes in 1787:—"Mr. Tate in Surat built here last season a ship which holds 400 bales of cotton, finished it in five months, sending the cotton to the Isle of France, whence it is exported to Europe."

John Forbes in 1792 represents the house of Messrs. Forbes and Co., and may have been its founder, as the future Sir Charles Forbes was now only nineteen years of age. Neither John nor Charles Forbes nor James Tate appear in the list of Civil Servants.

The Bombay Insurance Company seems to have offered in 1792 great attractions as an investment to our eminent citizens. This Company was unlimited, and lasted under the same name, we believe, until 1868. The subscribed capital was 15 lakhs, and may be the parent of a Company of the same name, established in 1870.

William Ashburner joined the East India Company in 1754, and was in 1792 the oldest Civil Servant in Bombay. His office was a high one, the holder of it being styled "Warehouse-keeper and member of the Committee of Accounts." Robert Henshaw, our readers will recognise the name in Henshaw's Buildings near the Bank of Bombay, was called to the chair in 1803 at the great meeting in honour of Arthur Wellesley. He had been about forty years in the country, and was undoubtedly the Nestor of our Society at this time.

James Tod may have given his name to our Tod Street. The Armenian houses which were then so numerous have disappeared, but the Persic, *ie.* Parsee houses, are as strong as ever. Some of the Hindoo firms may exist to-day, but we cannot identify any one of them, and such shroffs as we know from independent information existed before 1792, Jewraz Balloo and others do not find a place in this Directory.

The wonderful thing is the repetition in our own age of names so familiar in 1792. The names are common in the Civil and Military services of Bombay of Warden, Peil, Ramsden, Strachey, Ravenscroft, Rivett, Dickenson, Waddington, Michael Kennedy, Foreman, Nugent, and Sartorius.

Helenus Scott and Carnegie are among the Surgeons. And there was one man in the Bombay Harbour in 1792, to wit, the Commander of His Majesty ship Phœnix, 96 guns, Sir Richard Strahan, whose fame has been handed down to future ages in the following undying quatrain :—

"The Earl of Chatham with his sword drawn
Stood waiting for Sir Richard Strahan ;
Sir Richard, longing to be at him,
Stood waiting for the Earl of Chatham."

This is no doubt the redoutable hero, so meanwhile we bid good-bye to Bombay and its Honourable Mayor's Court and Aldermen all that we had then in lieu of our High Court of Law and Justice.

TWELVE VIEWS OF BOMBAY.

CHAPTER XXIII.

TWELVE VIEWS OF BOMBAY.

THE DOCTOR, 1673.

On the other side of the great inlet to the sea is a great point abutting against Old Woman's Island, and is called Malabar Hill, a rocky, woody mountain yet sends forth long grass.

A top of the hill is a Parsee Tomb lately raised, on its declivity towards the sea the remains of a stupendous Pagoda near a tank of fresh water, which the Malabars visit it most for.—*John Fryer's New Account of East India and Persia*, 1698.

THE PHILOSOPHER, 1804.

The Island of Bombay is beautiful and picturesque; it is of very varied surface, well wooded, with bold rocks and fine bays, studded with smaller islands. There is scarcely any part of the coast of England where the sea has better neighbours of every kind. But what avails all this in a cursed country where you cannot ramble amid such scenes, where for the greater part of the day you are confined to the house.—*Life of Sir James Mackintosh,* 1835.

THE TRAVELLER, 1812.

Of all places in the noble range of countries so happily called the Eastern World, from the pitch of the Cape to the Islands of Japan, from Bengal to Batavia, nearly every hole and corner of which I have visited in the course of my peregrinations, there are few which can compare with Bombay. If, indeed, I were consulted by any one who wished as expeditiously and economically as possible to see all that was characteristic of the Oriental world, I would say, without hesitation, "Take a run to Bombay."—*Basil Hall's Fragments,* 1832.

THE SOLDIER, 1818.

We next went by the road to Malabar Point, where the Governor has another house, and about half way to it stopped at the garden. The view was beautiful, and the road from it, shaded by innumerable cocoanut trees, delightful.—*Col. Fitzclarence (brother of Lady Falkland) Overland Journey to India*, 1819.

THE BISHOP, 1825.

Thy Towers, Bombay,
Gleam bright, they say,
Across the dark-blue sea.

—*Heber's Journey to Bombay*, 1828.

THE GOVERNOR, 1830.

Malabar Hill—to me—a most delightful residence, almost in the sea. To a man from Bombay, that noble harbour will suggest a comparison with that of Corfu, but to complete it, the noble range of western mountains, should, like those of Albania, be covered with snow.

In natural beauty the Bay of Naples and its vicinity are not so striking as either Corfu or Bombay.—*Kaye's Life of Malcolm*, 1856.

THE GEOLOGIST, 1855.

The Bombay Islands are, I should say, scarcely surpassed in picturesqueness and beauty anywhere in the world.—*Geological Papers on Western India.*

THE CICERONE, 1859.

The scenery, too, is among the most beautiful in the world.—*Mr. Eastwick in Murray's Hand Book*, 1859.

THE PRESBYTER, 1868.

As to the Native Town, no Irish village of the worst kind has a look of greater poverty, confusion, and utter discomfort. The low huts covered with palm leaves, the open drains, the naked children with their naked fathers and miserable looking mothers, together with the absence of all attempt to give a decent look to the houses, present a most remarkable contrast to the wealth and luxury of the neighbouring city.—*Peeps at the Far East : Norman Macleod,* 1871.

THE EDITOR FROM A BALLOON, 1877.

We were soon at an elevation of about six thousand feet. We were in a dead calm, and had ample leisure to look out, over Bombay, its groves and houses, the harbour with its tiny ships, and the narrow plain of the Konkan bounded by the Ghauts on the east and south. Looking straight down we saw underneath a large bunder, with its sheds and basin, like the farm yards which children make with a box of toys. Bombay looked, as it always looks from a height, beautiful as a fairy picture. The eye rested on the groves and trees, the houses and streets, the foliage predominating over the white stucco, even far into the native town. The Elphinstone College, Parell, and, in the distance, the splendid buildings beyond the bare and brown Esplanade, stood out clear and stately from the panorama below. The whole contour of the island with Trombay and other parts of Salsette were part of the picture. The Vehar Lake, embosomed in surrounding hills, we could almost look down into. Across the harbour lay Elephanta, looking very flat and insignificant when seen from this elevation. Butcher's Island, with its lines of barracks, though smaller, was more picturesque than the larger and far more interesting Elephanta.—*Abridged from Mr. Grattan Geary's Account of his Balloon Ascent on 1st December,* 1877.

THE AGRICULTURIST, 1879.

Bombay, take it all in all, is the most picturesque city in India. Viewed from Government House on the Sea Point of Malabar Hill I have seen nothing finer.—*James Caird in Nineteenth Century,* 1879.

SIR RICHARD TEMPLE, 1879.

Believe me that if our atmosphere were a little less hazy, the scenery of Bombay would be little inferior to that of Southern Italy, of Sicily, and of Greece, which has delighted so many generations of men, and this native city may fairly take its place with the finest cities of the East.

Not only is it superior to every other city of India, but it is almost equal to such cities as Cairo, Constantinople, Bagdad, Ispahan, and Canton.—*Sir Richard Temple's Speech*, 1879.

BOMBAY,

SOCIAL AND POLITICAL,

TWELVE VIEWS.

CHAPTER XXIV.

BOMBAY, SOCIAL AND POLITICAL, TWELVE VIEWS.

AN EYE-WITNESS, 1690.

I CANNOT, without horror, mention to what a pitch all vicious enormities were grown in this place.

Their principles of action and the consequent evil practices of the English forwarded their miseries and contributed to fill the air with those pestilential vapours that seized their vitals and speeded their hasty passage to the other world.

Luxury, immodesty, and a prostitute dissolution of manners found still new matters to work upon.—*Anderson's Western India,* 1854.

THE MUSLIM, 1694.

Mahomed Hashim Khafi Khan, author of the "History of Aurungzeb," was sent by the Viceroy of Guzerat to the English in Bombay on a mission, on which occasion, while commending them in other respects, he accuses them of levity in laughing more than befitted the solemnity of political intercourse.—*Elliot's Historians of India*, 1877.

THE STATESMAN, 1707.

When the English first settled in India they were mightily admired by the natives, believing they were as innocent as themselves; but since, by their example, they are grown very crafty and cautious, and no people understand better their own interest, so that it was easier to effect that in one year which you shan't do now in a century, and the more obliging your management, the more jealous they are of you.—*President Pitt of Madras, Grandfather of the Great Earl of Chatham.*

THE POLITICAL ECONOMIST, 1775.

It is a very singular Government in which every member of the administration wishes to get out of the country, and consequently have done with the Government as soon as he can, and to whose interest and long after he has left it, and carried his whole fortune, it is perfectly indifferent to him, though the whole country was swallowed by an earthquake.—*Smith's Wealth of Nations.*

THE CIVILIAN—CES GENS LA, 1765-83.

O my soul, come not thou into their secret, into their assembly mine honour be not thou united.—*Forbes' Oriental Memoirs,* 1813.

LA FEMME ANGLAISE.

La femme Anglaise est un etre fort extraordinaire. La plus passionnée, celle qui plantera la mari, enfans, consideration, pour courir apres un autre homme, celle-là même aura pour cet homme, à de nombreux égards, une réserve incompatible avec l' intimité francaise, qui est, a mon sens, la plus douce des formes de l' amitie. Il y a une barriere de glace entre elle et moi que la passion la plus ardente de ma part ne fondrait jamais entierement. Il est bien entendu que quand je dis *moi,* j entends un homme quelconque de France, et même d'Angleterre, et non Victor Jacquemont.—*Correspondance de Victor Jacquemont,* 1833.

MACKINTOSH'S BOMBAY, 1804-11.

The society of Bombay was not then so extensive as it has since become, and as to a certain degree it had become before he left it. It possessed, however, many able and estimable persons, some extremely intelligent merchants, several of them of uncommon natural powers, some brave military officers, experienced practitioners; and in the Civil Service, men well versed in the conduct of affairs. Men of talent occasionally visited it from all parts of India.—*Life of Sir James Mackintosh*, 1835.

THE MISSIONARY, 1811.

Dined at Farish's with a party of some very intelligent and well-behaved young men.

What a remarkable difference between the old inhabitants of India and the new comers. This is owing to the number of religious families in England.—*Sargent's Life of Henry Martyn*, 1819.

THE PERSIAN.

No wonder the Persian Ambassador on first witnessing a ball at Bombay, after seeing one dance and perceiving the ladies about to commence another, observed with great politeness turning round to the Governor, that he hoped that they would put themselves to no more trouble on his account.—*General Briggs' Letters to his Son*, 1828.

THE CHOTA SAHIB, 1830.

Society consisted chiefly of foolish *burra sahibs* (great folks) who gave dinners, and *chota sahibs* who ate them. The dinners were in execrable taste, considering the climate. But the food for the palate was scarcely more flavourless than the conversation. Nothing could be more vapid than the talk of the guests, except when some piece of scandal affecting a lady's reputation, or a gentleman's official integrity gave momentary piquancy to the dialogue.—*Bombay Courier*.

L' INDE OCCIDENTALE POONA, 1832.

Les Anglais de Poona ne sont pas amusans. Dans le nord de l' Indoustan ou chacun d' eux est une espece de pacha, ils grandissent avec leur dignité, selon le principe, que noblesse oblige ; et chose *mirabile dictu !* ils deviennent même aimables. Ici Je le retrouve au naturel, ce qui n'est pas un compliment a leur faire. Toutefois, comme Je suis accablé de besogne, il vaut mieux peut-être qu' il en soit ainsi. Je n'ai aucune tentation d' aller chercher du plaisir chez eux hors de mes paperasses. Ils me rappellent Milord *What Then de la Princesse de Babylone*, par leur prodigieuse indifference à tout ce qui est en dehors du cercle etroit et routinier de leur monotone existence. Je préfère les Cachemyriens qui formaient seuls ma société l' an passé. Je crois quils avaient plus de mouvement dans l' esprit que les mécaniques vivantes, en habits rouges et noirs, qui peuplent ce quartier-general de la puissance Anglaise dans l' Inde Occidentale.—*Victor Jacquemont,* 1833.

THE CENSORIOUS, 1854.

Anglo-Indian society was, as it has ever been, one degree worse than English.

Now that the world bears itself more morally, there is still rather a lower standard of principle, together with more shamelessness and disregard of propriety in Bombay than in England.—*Anderson's Western India.*

EXCELSIOR.

However we may regret much that is still common among Anglo-Indians, it is evident that a very marked improvement has taken place in the conduct of the higher classes, and the explanation of this lies not merely in the fact that India is now much nearer to England than she was a century or two ago.—*Bombay Guardian, 9th August,* 1879.